# CAPTIVE
# BODIES

## THE SUNY SERIES
### CULTURAL STUDIES IN CINEMA/VIDEO

Wheeler Winston Dixon, editor

# CAPTIVE BODIES

## Postcolonial Subjectivity in Cinema

### GWENDOLYN AUDREY FOSTER

STATE UNIVERSITY OF NEW YORK PRESS

Published by
State University of New York Press, Albany

© 1999 State University of New York

For information, address State University of New York Press,
State University Plaza, Albany, N.Y., 12246

Production by Marilyn P. Semerad
Marketing by Patrick Durocher

**Library of Congress Cataloging-in-Publication Data**

Foster, Gwendolyn Audrey.
    Captive bodies : postcolonial subjectivity in cinema / Gwendolyn
Audrey Foster.
        p.    cm. — (SUNY series, cultural studies in cinema/video)
    Includes bibliographical references and index.
    ISBN 0-7914-4155-5 (hardcover : alk. paper). — ISBN 0-7914-4156-3
(pbk. : alk. paper)
    1. Captivity in motion pictures.  2. Imperialism in motion
pictures.  3. Racism in motion pictures.  4. Sexism in motion
pictures.  5. Motion pictures—Political aspects.  6. Motion picture
industry—Political aspects—United States.  I. Title.  II. Series.
PN1995.9.C333F67  1999
791.43'658—dc21                                                      98-37251
                                                                              CIP

10  9  8  7  6  5  4  3  2  1

# CONTENTS

※

# LIST OF
# ILLUSTRATIONS

Cover Photo: *A Tale of Love*, the bound lovers. Courtesy Trinh T. Minh-ha.

# ACKNOWLEDGMENTS

Earlier versions of some of the chapters and materials in this book appeared in the following publications: My essay on Carol Clover's *Men, Women and Chainsaws* first appeared in *Prairie Schooner* 69.2 (Summer, 1995); reprinted from *Prairie Schooner* by permission of the University of Nebraska Press. Copyright 1995 by the University of Nebraska Press. My essays on *The Dalton Girls* and *High Noon* first appeared in *Film Criticism* 20.3 (Spring, 1996) and *Film Criticism* 28.3/29.1 (Spring/Fall, 1994) respectively; my thanks to editor Lloyd Michaels. My essay on frontal male nudity was first published in *The Mid-Atlantic Almanack* 4 (1995). My interview with Barbara Hammer first appeared in *Post Script*; my thanks to Gerald Duchovnay, editor. My comments on the new feminist cinema in chapter 4 originally appeared in *Angles*; my thanks to Elfrieda Abbe. My essay on Safi Faye's cinematic works first appeared in *Popular Culture Review*; my thanks to editor Felicia Campbell. Finally, my interview with Trinh T. Minh-ha was originally published in *Film Criticism* 21.3 (Spring, 1997); my thanks again to Lloyd Michaels. All of these materials have been extensively rewritten and modified for their inclusion here.

I would also like to thank the members of the Department of English of the University of Nebraska, Lincoln, for their support of my work, and particularly the Chair of the Department, Dr. Linda Ray Pratt. In addition, I would like to thank Trinh T. Minh-ha, Barbara Hammer, Judith Mayne, Sandy Flitterman-Lewis, Laurence Kardish, Deac Rossell, Marta Braun, Oyekan Owomoyela, Homi Bhabha, Fatimah Rony, Manthia Diawara, Susie Bright, Jacqueline Bobo, Donald Bogle, Carol Clover, Judith Butler, Lisa Cartwright, Sue-Ellen Case, Ana Castillo, Rey Chow,

Richard Dyer, Karen Finley, Hal Foster, Diana Fuss, Bill Nichols, Jane Gaines, Gloria Gibson, Sander Gilman, bell hooks, E. Ann Kaplan, Ed Guerrero, Eve Sedgwick, Ella Shohat, Linda Williams, and numerous other scholars for their encouragement and example during the creation of this text. I also wish to thank the librarians here at The University of Nebraska, Lincoln, including Brian Zillig, Kent H. Hendrickson, Kathleen A. Johnson, and Track Bicknell. Thanks also to the British Film Institute, The Walter Reade Theater at Lincoln Center, Film Forum, The Brooklyn Museum Film Department, The American Museum of the Moving Image, The Academy of Motion Picture Arts and Sciences, Women Make Movies, Inc., The Black Film Archive at Indiana University, and The Film Study Center at The Museum of Modern Art. Finally, sincere thanks to Dana Miller for typing the numerous drafts of this manuscript. All stills used throughout this volume are courtesy of The Jerry Ohlinger Archive, unless otherwise noted in the caption for each still.

# INTRODUCTION

❃

This is a study of bondage. Bondage to the image. A book about captivity and the captured body. A book as much about the captor as the captive. Even before the invention of the cinematograph, scientists and artists have attempted to capture images, especially images of the body. Though much has been written about the objectification of the body (especially the female body) in precinema, photography, and all facets of moving-image production, many questions still remain and are hotly debated in the fields of film studies, cultural studies, feminist studies, and elsewhere. Largely, these questions center around Foucaultian paradigmatics. Are we "subject" to others? Are we "bound" and "captive" in images? Are we "captive" bodies and "captive" audiences, held hostage to the spectacles of voyeuristic pleasure? Are those behind the camera involved in a process not unlike that of the slave system, enslaving the body in the image?

Looking at the language of photography and cinematography, one can see an astounding fascination with bondage and captivity. One "shoots" film, one "captures" images, and one is "captivated" by spectacles of celluloid: "I was glued to my seat." Furthermore, this taxonomy of capture, of captive bodies, extends beyond the systems of visual pleasure and spectacle. In this book, I wish to re/look at cinema, emphasizing captivity as a palimpsest that draws itself as a power/knowledge grid around the history of filmmaking, film study, and film spectatorship, distribution and the like. I will trace the discursive systems of the film factory, from its origins in "Inceville" and Edison's studios, through the lens of one familiar with the system of Plantocracy and slavery. I will move across boundaries of systems of film study, themselves "bound" to categorization and discursive mapping. I'm interested in the relationship between the image

1

of the bound body, usually (but not always) female and/or African, and Postcolonial problematizations of "Whiteness," gender, sexuality, and class. I hope not to be enslaved to the boundaries of captive criticism, which seems itself to be mired in the bondage of locating culture within a few large systems of acceptable practices of film criticism and cultural studies.

I wish to identify the system of captivity to narrative that we are now experiencing. As viewers, we are now faced with the "choice" of five screens at the local multiplex playing White retreads of captivity and slave narratives, remade as huge, uninvolving spectacles: John Woo's *Face/Off* (1997), Joel Schumacher's *Batman Forever* (1997), Simon West's *Con Air* (1997), and other similar films. I find the bondage of film narrative is equalled by the slavery to the film production system, in which "stars" are subject to the Plantocracy of Hollywood, a system that disciplines the body, not only within the narratorial structure of the films it produces, but in the star-slave system, which captures workers, and holds them captive, enslaved in certain roles (for example Sylvester Stallone, who is held captive by both audience demand and studio politics in the same role, a copy of himself in every film he makes), one can see countless exemplifications of all types of captivity, even of the films themselves. Turner Classic Movies bills their library of films as "the best movies in captivity," which indeed they are, but the statement resounds with a politics of representation that again involves a lack of agency and a predominance of captive bodies.

Look at the way we regard a film shot at a studio: it is commonly referred to as "studio bound," and these studio-bound pictures, in turn, are subject to hunting and harvesting. A long history of recycling images as stock footage attests to a system of captive stars, locations, animals, and so forth. This was especially true of the "jungle pictures," highly popular in the forties and fifties, but having roots in the primitive and silent era, and continuing to be revamped and restaged in films such as Frank Marshall's *Congo* (1995), John Pasquin's *Jungle 2 Jungle* (1997), Anthony Minghella's *The English Patient* (1996), and Steven Spielberg's *The Lost World* (1997).

I find it fascinating that so little has been written on jungle pictures, particularly because these films extend the Colonial practices of the nineteenth century. In these films, the viewer/maker seeks to "capture" the dark continent, and the Black body, defining Whiteness against the backdrop of this simulacrum of the dark body. These films may be viewed as a return to the captivity of Colonialist racist imagery. The Hottentot Venus, for example, was subjected to the gaze of Western audiences in person. In the name of science, an African woman, Saartje Baartman, was brought to London and Paris in the early nineteenth century to display her naked body and thus "prove" the supposed inferiority and difference of her race and gender. Without succumbing to reobjectifying and recolonizing Baartman and all she re/presents, I wish to resuscitate questions of subjectivity and objectivity around the trope of the body in captivity and, among other things, expand this project to revisit what possibility there is for agency on the part of the captive.

In addition, I hope to cut across comparative analogies about the captor, including Edweard Muybridge, whose "scientific" motion studies included archetypical displays of the captive body, especially bodies engaged in what was considered forbidden. I will specifically discuss two series of Muybridge serial plates: images of a White woman covering her body entitled "Turning Around in Surprise and Running Away," alternatively titled "Ashamed"; and "One Woman Disrobing Another," also titled "Inspecting a Slave (White)." These alternative titles were first discovered by cinema historian Marta Braun in her study of Muybridge's original notebooks; Braun also correctly identifies Muybridge as a creator of narratives, rather than a documentarist. I will also examine the use of captive bodies in the work of Etienne-Jules Marey. My study of captive bodies will also include a reexamination of captive sexualities and gender as they are rehearsed and simulated in the raced and classed images of American film, from Mary Pickford in William Beaudine's 1926 film, *Sparrows*, a White remake of a slave narrative, to early attempts at ethnography such as Robert Flaherty's *Nanook of the North* (1922), which exhibits all the properties of classical Colonialist practice in that it is a simulation, a copy without an original, of the lives of the Inuit people.

Capturing an/other is the project of narrative films, just as much as the "ethnographic" film and image making is an extension of the ethnographic practice of denial of subjectivity, and the privileging of the gaze of the captor over the "primitive," "exotic," "sexual," backwards, and romantic savage. The definition itself of the clean White body is maintained by the insistent prevalence of images of an/other. As others have observed, "Whiteness," as a category, is maintained by a constant supply of Colonialist imagery. Homosexuality is also consistently Othered in order to maintain its binary category of heterosexuality. The captive body is thus resuscitated and renarrated in order to maintain its binary: free-

4

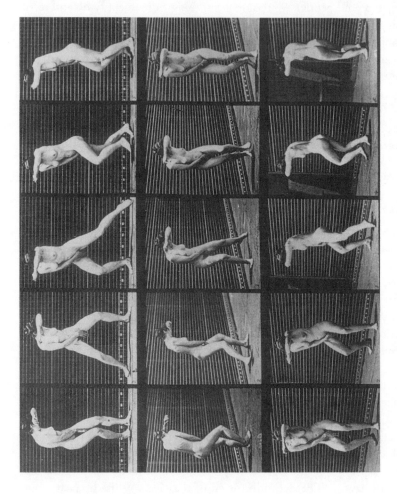

FIGURE 1. "Turning Around in Surprise and Running" aka "Ashamed" by Edweard Muybridge. Courtesy Jerry Ohlinger Archives.

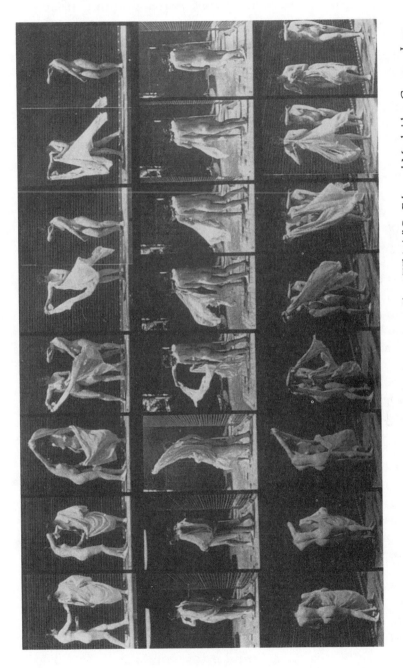

5

FIGURE 2. "One Woman Disrobing Another" aka "Inspecting a Slave (White)." By Edweard Muybridge. Courtesy Jerry Ohlinger Archives.

dom. To contain classed bodies, a whole system exists that attempts to erase class, as much as it reinterprets it and perpetuates it. The female body is tied to the tracks, bound and gagged, held captive, in order to maintain existing gender conditions, to define masculinity and femininity. We are in this fashion trapped in a scene of binaries that support our taxonomies of subjectivity and objectivity. The image production system itself is maintained in order to simulate reality (as Baudrillard and others remind us); the simulation of reality provides the binary to *experienced* reality. But is there a way out of this system and its systematizers?

I hope to take up these issues and examine them with the full knowledge that criticism itself is subject to capture and bondage. *Captive Bodies* seeks to revisualize American cinema through the lens of critical discourse on captivity narratives, slave narratives, and Postcolonial problematizations of filmic constructions of "Whiteness," "Blackness," gender, and sexuality. Reconstructing the manner in which Hollywood cinema is grounded in the absence and presence of Plantocratic ideology, *Captive Bodies* reads the Hollywood system as a Plantocracy. Drawing upon a wide range of critical methodologies, including Postcolonialist studies, feminist film criticism, anthropology, and phenomenology, I foreground the body and subjective corporeality as it is constructed as a site of struggle against Colonialist practice. Critics are remapping the landscape of cinema history as the center of struggle over ownership of the body, reminding us that cinema has been mired in the Master's discourse. Film imagery is rooted in both a presence and absence of images of slavery, Colonialist appropriation of Native American, African, and female bodies, and a whole range of signifiers of bound bodies, captive knowledge, holding desire and resistance hostage to its referents. In this book I locate a healthy hint of agency, a dialogic in the testimony of Hollywood filmmakers who have either signed on as Plantocratic overseers of Colonialism, or resisted as models of Postcolonial subjectivities. The book thus includes critical analysis of a wide range of films and filmmakers, whose films paralleled the cultural work of early American slave narratives and captivity narratives in their attempt to free the body from the chains of Colonialism.

Rereading early stereoscopic images, I will problematize knowledge and "truth" as they are staged in these early attempts to colonialize the Other. The text will also include an examination of recent "autoethnographies" by Postcolonial filmmakers such as Barbara Hammer, Isaac Julien, Sadie Benning, Su Friedrich, and Trinh T. Minh-ha. In addition,

I will seek to resituate film criticism and spectatorship at the margins of a filmic drive that is informed by slavery to narrative, commodification of the body, and is held hostage at the multiplex. Travelling across a critical landscape of free inquiry, I will question master narratives, which synthetically coalesce into an imaginary landscape. I will draw upon, yet question, Foucaultian representations of hegemonies of power/knowledge. This is a study of freedom as much as it is a study of bondage and captivity. Instead of setting out "boundaries" for myself here, I hope to open up discursive analysis, and allow myself and the reader a greater range of freedom of inquiry.

# CHAPTER ONE

## ⚜

# Images of Bondage:
# Captive Bodies

Recently I found myself in a debate with a colleague about the politics of a play about Saartje Baartman (or the "Hottentot Venus") which opened at the Joseph Papp Public Theater in New York. *Venus*, by Suzan-Lori Parks, is radical Black feminist theater in that it reinscribes agency in the form of Adina Porter, who plays the role of Baartman. As Michele Wallace writes, "Adina Porter does a moving job of endowing Baartman with humanity, [but] the play isn't necessarily about the empirical experience of the actual woman, what it was like for Saartje Baartman to be exhibited nude, to be stared at by White men fascinated with her buttocks. More important to Parks, I imagine, is to come to terms with the variables that created the situation (31). Wallace points out that the theater piece exposes the Colonialist practice of gazing at captive Africans, Indians, and Southeast Asians, who were "exhibited" in Europe and the Americas in the nineteenth century in order to support and inform racist ideologies; indeed race itself as a category depended upon such display, or, as Wallace notes, "You had to be able to see the difference" (31). What my friend and colleague and I were arguing about was the politics of restaging such a Colonialist practice. We got into a discussion of agency, and she was decidedly suspicious of the re/display of Baartman, even for the sake of political theater as a practice of decolonization of the image of Black female sexuality. I took the position that the only way to undo violence is with yet more violence itself. In other words, I agreed with Parks's choice of reinvoking the specter of violence (ocular violence and physical violence [the captive body on display]) as a means of performing the body in freedom, and revisiting the site of the emergence of the Western gaze of capture; such a strategy, I argued, seeks to transgressively reinscribe the Black female body.

Nevertheless, I could see her point. There is real danger in re-representing the colonized subject as a captive body on the twentieth-century stage. But what better way to embody a lost subjectivity than to have an actor perform a speaking subject as Saartje Baartman, the "Hottentot Venus?" But there is still an overriding degree of ambiguity in any work which questions control of one's own image. This ambiguity is shared by contemporary fashion models, as noted in Elizabeth Hollander's study, "Subject Matter: Models for Different Media." On the one hand, Hollander submits that the model has little or no control in her image making:

> the model who poses for him [the photographer] may or may not have something to do with conception, but because the camera reckons her relation to the picture plane mechanically, it is rarely in her control . . . the camera has no interest in embodied space. (14)

The model's body is sometimes seen to be in control of the model, the body to be captured by the lens, in the form of self-representation. As Hollander continues:

> The model's awareness of what her own body is doing is likewise deeply engaged in this process [of looking]. Each pose, whether it lasts for fifteen seconds or half an hour, proposes that something is there to be seen. (137)

Hollander also incorporates into her discussion her own experiences as a model. "My position could not be defined by them, even if my physical pose was" (137). I wish to explore this ambiguous assumption that both captor and captive have some degree of control over embodied space as I move into a closer examination of the captive body.

Lisa Cartwright's study of the origins of medicine's visual culture, *Screening the Body*, sheds light on the formidable Colonial confidence of members of the medical profession who began taking x-rays, photographs, films, and other forms of visual measurements of the body in order to discipline it. With full knowledge of the horrific effects of radiation poisoning, physicians in the nineteenth century repeatedly subjected themselves, their colleagues, and their constituents to deadly levels of radiation with the primitive x-ray machine. Perhaps the most gruesome and bizarre case covered by Cartwright is the case of Elihu Thomson, who, in 1896 tested his own body with the x-ray (or the Rontgen ray). The repulsive accounts of cases such as that of Thomson are equalled in scope by doctors who "tested" the ability of x-rays to "cure" men and various human maladies. But the overall project of the evolution of the x-ray was to capture the *inside* of the body, whether it be the body of the subject under the medical gaze of the physician, or the body of the physician her/himself.

As Cartwright notes, both the x-ray and the cinema date their "birth" from the year 1895. The early cinema shares a preoccupation with measuring and capturing images of the body: movement of the body in the motion studies of Marey and Muybridge, and deterioration and disfigurement of the body in early "medical" films, as well as Thomas Edison's *Electrocuting an Elephant* (1903) and Mutoscope/Biograph's *Female Facial Expressions* (1902). Cartwright links popular visual entertainment with "scientific" visual inquiries, noting their Foucaultian role

> [in the] emergence of a distinctly modernist mode of representation in Western scientific and public culture—a mode geared to the temporal and spatial decomposition and reconfiguration of bodies as dynamic fields of action in need of regulation and control. (xi)

Nevertheless, Cartwright insists that we "foreground most fully the crucial issue of agency on the part of living 'objects' of the disciplinary gaze" (109). But foregrounding agency becomes a rather problematic issue when it comes to certain images of precinema as well as early cinema.

## SEEING DOUBLE

Take, for example, the stereoscopic images of the nineteenth century, meant for popular consumption by a Colonialist and medicalized gaze. These stereographs, many of which are available in the study *Wonders of the Stereoscope*, represent another example of the Victorian preoccupation with reproduction of a semblance (or a resemblance) of reality in a process not entirely unlike 3D movie technology. Looking through these double images, when the stereoscope works, we can perceive the illusion of 3-dimensional depth of frame. As I look through these images, including many idyllic visions of family life such as *The Happy Homes of England* from the 1850s, I am myself captivated when I come upon a gruesome image in *Criminal Kneeling over His Own Grave—Japanese Executioner Beheading a Condemned Chinese, Tientsin, China* (photographed by James Ricalton and published in 1904). I fail to locate any agency on the part of the man about to be beheaded, yet I'm drawn to this repulsive, perhaps even pornographic image. How am I relating to the captive body in the photograph, much less the captors, who stand around looking almost bored by the "work" of political execution?

The identification process here is challenging because one identifies on a number of levels. Initially I was angered by the inhumanity of the photographer implicitly agreeing to photograph such a scene. But, as John Jones writes, "to direct criticism at the photographer is an evasive device" (110). I am disturbed by the images of aboriginal subjects depicted in *Ku-Ra-Tu at Rest*, photographed by Jack Hillers in 1874. Both dual images offer the Colonialist (and the Postcolonialist) a view of the theater of race as a tourist spectacle. To say that I am not implicated in this specter is to evade the questions of fetishistic pleasure.

My response seems to fall into the realm of fetishism as described in Linda Williams's influential essay "Film Body: An Implantation of Perversions." Expanding upon theories of Christian Metz, Williams describes fetishistic pleasure as a process in which the viewer is equally entranced with the abilities of machines to capture images as they are the images themselves. Nevertheless, Williams ascribes to the belief that such pleasure is tied to the historical moment:

> The fetish pleasure is strongest at the moment the "theatre of shadows" first emerges, when audiences—like the audiences who first viewed the projection of moving bodies by Muybridges' zoopraxiscope—are still capable of amazement at the magical abilities of the machine itself. (522)

Muybridge's apparatus, Williams argues, was more capable of inducing fetishistic pleasure when it was first invented. The stereoscopic photography discussed above supports Williams's conclusion that "the cinema became, even before its full 'invention,' one more discourse of sexuality, one more form of the 'implantation of perversions' extending power over the body" (532). While Williams's article contends that such power relations were predominantly regulated by the fact that the early photographers and cinematographers were men fetishizing women (and indeed, the evidence supports such a reading), I'd suggest that all subjects—men, women, and particularly non-Western "Others"—were also equally fetishized. Even the inside of the body, regardless of gender, was subject to fetishistic inquiry in the x-ray studies discussed above.

To return to the issue of the stereographic image of *Beheading a Condemned Chinese* and *Ku-Ra-Tu at Rest*, I am reminded by Marta Braun that photographers such as Muybridge used the camera "not as an analytical tool at all but . . . for narrative representation" (249). Thus, it is not simply the captured image on display in these stereoscopes, but the *narratives* that they offer which help us gain access to the ideology of their captors. In problematizing my own status as a Postcolonial viewer I am ultimately asking the question, With whom am I identifying? Captive or Captor? Or both? Furthermore, can either captive or captor even be a substitute for the self? Diana Fuss's study on the philosophy of identity, *Identification Papers*, leads me directly into confrontation with questions of identification as they relate to captive images and captured narratives such as *Beheading a Condemned Chinese*. I initially identified with the Chinese captive in the stereoscope. My attraction to the photograph was focused on a figure who is frozen in time at the moment of death. Nevertheless, after I stared at the figure at length, I shifted my gaze to his captors, trying to perceive anyone in the number of figures who may have questioned their own actions. I found none. In my attempts to understand my identification process, as I view the narrative produced by the stereograph, I am reminded by Fuss that

> Identification is both voluntary and involuntary, necessary and difficult, dangerous and effectual, naturalizing and denaturalizing. Identification is the point where the physical/social distinction becomes impossibly confused and finally untenable. (10)

Identification is therefore a murky process of internalization of narratives of an/other. Though I am more inclined toward philosophical "answers" about identification questions, I cannot dismiss psychoanalytic theories out of hand, especially as a subject of the discursive field of film studies.

14

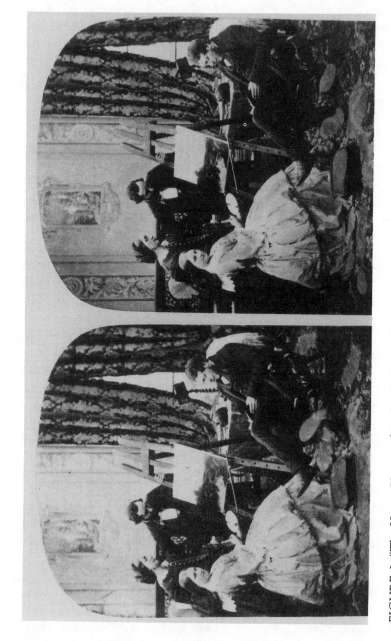

FIGURE 3. "The Happy Homes of England"; the privilege and romanticism of British Colonial Life. Courtesy Jerry Ohlinger Archives.

FIGURE 4. "Criminal Kneeling Over His Own Grave—Japanese Executioner Beheading A Condemned Chinese, Tientsin, China"; the alliance of the display of the Other with the dispassionate camera eye. Courtesy Jerry Ohlinger Archives.

Film narratives themselves are in many ways preoccupied with psychoanalytic identification theories. Identification entails more than fetishistic pleasure. It entails fear, fascination, dread, pleasure, and pain. Yet perhaps what upsets me most about my fascination with the stereograph of the beheading of a non-European Other by a non-European Other is that the visual narrative seems to be packaged for the consumption of the tourist in her/his Victorian home. As Fuss comments, "Identification is not only how we accede to power, it is also how we learn submission" (14). Secure in the domestic sphere, the Victorian consumer of these images views them without physical risk to her/himself, much in the same way that millions of viewers were transfixed by the tragic spectacle of the death of Princess Diana, repeated and repeated on CNN and CNBC as an endless loop of images of death and destruction, made stereoscopic through repetition alone.

## REPEATING THE PAST

Indeed, one of the most remarkable and obvious traits of the Victorian stereoscopic photographers is their obsession with serial repetition. They repeatedly photographed images of the captive body, and these images were enormously popular with the public. Just as the gruesome *Electrocuting an Elephant* was popular as a moving picture, so were the stereographic images of the subaltern, the mysterious figures of the Orient. The link between seriality and the Colonialist preoccupation with capture and domination is clear. Seriality is usually linked with minimalism and pop art of the twentieth century, but there is certainly an element of seriality to be found in the imagery of the turn of the century. Nowhere is this serial repetition more apparent than the case of the statue of "The Greek Slave" by Hiram Power, which was reproduced in many formats, including the stereoscopic photograph.

The interest in viewing the White female body as a slave is pernicious during this period, as in the case of Muybridge's "Inspecting a Slave (White)." The story behind the popularity of these images deserves further scrutiny. Hiram Power's "The Greek Slave" was originally carved in 1845 but became popularized through photographs and exhibitions into an international phenomenon. The similarity to a modern S/M pinup is obvious, but what intrigues me here are the limitless capabilities of serial captivity of images. Seriality tends to move the image toward abstractedness as

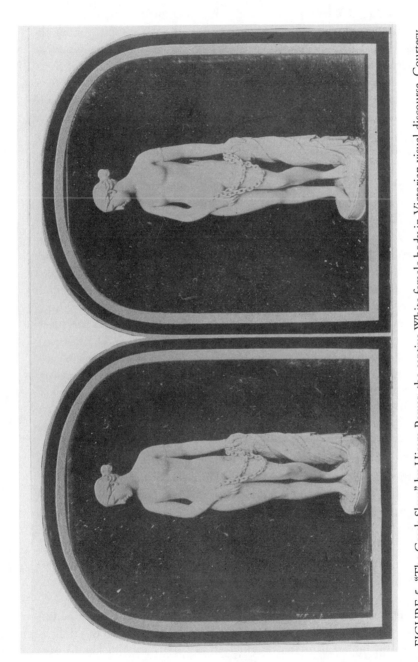

FIGURE 5. "The Greek Slave" by Hiram Power; the captive White female body in Victorian visual discourse. Courtesy Jerry Ohlinger Archives.

it moves the subject into a state of disembodied subjectivity. This changes the narrative capabilities of the stereoscope or photograph, for, in the words of Hal Foster, "abstraction tends only to *sublate* representation, to preserve it in cancellation, whereas repetition, the (re)production of simulacra, tends to *subvert* representation, to undercut its referential logic" (63). The slippage of narrative of *The Greek Slave* is apparent when we try to recapture the possibilities of narratives that this captive body (actually a simulacra of a captive body) may have supported or informed. The secret of the popularity of the female slave is certainly multifaceted. It would be far too easy to dismiss it as another example of the primacy of the White male gaze. It is certainly that, but it must have meant much more to contemporaneous audiences. Women, in particular, were drawn to the statue. John Jones recounts how feminist Frederika Bremer stated "this captive woman with her fettered hands seized upon me with unusual power" (Jones, 36). I'd suggest that the popularity of the White female slave image attests to a pattern of White appropriation of the slave narrative itself. I think in many ways this phenomena repeats itself in the representation of White women as slaves, captives, victims, and hostages in popular culture. Scholars are beginning to look at the connections between slave narratives, captivity narratives, and other Western narratives. But, for the most part, slave narratives and captivity narratives have been traditionally treated as if they existed in a vacuum, as if they were not influenced by Eurocentric popular culture and as if they had little influence, in turn, on popular culture and popular literary narrative. Perhaps the "pop-star" fame of *The Greek Slave* marks a code-switching in which White women were in a sense fetishized by their renarration into the (absent) slave narrative. Slave narratives were very popular in the late nineteenth century, and it seems to me that the case could be made for this possibility. There is the distinct possibility that White women were drawn to the sculpture for any number of reasons, including fetishistic pleasure in viewing the scopophilic subject, a simulacra of herself in bondage. The viewer could have identified with the captive or the disembodied absent captor, or both. Nancy K. Miller's work with regard to the dismantling of the universal female subject reveals the question as a site of contestatory feminist politics. Miller writes:

> The 1980s revealed that the universal female subject could be just as oppressive as her male counterpart and under accusations of first-world imperialism and essentialism her reign was quickly dismantled. (17)

Keeping these remarks in mind, we may be able to read any number of narratives across the specter of *The Greek Slave*. She may stand in
as a captive of class, race, gender, or sexuality, and with each active gaze
that falls upon her, whether in a stereograph, a lithograph, a postcard, or
any reproduction, she invokes the panoply of desires and narratives of
possible audiences. The compulsion to contain the body, in this case the
female body, is indicative of a culture dedicated to containment, discipline, and narratives of captivity, but the readings of these remnants
(resemblances) of culture such as the stereoscopic image of *The Greek
Slave* are subject to a critical guessing game, one in which I am perfectly
happy to engage. Scientific containment moves across the images of popular culture. Just as physicians attempt to capture the interior of the body,
so do popular image makers trade in taxonomy and containment, yet
often there is a problem knowing the container from the contained.

## IMAGES OF EMPIRE

Take the case of the widely popular images of Egypt and other Mideast-
ern countries. They coincide with the crest of the legacy of Colonialism.
They may be taken simply at face value; as artifacts or testimony of the
political means of ownership through taxonomy. By capturing the
exotic Other in photographs, stereoscopes, and other visual media, men
of Empire advanced the fantasies and realities of quest and Othering the
subaltern. But is the subject always the object in these cases? Certainly
at one level the captured is objectified *Delights of Summer in the Vale of
Cashmere—Music for a House-Boat Party on Jhelum River* (1903), a
stereoscopic photo from the Underwood Library (a company which
sold their stereographs door to door). In this stereoscopic image, a
young man plays a sitar in the foreground (which is set off by the three-
dimensional process to great effect). He looks directly at the viewer, as
do several other figures in the background. The setting provides an idyllic fantasy of the travel narrative. The Underwood Brothers, who,
according to John Jones were very successful salesmen, would use the
stereoscope as part of a sort of package or travel guide. The stereographs
were packaged much like books, and on their reverse side one could
read information on travel. For example, the back of the card *The
Delights of Summer in the Vale of Cashmere* "was packed with information about the buildings in the background, how to hire houseboats and

FIGURE 6. "Delights of Summer in the Vale of Cashmere—Music for a House-Boat Party on Jhelum River": the "look back" or Third Eye of the subaltern in travel exotica. Courtesy Jerry Ohlinger Archives.

servants, the sitar and how to play it, and general observations on Hindu music" (Jones, 102).

The stereoscope thus exemplifies the articulation of Colonial mastery in all its glory. The figures and the land are captured and frozen in time in a performance of obeisance to the eye of the Western camera. But this is merely a performance of self and identity. One doesn't have to look very hard for the returned gaze of the subaltern, who effectively marks the *viewer* as subject. As Fatimah Tobing Rony writes, "it is the returned gaze of the colonized Native" (Rony, 43) that constitutes what she terms "the Third Eye." Rony's study *The Third Eye: Race, Cinema, and Ethnographic Practice* is remarkable for its insights into the "Third Eye." Drawing on the work of Franz Fanon, Rony describes how the Third Eye, otherwise known as "the look back," or "the returned gaze" (Dixon, 47–53), breaks down the Foucaultian paradigmatic of subjectivity and objectification in numerous disparate works and acts such as the Hottentot Venus, Josephine Baker's filmed performances, Félix-Louis Regnault's "ethnographic" cinematographs such as "Jump by Three Negroes" (1895), and many other ethnographic spectacles.

The viewer of *The Delights of Summer in the Vale of Cashmere* might find some discomfort in the Third Eye of the stereograph. The performers in the stereograph are quite aware of being viewed (and captured by the camera) as objects of ethnographic spectacle, and the look back testifies to their resistance to the objectification process. There is more than resistance to the identification process; there is, in a sense, Othering by the Other. The Western viewer is tantalized by the "taxidermic image of romantic ethnography," to invoke Rony's phrase (100), yet the viewer is also being observed and made captive to an identity constituted by an/other. Rony identifies this "predicament" as that moment when the viewer "who, recognizing that he or she is racially aligned with the ethnographic Other yet unable to identify fully with the image, is left in uncomfortable suspension" (17).

What is suspended here goes beyond recognition towards identification, and identification would suggest a desire on the part of the Western viewer to become the Other, to suspend knowledge of the self through the Other. As Margaret Chatterjee noted in 1963, our knowledge of ourselves is problematic and performative, and intersubjective processes govern identity itself: "We are involved in a mutual process in which knower and known modify each other" (Chatterjee, 18). Thus, the performance of self in the captivity narrative of a stereograph such as *Delights of Sum-*

*mer in the Vale of Cashmere* is volatile and reciprocal. The captive audience is confronted with knowledge of self that is being modified by the subject, and in turn, the sitar player is a captive body working in the realm of subjectivity that modifies his sense of self by performing for the stereograph. Both viewer and subject are captives and captors, both are involved in mediating the image of self between the known and unknown, both are coperforming a narrative of selfhood.

Coperformance of selfhood or subjectivity would obviously not fit into the goals of the Colonialist process, yet the Colonialist process was not always successful in the governance or maintenance of disciplined bodies. Certainly the cultural production and captivity of the "other" successfully produced and defined notions of travel fantasy, conquest, and the taxonomies of evolution, race, gender, class, and sexuality. However, each "success" was marked by elements of resistance, subterfuge, and other manifestations of the Third Eye, such as parody or transgressive reinscription of identity. Because knowledge of the self is subject to transgressive reinscription and mutability through performativity, it is important to see the value of gaps and markers of determinacy in viewing these precinematic records. One example of such transgressive reinscription can be seen in another stereograph designed for the Colonial tourist gaze: *View of the Rock Temple of Derr, Now the Chief Town in Nubia* (1856), by Francis Frith. Frith worked with the Wet Collodion process and met with great difficulties; travelling to Egypt, he attempted to use a wicker van for his darkroom. As John Jones wrote, "the heat filled the interior of the van with fumes of ether, boiled the collodion as it was poured and drove Frith to work in dark rock-tombs and caves, only to be forced back to the van because sand and dust ruined the wet plates" (40).

Like Flaherty in *Nanook of the North* (1922), Frith was intent on capturing a bygone era, precontact Egypt, but his efforts were to be as fraught with difficulty (if not impossibility) as that of Flaherty who tried to (re)capture Inuit culture as a romanticized precontact idyllic lost paradise. Both Frith and Flaherty were distraught by the signs of modernity, signs of Colonialism, signs of themselves, indeed essences of the Colonial self as it marked the subaltern countryside. What distressed both Frith and Flaherty was a mirroring of the self, though they did not name it as such. They convinced themselves that the Colonialist process was the sole responsibility of the Colonialist subject. In disowning responsibility, the Colonialist essentially attempts to transgressively reinscribe his identity *as* the Other. Similarly, in William Beaudine's *Sparrows*, a Mary Pickford

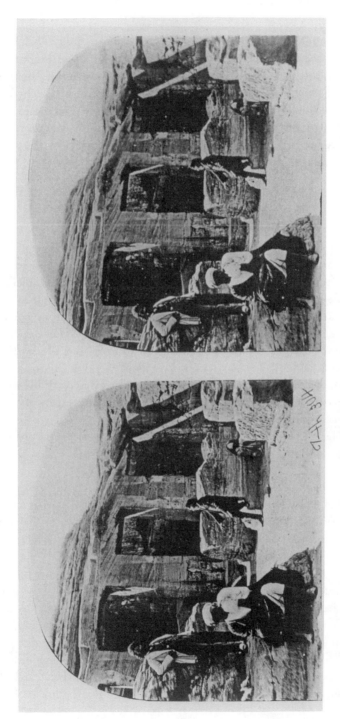

FIGURE 7. "View of the Rock Cave of Derr, Now The Chief Town in Nubia." Courtesy Jerry Ohlinger Archives.

vehicle from 1926, Beaudine constructs a phantom jungle hell in the swamps of the South, where Mary presides over a group of orphans who are forced into slave labor on a rural farm. Pickford's eternal "little girl" character finally finds safety in the arms of the adoptive patriarchy in the final reel of the film, but not before Beaudine stages a horrific and brutal chase through the "savage swamp" surrounding the work encampment, as Mary and her orphan band are exposed to the dangers of the natural world (snakes, alligators) at every turn.

## CONTEMPORARY COLONIALISM

Such a process seems endemic to postcontact cultures and is popularized in the constant preoccupation for the search for the edenic lost paradise that still captivates audiences today with such films as Steven Spielberg's *Jurassic Park* (1994) and *The Lost World* (1995), and many, other Colonialist enterprises. Frith failed to capture the lost phantom paradise. Looking at *View of the Rock Temple of Derr, Now the Chief Town in Nubia,* one is confronted by the ruins of the dream of Empire, a dream dependent on packaging a lie that removes responsibility for Colonialization and at the same time betrays a pathetic obsession for a lost Eden that, if it ever existed even in a metaphoric sense, was destroyed by the same Colonialist efforts that attempt to reclaim it.

A clue to the self-knowledge of resigned failure on the part of Francis Frith comes in the label of the stereograph for *View:*

> Of the time of Ramses the Great, in whose long and prosperous reign a very large proportion of the now existing Egyptian temples were built. This temple penetrates the rock to a depth of 110 ft; the interior walls being somewhat rudely sculptured. (Jones, 41)

Like the Western male in the photograph, who averts his gaze, the caption utterly ignores the presence of the living subjects, all of whom stare at the subject with a distinctively Third Eye, as well as the oddly posed Western interloper, who seems to be posed as a Byronic tourist, cane in hand, beholding the majesty of a lost Egyptian paradise, now available only as a graphic tracing, a memory picture of the time in which the temples were built. The figure in the foreground is entirely cloaked in fabric, and sits in a posture that seems to indicate that he has no intention of posing for the photograph. A standing figure behind him has his arm on his waist in a performance of resistance, and a crouching veiled figure, most likely female, hides herself from the scientific/tourist gaze of the camera entirely. Indeed, the only figure who seems to be performing for the photographer is the Western male, who seems lost in a trance of romantic misguidance. Nevertheless, a reviewer of the *Illustrated Times* (26 December 1851) wrote of Frith's photographs:

> We, looking through the lens of the stereoscope at Mr. Frith's aston-
> ishing photographs [see] straightaway, by virtue of binocular glam-
> our—not that modern Egypt . . . intersected by railways, converted
> for the purpose of canalization by M. De Lesseps, whose pyramids
> are now elbowed by overland route hotels and posting houses,
> whose deserts are now traversed by omnibuses bearing bilious
> majors and "beardless griffins," and whose arid sands are strewn
> with soda-water bottles and the corks of bygone flagons of Bass and
> Allsopp's pale ale . . . (Jones, 40)

In short, Colonialist confidence is ultimately undercut by the denar-rated tale of the path of Colonialist destruction itself. The stereoscope becomes an indictment of the viewer, and the reviewer's comments cited above inadvertently underscore the failure of Frith to recapture what is lost because of the reviewer's remarkably good ability to describe what is *not* in the picture—that which is denarrated (a term I borrow from Zavarzadeh). That is, the reader can certainly imagine the scrapheap described and participate in evoking a vision in his/her head of that which has been carefully, if not effectively, denarrated in *The View of the Rock Temple of Derr.*

The tension between Frith's performance of the self as photographer of lost Eden, in competition with the disruptive Third Eye of the pictures' subjects, as ultimately interpreted for Colonialist consumption by the reviewer for the *Illustrated Times,* locates a Colonialist subject that is indeed nothing like the universal subject usually identified as the White male British Colonialist. The reflected gazes, the visual and written record, and the politics of transidentity making point to a multiplicity of identities and subjectivities of the Colonialist gaze bearer. Yet the same records testify to the urge to consolidate identity of the Colonial.

The stereoscope itself, perhaps, provides the most compelling evi-dence of both self-delusion and complicity in maintaining a semblance of a universalized subject of the Colonialist self. That self, represented by the Byronic European figure, seeks to perform the delusion of Empiric destiny as a stand-in for the essential Colonialist, yet his performance betrays his discomfort in his gait and posture, which seem every bit as uncomfortable as Frith must have been in his makeshift van. The temple itself stands as a mockery in its weighted physicality and immobility, as do the subaltern subjects who, though they do not speak literally, confront the viewer with the gaze of an active Third Eye and their grudging forbearance. The master's discourse, then, here turns against itself to create a Third Eye for the Colonialist, the eye that views with discomfort the refracted image of Colonialist selves.

## WORKING BEYOND THE IMAGE

Ultimately, then, a Postcolonial reading of these artifacts moves us into a realm of multiplicities, of possible identities and performed knowledge of selves. This problematizes binaries of subject and object as we routinely comprehend them, for, as Chatterjee states, "the notion that the subject can be an object of knowledge for another subject is self-contradictory" (29). What is clear, however, is that these precinema images of which I speak do not exist in a vacuum of meanings that are easily "unpacked." Instead, they are like *camera obscuras* through which we can see the beginning stages of the Plantocracy of image-making systems. There is no "master shot" that we may "release" or "remaster" that captures the complexities of the master narratives of captives and captors. If it is true, as Éric Alliez holds, that "knowledge is comprehended as a unilateral action of the subject in reference to represented images" (238), then we must return to these images repeatedly, almost as a serial modern artist might, in order to seek through their abstractedness, forms that lie in the fold and expose elements of manipulable signifiers. Like a Daguerreotype, the fold is formed in something of a measurable time, thus capturing time and narrative in a graphic method, to create a resemblance or facsimile of real time.

Since "to be is *to be experienced* by means of representation" (Alliez, 238), active Postcolonial spectatorship and decolonization of the specters and folds of seemingly impenetrable master narratives are not only a workable means of mediating and locating culture, but also an ongoing recovery process that is not limited by time. This process stands outside the Cartesian order of time, captive and captor to our critical systems of logic and renarration. We can thus jump through time and space configurations toward images that are like auras of the early motion studies and stereoscopic narrative folds. Since all of motion picture history is based on trickery of light and movement, we should embrace the possibility of using games and visual trickery to dis/order the master narrative of moving image study.

In thinking about such a possibility, I am reminded of the words of Hélène Cixous, who writes in *Root Prints*:

> How can we see what we no longer see? We can devise "tricks": my grandmother's room which I looked at through the keyhole; because of focalization, I had never seen a room that was so much of a room. The city of Algiers which I looked at in the bus windows. The person we love made to appear as an aura. Microscopes, telescopes, myopias, magnifying glasses. To think, I knit my brows, I close my eyes, and I look. (4)

In the spirit of Cixous, then, I'd like to look forward many years in cinema history to a time which, for me, will actually be looking backward to the image of Marlo Thomas as *That Girl* in an episode of the series interchangeable with so many identical narrative trajectories in which the plot includes a sequence in which "That Girl" is bound and gagged. We have seen so many images of women and men bound and gagged that the image becomes almost undistinguished, yet to me, there is something striking about the banality of yet another image of captivity centered around the corpus of Marlo Thomas. How do we account for the image of the veil or the blindfold in *That Girl* when we compare, say, Marlo Thomas in a gag with Muybridge's "Inspecting a Slave (White)," or "Ashamed," or even the image of "The Greek Slave?"

What is telling and perhaps even measurable is the time gap between the early precinema images just described and the televisual image of "That Girl," but are they really so far apart, spatially or thematically? Is Marlo Thomas's gagged image, suspended in time, that far from the images of the clinicians who x-rayed themselves and then photographed the captive evidence? If we look closely, can we not see "That Girl" as a simulacrum of the subjects of the travel narrative in *Delights of Summer in the Vale of Cashmere*, or *View of the Rock Temple of Derr, Now the Chief Town in Nubia*, for that matter? To do so suggests a radical

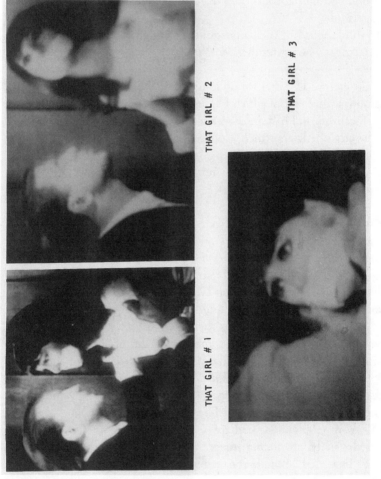

THAT GIRL # 1

THAT GIRL # 2

THAT GIRL # 3

FIGURE 8. Bondage as "play" and image of distress in *That Girl*, three video frame grabs. Courtesy Jerry Ohlinger Archives.

reworking of Postcolonial looking at the colonizer becoming the colonized, fetishizing his/her own subjects, his/her self, through the aura of the captive body revealed in the fold; the captive corpus of Marlo Thomas performing the captive body.


## I LOVE TO YOU


Luce Irigaray's *I Love To You*, sheds light on the complexities of looking across cultures and genders. While much of the work insists upon a seemingly essentialized return to binaristic categories of male and female, Irigaray's specific ideas with reference to sexed subjectivity are fascinating when we emphasize the sexed identity of Marlo Thomas as a woman who performed the female body in captivity for the pleasure of a mixed television audience. It is tempting to read this image as an archetype of *the* image of White woman in television and film history, a testament to the determinacy of gender power relations, a display of dominance over the female in patriarchal society. Indeed, the image stands for this as much as the earlier precinema images stand as trophies of capture, but it is important to look deeper, peer into the fold, and see the multivalent planes of narratives that such an image holds and beholds. As Irigaray writes, "in order to constitute a free and active temporality, the I-woman needs a *she* that is valorized as a pole of intentionality between *she* and *she*, I-*she* and *she-herself*" (67). What Irigaray is working out here is a means of transcending patriarchalization.

I'm interested in how I can adapt these ideas to a new unfixed way of looking at female subjectivity, particularly in the case of this image of Marlo Thomas in a close-up, wearing a White gag and "performing gender" (in the sense that Judith Butler uses the phrase). To read her as a victim is to read her in patriarchal terms, just as to read precinematographic Colonial subjects as disembodied subjects is to foster Colonialism's project by refusing to reject Colonialism's terms. But how else can we read her, or let her read us? As a subject of her own making, a playful ludic embodiment of a riff on sexuality? Perceived from a Postmodernist perspective as a playful image of S/M seduction, the image is not all that far from the self-representations of Betty Page or Robert Mapplethorpe. Irigaray's project is thus to move to a new plane in discussing sexual difference in which women and men avoid reducing the other to the status of object, as does contemporary S/M theory. This is particularly true of

Queer theories that treat images of bondage in a relatively new manner, outside and against the history of the repression and pathologicalization of sexuality. Certainly there is one level on which the image of "That Girl" may be viewed as another example of the captive embodiment of sexuality, and visual fetishism of the female body for the pleasure of a patriarchal audience.

Yet the image is not bound to that reading, or to that time when it was produced. It keeps on (re)presenting and (re)narrating itself in a performative gesture that defies patriarchy, Colonialism, or the history of penalization of sexuality, most especially any sexuality that is deemed aberrant, Queer, pathological, or impure. As Valerie Steele writes in *Fetish: Fashion, Sex and Power*, "the image of the 'bad girl' also appeals to women" (43). Certainly many viewers, whether heterosexual, lesbian, or bisexual, might have consumed the image of "That Girl" in light bondage in a transgressive manner. In this fashion, one might identify with "That Girl" as the archetypal captive good girl, just as one might identify with the generic malefactors in an episode of an action TV show, rather than the ostensible "good guys." To say that Victorian audiences couldn't transgressively identify with the image of a captive White women in *The Greek Slave* and "Inspecting a Slave (White)" is to deny their sexualities in a matter not unlike that described in Foucault's *Discipline and Punish*. What is at stake, then, is that we guard against attempts to recolonialize the past and its images. We must avoid systems that participate in the regulation of the body and sexuality, and attempt to discipline the body without our consent.

## THE RECONSTRUCTED BODY

The captive images I have been speaking about bring up some of the same issues of the captive female body in the slasher film. Carol Clover's work in this area has quietly revolutionized the way film theorists think about spectatorship, gender roles, and sexuality. Clover, a Professor of Scandinavian and Comparative Literature at Berkeley, became fascinated by slasher movies after a friend "dared" her to see *The Texas Chainsaw Massacre*. The "jolting experience" moved her into speculations about the role of the female body in male spectatorship of films such as *I Spit on Your Grave*, *The Silence of the Lambs* and other movies, whose video box covers included "screaming women, poised knives, and terrified eyeballs." Clover questions the notion that audience males identify solely with male heroes and argues convincingly for a rereading of the popular image of the final female survivor, with whom, Clover concludes, men identify with in a psychologically complex manner. She never flinches in this study of the "low" tradition in filmmaking in which women are often the center of psychologically "thrilling" bloodbaths of horror. Clover covers slasher films, satanic possession films, rape-revenge films, and female-hero films, and considers the issues of spectatorship, gender identification, sado-masochism, and desire in an often fresh and insightful manner.

Clover's discussion of "The Final Girl" illuminates an often missed gendered trope in popular slasher movies. Until now, the possibility of cross-gender identification has been identified in only the female specta-tor. Clover contemplates the notion that men might "elect to betray their sex and identify with screen females" (43). As male characters are quickly and easily killed off from a slasher movie, men are often left with one strong female character with whom to identify. As Clover continually demonstrates, "policemen, fathers, and sheriffs appear only long enough to demonstrate visible incomprehension and incompetence . . . the killer is himself eventually killed or otherwise evacuated from the narrative. No male character of any stature lives to tell the tale" (44). The Final Girl, for example Ripley in *Alien*, carries the narrative forward. The Final Girl is also the "first character to sense something amiss and the only one to deduce from the accumulating evidence the pattern and extent of threat; the only one, in other words, whose perspective approaches our own priv-ileged understanding of the situation" (44). Clover notes that our identi-fication with the Final Girl is often marked by a shift in point-of-view camera narration; from the perspective of the killer to that of the Final Girl, with whom we are in the closet, watching for the killer. Clover sup-ports her claims with audience studies that note that the audience cheers when the Final Girl finally destroys the killer. But Clover is not content with a simplistically gendered reading of Killer and Final Girl, whose gen-der is, she contends, often mutable. "What filmmakers seem to know bet-ter than film critics is that gender is less than a wall than a permeable membrane" (4), argues the author. While the Killer is often dressed as a female, the Final Girl is often "masculinized" by her name, clothing, and "active investigative gaze, normally reserved for males" (48). Clover sug-gests that the Final Girl signifies male lack; as an "homoerotic stand-in" (53), she is a "male surrogate in things oedipal," and Clover concludes, she is "an agreed-upon fiction [for] male-viewer's use of her as a vehicle for his own sadomasochistic fantasies" (153).

Gendered violence is at the center of debate over *I Spit on Your Grave* (1977), a rape-revenge film in which a woman is brutally raped and takes revenge upon her attackers. Other rape-revenge films include *Lipstick, The Accused, Sudden Impact,* and *Extremities.* Clover makes no apologies for a critical examination of such a sensationalist violent film as *I Spit on Your Grave,* arguing that "its brutal simplicity exposes a mainspring of popular culture" (116). *I Spit on Your Grave,* according to Clover, exposes gang rape as a male bloodsport, having more to do with male spectatorship than sex. Jennifer, the Final Girl of the film, turns the tables on her attackers and is "just as vicious" (123) in her retribution.

I would argue that Jennifer's killings are presented in lengthier, grislier detail, suggesting that the vengeful female is more responsible for her actions. She is able to prethink her acts with care, while the group of men act upon a seemingly instinctual impulse. Clover might also have considered more carefully the fact that Jennifer prays to, and is possibly metaphorically sanctioned by, the Virgin Mary, before she begins her revenge. She hangs one male, after seducing him, knives another in the genitals, again, after seducing him, axe murders another, and uses a boat propeller to dismember another. Clover's reading of spectatorial pleasure/pain for the male spectator allows for an oscillatory model of spectator identification.

While *I Spit on Your Grave* is seen as an analysis of group male behavior, Clover notes that *MS 45* takes male behavior on an individual basis. Each rape adds up to one more "act of domination" of women that "add up to pervasive structural misogyny" (144). *MS 45* opens with two rapes, but the central female figure, Thana, kills "for the figurative rape of all women" (144). Clover again questions the dominant theories of male spectatorship in her discussion of *MS 45.* Gerald Peary, for example, has noted that men silently view the film as a sort of punishment for identification with the early rape scenes. Why, asks Clover, would men silently watch the remainder of the film if there is not identification with the Final Girl? Clover pushes the identifactorial model further by postulating that the male spectator identifies with the female, to some extent, during the rape sequence. "However you cut it," says Clover, "the male spectator of this film is masochistically implicated" (142). Clover's logic is that the spectator must have identified during the rape, because he stays to watch the revenge sequences, which include dismemberment of the male body.

*Men, Women, and Chain Saws* does not limit itself to discussion of female rape-revenge films. The discussion of *Deliverance* and *Hunter's Blood* in the section "The Body in Question" theorizes that commercial films repeatedly associated the vagina with the male anus. They operate in a narrative universe in which "men are sodomized in much the same way that women are rapable and with much the same meaning and consequences" (158). Clover poses a model for reading rape-revenge movies from the point of view of the "one-sex" logic elaborated upon by Thomas Laqueur. Until the late eighteenth century, Laqueur notes, medical literature insisted that male and female bodies were merely different by nature of a system of analogues, with virtually the same genital system. In this way, the male anus is analogous to the female vagina.

For Clover, the one-sex model is helpful in looking at rape-revenge films, because it becomes obvious that it is the common body that is at "stake." Clover does not go so far as to suggest that the male spectator feels or identifies with Bobby's or Jennifer's rapes in exactly the same manner. She merely suggests that perhaps *all* viewers "feel" violation similarly, whether the subject is male or female. The issue of homophobia is not sufficiently addressed in Clover's discussion of male rape-revenge films such as *Deliverance* and *Hunter's Blood*, but this is hardly a significant omission because it is in keeping with Clover's challenges to simplistic models of horror film criticism. For Clover, it goes without saying that these exploitational vehicles are despicably misogynist and homophobic. Clover's use of the one-sex model is not meant to be a rigid marker of sexual unification. It is simply useful in drawing comparisons between male and female rape-revenge films.

Clover questions dominant critical readings of horror films throughout *Men, Women, and Chain Saws*. She argues that the emphasis on readings of the "assaultive" gaze is "defective," (182) and "fails to account for the larger system of looking to which assaultive gazing is inevitably subordinated" (182). Certainly, Clover agrees, the "I-camera" stalks the audience/victim in films such as *The Eyes of Laura Mars* (1978) and countless others, but, Clover argues, there is also a "reactive" gaze at work in many horror films. In Clover's reading of *Peeping Tom* (1960), for example, "the eye of horror works both ways. It may penetrate, but it is also penetrated" (191). The reactive gaze is often missed by critics who are more interested in the assaultive gaze. Clover argues against Laura Mulvey's original model of sadistic voyeurism, in which "the gazer salves his unpleasure at female lack by seeing the woman punished" (206), overlooks the masochistic element of scopophilia.

Connecting masochistic desires for passivity and beatings to the reactive gaze, Clover sees the long silence about masochism as "evidence that something crucial to the system of cultural representation is at stake" (227). This absence has, according to Clover, culminated in oversimplified readings of the psychoanalytic mechanics of male scopophilia, and concomitantly clouded our ability to see how female figures "are made to stand for, and act out, a psychosexual posture that in fact knows no sex" (228), in a scenario in which men can experience both the pleasure and pain of a rape fantasy. Clover also discusses the theories of Laura Mulvey and Christian Metz on feminine masochism, pointing out that their work provides a basis for a two-way, assaultive/reactive sadomasochistic model. Clover contends that critics, "rather than exposing the cultural lie on which higher forms of cinema are based, [have] unwittingly colluded with it" (230).

Amazingly, Clover ends her book with a call for more low-budget horror films. It would seem as if she has been converted since her initial cool reception to the low art form. Clover is probably partially correct in her assertion that big-budgeted films will take few risks and offer less of the "bizarre and brilliant themes that bubble up from the bottom" (236), of the seventies and eighties. However, the contemporary spate of high-budgeted Steven Seagal movies, macho kick-boxer fare, and the continual stream of current rape-revenge films will offer critics plenty of psychoanalytic fodder. Tania Modleski's analysis of the *Lethal Weapon* series in *Feminism without Men* (1991) attests to recent critical approaches to male sadomasochism and homoeroticism in even the most standard Hollywood fare. Clover's estimations of low-budgeted exploitation vehicles as worthy of critical examination is a good point, but it is also a point that argues for a more comprehensive analysis of those low-budget films that do "bubble up" with themes scarcely addressed in mainstream cinema. Clover's work might have benefitted from a screening of films such as *Ilsa: She-Wolf of the S.S.*, a film that revels in sadomasochistic treatment of the male body, and is generally relegated to the world of "camp." Though the film does not immediately fall into the Final Girl category, or the rape-revenge model, it certainly treats the spectator to a misandrist attack on men through the element of a female dominatrix, who kills all the men who cannot satisfy her sexually.

Clover's reading of these difficult texts gathers strength primarily from her ability to build upon and expand previous genre scholarship, as well as her inclusion of remarks of the genre's "auteurs" themselves, such as Steven King and John Carpenter. *Carrie* (1976) was, according to its author, a feminist film. Clover's inclusion of King's remarks adds to the critical discussion of *Carrie*, particularly with regard to the treatment of the central female character as both monster and victim. King's remarks also underscore the mutability of gender in the figure of Carrie, who he says is "Woman, feeling her powers for the first time," and "any student who has ever had *his* gym shorts pulled down" (4). Carrie's flexible gender, rendered by King's remarks, further supports an oscillatory model of spectatorship. Gale Anne Hurd, who produced *Alien*, makes a remark that also supports the theory of cross-gender identification: "you don't have to be a liberal ERA supporter to root for Ripley" [Sigourney Weaver's character in the film] (46).

John Carpenter's remarks support Clover's theoretical presumption that consistent themes and topics exist in these films, because, as Carpenter notes, they are essentially archetypal. "That's what people want to see. They want to see the same movie again" (10). Clover notes that interviews with horror directors often include mentions of myths and archetypes, as well as dreams and the unconscious, and can be very useful to film criticism. William Castle, a director of a number of intriguing horror films of the fifties and sixties, admits "I definitely feel that possibly in my unconsciousness I was trying to say something" (10). Clover's interspersal of the comments of horror film creators with those of audience members, and film theoreticians offers a dialogic that is rigorously active, as well as flexible.

*Men, Women and Chain Saws* repositions sadism as the less important of a binary structure of sadomasochism. The male body and the female-hero are refigured in oscillatory models of gender and spectatorship. While the horror film often acts out a spectacle on the female body, Clover convinces the reader that this does not mean that they are mainly about female objectification. Instead, they are battlegrounds of male desire/fear for punishment and aggression. The female body becomes a mirror for the male spectator to feel through, as well as objectify. *Men, Women and Chain Saws* is, in a way, a "jolting experience" to the feminist reader conversant with theoretical models that support more simplistic ways of looking at horror movies. Clover's study also inherently answers the question of the popularity of such movies, especially those "bad," grade "Z" films, such as *I Spit on Your Grave*. Filmgoers are apparently enjoying the sadomasochistic pleasures of films that transcend gender and reunite the viewer with his/her base desires. If there is one basis gap in Clover's book it is the absence of discussion of the female viewer of the splatter horror genre. I have female friends who anxiously await the next

*Friday the Thirteenth* or *Nightmare on Elm Street* with perhaps more or equal vigor than that of their albeit overwhelmingly male audience. Perhaps theirs is still an instance of forbidden female looking? Or are we to extend Clover's model of sadomasochistic involvement in male viewers to that of women audience members? Surely this is an area worthy of further critical discussion.

I disagree with Clover's dismissal of studies of individual horror auteurs. While it is true that horror films are much like folk tales, telling the same stories repeatedly, as Clover notes, these stories can be rendered with remarkably different emphasis (toward the sadistic or masochistic impulse). Hitchcock, for example, often seems to embrace the point of view of the sadistic, while John Carpenter revels in the masochistic. Clover's knowledge of myth and folk tale, however, allows for interdisciplinary textual comparison between, for example, the Final Girl and the female avenger in Greek myth and Germanic legend. Another example of the Final Girl scenario is *Thelma and Louise* (1991) which Clover calls a "very safe movie" (235), in comparison to a film such as *I Spit on Your Grave.*

In *Men, Women, and Chain Saws,* Carol Clover builds upon studies such as Kaja Silverman's *The Acoustic Mirror* (1988), Mary Ann Doane's *The Desire To Desire* (1987), Judith Butler's *Gender Trouble* (1990) and Gilles Deleuze's *Masochism, Coldness and Cruelty* (1989), among many critical sources. But Clover's deft analysis of the Final Girl, gender flexibility in spectatorship models, and the importance of masochistic pleasure in the horror movie audience revises much simplistic thinking about horror movies. Clover argues persuasively for an opening of canon-driven scholarship to the "low" genres of slasher, possession, and rape-revenge film. Clover's conclusions about male sadomasochistic pleasures argue against censorship advocates, who oversimplify the mechanics of gendered spectatorship models.

## THE CORRUPT JUNGLE

Rape-revenge films share with jungle films the ability to construct forms of Whiteness. Existing in an all-White jungle of monstrous fantasies, films such as *Halloween, I Spit on Your Grave,* and the now popular and increasingly numerous grisly White serial rapist/killer films (such as *Kalifornia, Henry, Portrait of a Serial Killer,* and too many other films to name) call attention to Whiteness and White power. Annalee Newitz in her essay "White Savagery and Humiliation" asserts that such films as *Kalifornia, Natural Born Killers,* and *Cape Fear racialize Whiteness.* Newitz writes:

> Clearly civilized Whiteness is middle and upper-class Whiteness, which does not bear the degrading mark of race after being sloughed off a low class White other who is both criminally violent and the embodiment of judicial corruption. Whites who are not "trash" here seem innocent of racially marked Whiteness and its attendant brutality. (138)

The depiction of White on White violence, often located in Southern states, conjures up a reinvocation of the primal scene of the Plantocracy. It is no longer the threat of Black male rapist against White women, as articulated most notoriously by D. W. Griffith in *Birth of a Nation* (1915). Instead, through resynthesis and representational contiguity, the White racialized male becomes the threatening menace who threatens the White civilized classed male, he who is in turn racialized as the Whiter male. This phenomena suggests a resurgence of the attempt to resexualize and reenergize White supremacy as the unachievable phallus of the White race.

As it becomes increasingly noticeable and problematic to code Black men as monstrous sex criminals, recent films mark White trash males as the embodiment of the feared Dark Continent. Narratives of captivity and threat are increasingly White on White. What is behind the current popularity of serial killer films? Why do predominantly White audiences find the reinscription of White supremacy in the performatives of tropes of the serial murderer so funny? Are Whites attempting to sexualize and remark Whiteness at the expense of those who are economically disenfranchised? How can we account for the sudden cultish embrace of Quentin Tarantino, whose *Pulp Fiction* resuscitates White supremacy, homophobia, and misogyny? As bell hooks writes in *Reel to Real:*

> Tarantino's films are the ultimate in sexy cover-ups of very unsexy mind-fuck. They titillate with subversive possibility . . . but then everything kinda comes right back to normal. And normal is finally a multicultural world with White supremacy intact. . . . But it's fine to remain silent when the cool straight White boy from the wrong side of the tracks offers a movie that depicts the brutal slaughter

and/or bashing of butt-fuckers and their playmates. If this isn't symbolic genocide of gay men what is? Yet everyone has to pretend there's some hidden subversive message in the scenes. Hello! But that's the Tarantino message: everybody is in the corrupt jungle doing their own sweet version of the domination dance. (48–49)

I'd suggest that serial murder films and Tarantino-esque films mark a deliberate stance against conscriptions of cultural norms of male Whiteness, which date back to the sexless "Imperial Man" of the British Colonial cinema, in such films as *Sanders of the River* (1935). Kenneth Cameron writes that the Imperial Man differed from the American jungle explorer in that he "had no sex. He was socially of the privileged class (or, so his accent told us). His manner was sophisticated and urbane" (66). The Imperial Man originates in the writing of Edgar Wallace, a hugely popular writer (both in England and America) of novels such as *Sanders of the River* (1911), and in the earlier popular novels of Henry Rider Haggard, such as *Allan Quatermain* (1887) and *King Solomon's Mines* (1885), all of which were made (and remade) into successful films that were to leave a distinctive mark on the popular imagination of both British and American audiences. As captives and captors of the British Empire, Imperial Men had far more important conquests (and plunders) to engage themselves with than the opposite sex. Abstinence was equated with Colonial White power. As Cameron writes:

> One effect of the imperial films, then, was to suggest that imperial men do not have sexual selves—that they are eunuchs of empire. Indeed, so severe is their sexism that the *absence* of women can be taken as an identifying mark of the imperial film . . . the view of imperial civil servant and soldier sees manhood as merely a projection of boyhood, the man all the better imperialist for preserving the boy's naivete, racial prejudice, and misogyny. (74)

A typical example of the Imperial genre, *Sanders of the River* starred Leslie Banks as Sanders, a busy British district commissioner whose job is to govern Africans under British rule. *Sanders* is also of interest in that it depicts the stereotypically Colonialist overdetermined image of an African couple, Bosambo (played by Paul Robeson) and his wife (played by Nina Mae McKinney). Amazingly enough, *Sanders's* author, Edgar Wallace, had originally considered using Charles Laughton in Blackface in the role

FIGURE 9. Paul Robeson and Nina Mae McKinney in *Sanders of the River*; the fetish display of British Colonialism. Courtesy Jerry Ohlinger Archives.

of Bosambo. Laughton understandably declined the role, despite the actor's past association with Wallace in the author's stage production of *On the Spot*, in which Laughton played an Italian gangster under Wallace's direction. Robeson, finally cast as Bosambo, was appalled by the result, and walked out during the premiere in disgust (Cameron, 65). The plot of *Sanders* revolves around a false economy of racial politics, inverting and exploiting the rape and capture of African bodies in a ghastly plot contrivance that finds Sanders *saving* Bosambo. Bosambo is, in turn, an embodiment of the good Black as it is constructed against Sanders's Whiteness. The Imperial Man is thus the penultimate businesslike White Hunter of Haggard's *King Solomon's Mines* (1937) and *Allan Quatermain and the Lost City of Gold* (1919).

## VISIONS OF OBLIVION

If Edgar Wallace's Imperial Man represented the abstinent, hard-working Colonial worker, Haggard's Imperial Man connotes the Great White Hunter, the mythologization of the plunderer who is resuscitated in films such as the Indiana Jones series, *The Lost World* (1997), *The English Patient* (1996), and countless earlier films such as *The Most Dangerous Game* (1932), *Hell's Headquarters* (1932), *The Lost Jungle* (1934), *Rhodes of Africa* (1936), *Queen of the Amazons* (1946), *Blonde Savage* (1947), *Forbidden Jungle* (1950), *Perils of the Jungle* (1951), *Wild Women* (1953), *Walk into Hell* (1957), *Liane, Jungle Goddess* (1956), and many others, not to mention the many incarnations of *Tarzan* and more recently *Congo* (1995). *Congo* has the distinction of introducing Ernie Hudson as the first Black version of the "Great White Hunter" with the deftly delivered line, "Well, *I'm* your Great White Hunter, but today I just happen to be Black."

These largely all-male expeditions usually encounter White women in specific tropes: as doctors, daughters, goddesses, or waiting women. White Jungle Goddesses often encounter their "first" White men in the jungle, in much the same manner that White Amazonian rulers of sci-fi films (often jungles in space) meet their Imperial mate as in films such as *Queen of Outer Space* (1958), *The Lost Continent* (1951), *Cat Women of the Moon* (1953), *Prehistoric Women* (1950), and *When Women Had Tails* (1970). Serials almost always featured some components of the fantasy of the Imperial Male and the White Jungle Goddess.

FIGURE 10. Frances Gifford as *Jungle Girl*: White Queen of An Imaginary Colonial Domain. Courtesy Jerry Ohlinger Archives.

In the fifteen-part serial film *Jungle Girl* (1941), the film's plot hinges on the threat of a replaced Imperialist Father, Dr. Meredith. Nyoka, played by Frances Gifford, is the daughter of Dr. Meredith, but unbeknownst to Nyoka, the real Dr. Meredith has been replaced by his evil twin brother. The American jungle films of the forties often demonstrate a distrust of the British Imperial Man and his plundering of the jungle; the evil Imperial doppelganger in *Jungle Girl*, for example, is interested only in stealing diamonds. *Manhunt of Mystery Island*, a Republic serial of 1945, suggests a literal and figurative reimaging of the Imperial Man. The "man hunt" of Mystery Island is a veritable hunt for authenticity of Colonialist imperative and practice, not to mention a displacement of the primacy of the Imperial Man. Dr. Forrest is the inventor of a transmitter of atomic power who disappears on Mystery Island, a tropical paradise ruled by the evil Dr. Mephisto and his minions. Dr. Forrest's daughter, Claire, played by Linda Stirling, searches for him for most of the serial's 265-minute running time. The daughter's often imperiled search for the lost father, almost always a well-meaning philanthropic man of science, constitutes another pronounced fissure in the representation of the Imperial Man, whose power is increasingly threatened by science, capitalism, world wars, and social change.

One intriguing aspect of *Manhunt of Mystery Island* is the introduction of a "Transformation Chair," which allows the dark-clad, evil figure of Captain Mephisto to change his molecular structure (and hide in the body of another person) in order to evade Clair and Dr. Forrest. The Transformation Chair suggests most strongly to me a fear and fantasy of the increasingly mutable lines of gender, class, race, and sexualities as they were reflected and coproduced in American society and popular culture. Forties serials constitute and perpetuate fantasies of Colonial conquest, but such fantasies increasingly depend upon transmutational machines and obliging cyborgs: men need more strength and cunning than nature provides.

The Purple Monster, for example (in the 1945 Republic Serial *The Purple Monster Strikes*), crash lands on Earth while leading the vanguard of an invasion from Mars. To effect this, the Purple Monster needs to enslave the body of an unwilling scientist and impersonate him. Further, to make his rocketship a success, he is dependent upon locating a special rocket fuel and an "electroannihilator beam" (which destroys anything in its path). For most of the serial's duration, an archetypal serial hero continually thwarts the Purple Monster's plans. If the Imperial British colonizer was hard working and nonsexual, the Americanized Imperial Serial Hero is ground down by endless and increasingly difficult tasks. His world is not all-male. He almost always shares his workload with his trusted female companion, usually the daughter of the man of science. This relationship reflected the contemporaneous realities of the American workplace, but I would argue that the serial films of the forties locate a radical refashioning of the boy's stories hero, who is no longer simply the Imperial Great White Hunter but now a fearless protector against Nazi invasion and the rise of atomic power. *Lost City of the Jungle* (1946), set at the end of World War II, directly addresses the moral decay of the Great White Hunter. Sir Eric Hazarius, played by Lionel Atwill, greedily plans to rule the world by searching for "Meteorum 245," an atomic substance capable of destroying atomic bombs. In the course of his criminal endeavors, he accidentally starts World War III by releasing the substance, which remains in a chest deep in yet another Lost City.

Another Imperialist Man turned evil rears his head as Dr. Vulcan in *King of the Rocket Men* (1949), in which the Rocket Man reconstructs American masculinity by intercepting Dr. Vulcan's "decimator," with which Vulcan plans to destroy New York City, by causing an earthquake and tidal wave. Rocket Man's costume suggests a body captive in Whiteness and bound in male subjectivity. The body of the Rocket Man, enslaved by a legacy of Colonial conquest, is an acute example of the fetishized Imperial Male. His sadomasochistic imagery bespeaks the manner in which "the cult of gender" (40), as Kate Bornstein terms it, perpetuates and reinvents itself. Rocket Man is unquestionably fashioned as a homo/erotic "bottom," which makes sense when we take into account the increasing demands placed upon the serial hero. Thus, Rocket Man marks a return to the order of the Imperial Man who was equally burdened by the tasks of Colonial conquest. The Imperial Man is, after all, a Bottom. Responsible for others, obedient, and faithful, he carries out orders without question. He is the butch femme who can be counted upon, and who, in turn, counts upon the primacy of the top, the legacy of Colonial conquest.

White Jungle Goddesses tend to move back and forth in the continuum of sado-masochistic polarities. Often, they play the "bottom" femme role. Tied to stakes, threatened by "savages," dangling from cliffs, and bound in roles of submission, White Jungle Goddesses evoke a spectacle that invites mastery of the female body. However, the White Jungle Goddess is *largely* invoked to inscribe the White female Imperialist as a

FIGURE 11. The ultimate "bottom": the eponymous hero of *King of the Rocket Men*. Courtesy Jerry Ohlinger Archives.

figure of mastery, a "top" who embodies White female supremacy. For example, in the serial *Jungle Girl,* Frances Gifford as Nyoka rules over the African jungle and its peoples. She swings through the trees and communicates with animals. She has a special jungle "call," and she parades across the screen on the back of an elephant. Her White female supremacy is maintained by her ownership of an amulet that allows her to rule a constructed "Aboriginal" tribe of people, who are dependent upon her as a "civilizer" and a Colonizer. She is not unlike Ayesha, or She Who Must Be Obeyed, in various incarnations from *She* to *Xena, Warrior Princess.* The process is not, therefore, confined to the domain of the masculine, but moves equally across both feminine and masculine White Colonial discourse.

# CHAPTER TWO

## ❧

# A Plantocracy of Images

The moving-picture industry evolved from, and perpetuated, the ideologies and many of the practices of the Plantation. A quick glance at the early maps and layouts of the first studios demonstrates a striking resemblance to the antebellum South. The studios, like the Plantocracies before them, were closed systems ruled by overseers. The primary objective in both camps is profit. A description of the slave camp shows remarkably similar patterns of labor management. As John Blassingame writes:

> In order to obtain the maximum labor at the cheapest cost the planter had to construct healthy cabins, provide adequate wholesome food and proper clothing, permit recreation and provide medical attention for his slaves. If the slaves adhered to certain moral precepts, rested during the hottest part of the day, spent all their time on the plantation, marched to the fields, ate, and went to bed at the sound of bugles or bells, and were kept under proper subjection, they would be healthy and industrious. (144–45)

The insularity of these systems, coupled with many other attributes, suggests a compelling reason for an analysis of Hollywood through the lens and the language of the Plantocracy, from its roots in the commodification of the body to its perpetration of the narratives and power/knowledge systems of hierarchy in terms of race, class, gender, and sexualities.

From the outset, I wish to emphasize that in *no* way do I suggest that the lived experiences of slaves under subjugation in the realities of Plantation America are in any sense comparable with Hollywood workers. There are clear-cut differences in exploitative labor practices and actual slavery. Barbara Crossette, in *The New York Times*, in an article on the modern abuse of the term *slavery*, cites Mike Dottridge, the director of the Anti-Slavery society: "Slavery is identified by an element of ownership or control over another's life, coercion and the restriction of movement—by the fact that 'someone is not free to leave, change an employer'" (1).

While the bondage of slavery is dependent upon *literally* captive bodies, I suggest the Hollywood Plantocracy is dependent upon *theoretically* captive bodies and I want to strongly emphasize that difference. Nevertheless, as cultural critics, are we not morally obligated at some level to speak the unspeakable, to deconstruct parallel systems of imperialism through their own languages and practices? Or, in the words of Edward Said, are we, as cultural critics not only bound to questioning "politics as given, but [also] to show how all representations are constructed, for what purpose, by whom, and with what compliments" (1993, 314)? In attempting to contain all discussion of slavery and Plantocratic method within the boundaries of purely historically discursive methodologies and projects, are we not once again erasing difference, and furthering the project of American racism, which is, to a large degree perpetuated by silencing discussion of its own past? I think, instead, we should actively seek out the history of the construction of Whiteness in the spirit of the work of Toni Morrison, who, in *Playing in the Dark: Whiteness and the Literary Imagination*, demonstrates that there is an African American cultural presence in all American literatures and cultures, even, and most importantly, in its absence.

Absence can only be maintained by acts of erasure and silencing, and it is imperative that we move against critical silencing as much as we move toward the embrasure of transformative processes of listening to language, especially language that we find uncomfortable or unspeakable. Above all, we must resist the urge to contain language. "Containment," as Jonathan Dollimore writes, "destroys difference through a coerced conformity masquerading as voluntary submission" (94). Difference is shared, thus the responsibility to speak of differences, no matter the consequences, is also imperative. "The intellectual's solution is not to abstain from representation," writes Gayatri Spivak (1988, 285). To do so fails to examine "what makes intellectual domination possible, how knowledge is transformed from invasion to conquest to revelation and choice; what ignites and informs the literary imagination, and what forces help establish the parameters of criticism" (Morrison, 8). In most studies of early Hollywood and its practices, the parameters of criticism have not included a comparison with the Plantocratic methods, language, and ideologies, with the exception of Mark Reid's recent study of the subject (1992).

We can begin with the issue of naming. The Hollywood Plantocrats realized that in order to sublimate a star, one must rename her/him. As the slaves were renamed, so the earliest "stars" became *metaphorically* property of the producers. In the beginnings of the star system, Florence Lawrence, for example, became "The Biograph Girl," effectively having her identity absorbed and held captive by the publicity campaign which at once erased her, and simultaneously catapulted her into a new, phantom identity. In the same way that Lawrence became "The Biograph Girl," most early performers were not known by their real names, but instead by the characters they played. Thus, the rise of the star system was dependent upon the Plantocratic methods of erasure and renaming. Even as late as the nineteen forties, the studios insisted upon image ownership. As Danae Clark observes in *Negotiating Hollywood,* contractual obligations meant that "The studios' power of creation and naming assured them economic and ideological, if not legal, ownership over the actor's body. . . . An actor's signature meanwhile permitted his or her 'image' to become the legal property of the studio" (23).

In the exploitation of captive bodies, whether in the slave system of actuality, or in the Hollywood system that came to resemble it in so many ways, it was important to the overseers that the workers should not be made to feel enslaved, or, as Tony Bennett states (cited by Clark), "They must be induced to 'live' their exploitation and oppression in such a way that they do not experience or represent to themselves their position as one in which they are exploited" (21). Similarly, the plantation ideology was dependent upon the insistent and consistent perpetuation of the stereotype of the happy benevolent slave, a stereotype that still persists albeit in a transformed state, in Plantocratic images of Blackness on the silver screen.

## THE HOLLYWOOD PLANTOCRACY

The movie industry has always been a Plantocracy, from the early days of Edison's New Jersey studio, "The Black Maria," where Edison pressed his workers into appearing in his early films without extra compensation, to Edison's later assembly-line studios in the Bronx, which were opened in 1907. Thomas Ince's eponymous studio city, Inceville, sprawled over numerous acres in the Santa Ynez Canyon of California, constructed by Ince in 1912 as a gigantic studio "plantation" where workers would sleep, eat, and grind out Ince's preplanned films from the producer's meticulously detailed storyboards, from which Ince would permit no deviation upon pain of termination of employment. This stands in direct contrast to the atmosphere encouraged by Alice Guy in her Solax Studios in Fort Lee, New Jersey, in the first years of the twentieth century, where her actors were encouraged to "ad lib," and a large sign which hung over the principal staging area encouraged all of her performers to "BE NATURAL." At the other end of the spectrum, in the early 1930s, at the peak (or depth) of the Depression, producer Nat Levine of Mascot Studios would work his employees for twenty, thirty, even forty hours at a clip, fueled by coffee and cheap food, until they were allowed to collapse in a huge dormitory filled with surplus World War I Army cots for a few hours rest, before being revived, zombielike, to renew their labors.

None of these studio workers were "slaves" in the proper sense of the word; if they were not happy in their work, they could, in theory, go elsewhere. And when film production was spread out between New York, New Jersey, and California in the first years of the cinema's existence, such lateral moves were possible. Then, too, early filmmaking (particularly one-reel subjects) were relatively inexpensive to make: Edison's 1903 *The Great Train Robbery* cost less than $400. But as filmmaking became centralized in Hollywood in the early teens, labor mobility became less of a practical option. If one wanted to work within the industry, one *had* to work in Hollywood, and the studio owners, like plantation owners, kept track of those workers who were dependable, and those who caused strikes, walkouts, and labor disputes. If you wanted a job in Hollywood, you had to play by the master's rules.

Thus, although superficial freedom was allowed to early workers (on both sides of the camera) in the cinema, a closer inspection of their actual status reveals stars and grips alike as captive bodies; captive within storyboards, publicity layouts, clichéd roles, racial and sexual stereotypes, and above all studio contracts. Until the De Havilland decision in 1948, these contracts amounted to perpetual indentured servitude for performers in films, who could be fired at the studio's pleasure, or put on suspension without pay for refusing to appear in films they felt were unsuitable. But the studios retained the right to add those suspensions on to the term of their original seven-year obligation, thus resulting in a contract that could literally be without end.

Yet the film industry, like the Plantocracy, was subject to self-scrutiny and resistance. As Danae Clark recounts, for example, "by 1935 the Screen Actors Guild was so distressed by the treatment of extras that it ran a feature in its magazine titled Are Extras People?" Hollywood legend is rife with examples of its brutality toward human (and animal) subjects, all in the service of profitability. During the shoot of *Riffraff*, as recounted in Clark, a group of extras worked twelve hours at a clip, and in one case were subjected to particularly harsh and cruel wind and rain machines, so strong that

> a number of women were forcibly knocked down and bruised in each take. One woman was knocked unconscious while another, who took the full force of the stream of water on her back, was paralyzed from her hips down for several hours. Four women were temporarily blinded when the water hit them full force in the eyes. (Clark, 115)

Such incidences were usually hushed up, because, as the Plantocrat relied on obedience and silence, so too did the Hollywood Plantocrats' attempt to have complete control over the representation of Hollywood and its supposedly happy "colonies" of happy workers. The reality was a different story. As Harry Fraser, a serial director who worked briefly for Nat Levine of Mascot Pictures, noted:

> Nat Levine [. . .] was the real Simon Legree without a whip. I recall doing a Rin-Tin-Tin serial for him [ *The Wolf Dog* (1933)]. I had an *eighty* [my emphasis] scene schedule one day, with the dog as the star [. . .] in addition to [D. W. Griffith regular] Henry B. Walthal [and] a long list of supporting actors [. . .]. Well, I came out with seventy scenes at the end of the day, but pushing everyone to the limit [. . .] when the Serial King [Levine] heard I was behind schedule by ten scenes, he practically accused me of causing the company to go bankrupt. (Dixon and Fraser, 102)

As this example demonstrates, the studio system was dependent upon the fact that the laborers were made to identify with the interests of the studios. In the same way, as John Blassingame explains, in the case of the slave system:

> This was the kind of slave the master *wanted*: a laborer who identified so closely with his master's interests that he would repair a bro-

ken fence rail without being ordered to do so. Systematic labor, implicit obedience, and unconditional submission (as child to parent or soldier to general) was expected of slaves. (148)

But like slaves, movie workers were often quite capable of seeing through the charade of the happy Plantocracy, and many directors, stars, and extras have spoken of the ways they resisted being made into captive bodies, often through the simple device of working for "runaway studios," acting in the African American tradition of Nat, the runaway rebel. Just as African/American literature and oral culture celebrates Nat for his bravery, and resistance, so too does the lore of Hollywood embrace mythic runaway directors such as Orson Welles and Erich Von Stroheim. Another stereotypical "type" of slave character that is reinscribed in the legends of Hollywood is the "Jack" type, who avoided the producers, was deferential in his presence, yet, like the slaves described by Blassingame, "could not always keep up the facade of deference" (133). Edwin S. Porter could be construed as a "Jack" type of director, an early prototype for many who would follow him. Porter embraced artistic integrity at the expense of his life work. As Charles Musser asserts, Porter was not willing to abide by the rules of his employer, Edison Films, whose rate of production was increasingly dependent on the needs of the changing distribution system. By 1908, "the whole approach to filmmaking shifted . . . [previously] distribution was determined by the production schedule" (391), but suddenly the producers were obligated to the licensors, obligated to produce product at a furious pace. Porter was unhappy with the frantic pace with which he was expected to turn out films, and like the archetypical "Jack" of Southern literature and African American oral culture, Porter seems to have attempted to mask his true feelings and "judiciously stayed away from the Bronx studio" (Musser, 453), eventually only to be fired because his "methods of production and representation were at odds with developments both at Edison and in the industry as a whole" (458). Porter found work in the runaway independent studios, knowing full well that the larger studios, like the Southern Plantations, had agreements between one another to not aid, hire, or help the "Nat" type of runaway.

The Edison studios, like the later studio built by Thomas Ince, were built on models of containment and control of disciplined bodies. Edison built his new Bronx studio in 1907, and emphasized that every bit of architectural planning was devoted to environmental and bodily control.

The imperialist notions and preoccupations of such a venture are clearly evident in a studio document reprinted by Charles Musser in *Before the Nickelodeon*, which notes that the building stands "like a rockhewn temple" (386). Here "every convenience and necessity is provided, except, indeed, easy chairs, for there is no lounging whatever in the Edison studio" (387). The building also has certain elements of Jeremy Bentham's panopticon in its construction, as offices and studios were constructed with few obstructions, the better to aid Edison's surveillance of his employees. Indeed, Edison was primarily preoccupied with discipline and Foucaultian order in all his business dealings.

Thomas Ince was to emulate Edison with his building of "Inceville" in 1912. David Cook asserts that Inceville was the "first recognizably modern Hollywood studio" (208), where Ince himself had complete control over each production in a system very much like a celluloid plantation. Directors who worked under Ince were much like plantation "overseers" or slavedrivers, who were discouraged from having any artistic input in their films. All the projects were carefully storyboarded, much in the style of Alfred Hitchcock, and then executed exactly according to plan by Ince's "directors." Nevertheless, many of the directors who began at Ince's factory, including Frank Borzage and Fred Niblo, were able to develop their own styles later on in their careers. The grinding labor was a good training ground, if nothing else. Working on serials, particularly, directors were faced with nearly impossible production schedules. One director described the script for a serial he had been hired to direct as "looking like the Manhattan and Los Angeles telephone directories tied together" (Dixon and Fraser, 113). Schedules for an average silent Western "B" feature could run as little as two days; even as late as the 1940s, companies such as PRC and Republic could complete an entire feature on budgets as low as $12,000 in four to five days, but only by exploiting their workers, both behind and in front of the camera, to the limits of their endurance.

Another parallel that exists between the studio system and the slave system is the introduction of enforced morality. Just as planters and overseers enforced Christian moral virtues upon their subjects, so did Hollywood attempt to regulate morality, particularly sexual morality, in the closed systems of the Hollywood Plantocracies. Whenever the Americans read of the "scandalous" behavior of Hollywood subjects, the studios responded by attempting to regulate behavior, through legal sanctions and motion picture codes that suppressed sexuality. The studio heads would, for example, commonly publish pieces in the trades that blamed the star system for the decay of morals, such as "The Price They Pay for Fame," published in *Silver Screen* (Clark, 76). Another manner in which studio Plantocrats maintained control was to fabricate lies, convenient marriages, love affairs, feuds, and the like, and then publicize them in their own trade newspapers and newsreels. But the Plantocracies could not sublimate acts of resistance entirely. Solidarity brought workers together, and led to changes in the system through unionization. The workers at the Disney studios, for example, blew off steam through disruptive humor when animators secretly drew a pornographic Mickey Mouse cartoon in direct response to Walt Disney's Plantocratic disciplinary harshness. When the finished cartoon was screened for Disney at a company dinner, he immediately fired those responsible and suppressed the negative (Eliot, 90). Yet the disciplined bodies of the studio systems could not be under constant surveillance and stars and directors were quite capable of playing the role of subordinate. Being so fully immersed in the capture of performed roles, they were always reminded that everyday performance is a fabrication and construct.

## THE CONSTRUCTION OF WHITENESS

The Hollywood Plantocracy was not only patterned after the slave system, but it also acted as an ethnographer of its own domain. As Ana López astutely terms it, the film producers were really "socioculturally bound ethnographers" (404), and thus "co-producers of cultural texts" (405). These texts include the birth of Whiteness, the cult of gender, definitions of class and ethnicity, narratives of allowable sexual representation, and the renarration of the experience of African (American)ness in American history. In doing so, the American cinema created a generic "sameness" of narrative structure, characterized by Jean-François Lyotard as "the paradox of immobilization" (357), in which narratives, spectators, and directors all seem trapped in immobility. This immobilization is coupled with its own palimpsest of movement and resistances, but one is still struck by the homogeneity of Hollywood product as it developed into an industry in the early 1900s. Lyotard writes in the cinema, for example, "all endings are happy endings, just by being endings" (353). As Zavardezeh emphasizes that reading what is *not* onscreen is just as important as what is allowed onscreen, so too does Lyotard see film directing as an ecclesiastic occupation, one that entails "a technique of exclusions and effacements" (355). One must keep these ideas in mind when we reexamine narratives, renarrations, and denarrations in the ethnographies of Hollywood's dream factory.

The Baudrillardinian powers of seduction implicit in film narrative are powerful enough to seemingly "naturalize" orders and regimes, and film audiences serve as coproducers of these seductive images, instead of being subjectified captive bodies. Far from being zombified captives, cinema audiences share responsibility with Plantocratic producers for the categorical definitions of cultures that have created the American cinematic landscape of phantasmal desire. Though D. W. Griffith may be the cinematographic father of racism (and gendered White supremacy) in American cinema, we should remember that it was audiences and critics that made his cultural ethnographic practices possible. Griffith has not popularized his racist and sexist ideologies without dependency upon a culture willing to accept (and coproduce) such images and narratives. The violence and repugnance of the narratives of the pro-Klan *Birth of a Nation* (1915) and the racially "Othering" *Broken Blossoms* (1919) were not aberrations, as one might be misled into thinking in looking through film history. Daniel Bernardi notes that Griffith's early works were deeply involved in the construction of Whiteness, race, ethnicity, and gender roles.

Such Griffith films as *The Chink of Golden Gulch* (1910), *A Romance of the Western Hills* (1910), *The Call of the Wild* (1908), *The Zulu's Heart* (1908), and *The Girls and Daddy* (1909) reinscribe the racist imagery begun in the much earlier films *Watermelon Patch* (Edwin S. Porter, 1905) and *Nigger in the Woodpile* (Biograph, 1904), which construct "Whiteness" in opposition to "Blackness," with all that is "White" being artificially and synthetically elevated, and "Blackness" aligned solely with a series of negative and/or childlike characteristics. This inscription and reinscription models the KKK as both a "paternal" order and an agency of social and cultural enforcement. The cultural "work" of articulating White supremacy depended on inclusions and exclusions, narrations and denarrations, but this Colonialist project was not possible without public approval and cooperation. Refreshingly, Bernardi insists that "Griffith's articulation of style and race are involved in the same cinematic and discursive processes [as his other stylistic innovations]; pragmatically, they constitute the filmmaker's narrative system" (104). In other words, we should not set up Griffith's legacy as a binary that suggests that Griffith's development of parallel editing and narrative storytelling (in such films as *The Lonedale Operator* [1911], *A Corner in Wheat* [1909], and *The Musketeers of Big Alley* [1912]) have nothing to do with his abilities to script "Whiteness" as the desired normative state, and "non-Whiteness" as that which is "Other." Whiteness, as coproduced by Griffith, other producers and directors, and audiences, is present both onscreen and off, but is always dependent upon Blackness and non-Whiteness for its mirroring and Othering process.

African American pioneer filmmaker Oscar Micheaux was to turn the trope of the captor against itself with his prolific output of films for Black audiences. *The Symbol of the Unconquered* (1920), Micheaux's attack on the Ku Klux Klan, typified his skill at using the master's tools against narratives that perpetuated racist American ideologies. Pearl Bowser and Louise Spence note that Micheaux often ignored or undermined the authority of censor boards by "showing a film without submitting it [to various censorship boards] for a license or [subsequently to audiences] without eliminating offensive passages" (57). In fact, Micheaux used censorship and fears of "miscegenation" to lure audiences to his films. With regard to the publicity around his film *The Homesteader* (1919), Micheaux wrote, "Nothing would make more people anxious to see a picture than a litho reading: SHALL RACES INTERMARRY?" (Bowser and Spence, 61).

Micheaux thus traded in inversions of stasis, fracturing and hybridizing a commonly held Colonial space of fear and fantasy. In mimesis and repetition of the fear/fantasy, Micheaux codes its myth as fallacious, or as Homi K. Bhabha states, in *The Location of Culture*:

> Despite appearances, the text of transparency inscribes a double vision: The field of the "true" emerges as a visible sign of authority only after the regulatory and displacing division of the true and the false. . . . Such a bringing to light is a question of the provision of visibility as a capacity, a strategy, an agency. (110)

*The Symbol of the Unconquered* should perhaps also be known as "The Signifier of the Unconquered," for Micheaux was an able code-switcher in the narratives of publicity for his own films. He announced the film's premiere with such tag lines as "SEE THE KU KLUX KLAN IN ACTION AND THEIR ANNIHILATION," and "SEE THE MURDEROUS RIDE OF THE INSIDIOUS KU KLUX KLAN in their effort to drive a BLACK BOY off Valuable Oil Lands—and the wonderful heroism of a traveler to save him" (Bowser and Spence, 62).

As Richard Dyer notes in his study of Whiteness, White people are hard to identify, and Whiteness needs to be "kept up" as a category or it risks failure. The invisibility of Whiteness "secures White power by making it hard, especially for White people and their media, to 'see' Whiteness" (1988b, 46), but, as Annalee Newitz comments, it is equally important to remember that White Supremacy is "the 'phallus' of the White race. It is an ideal which cannot even be achieved in a total sense" (146). Elusive and unachievable as it is, it is also by definition highly eroticized and fetishized. Like the captive zones or "dark bodies" of the "dark continent," the cinematic machine and its captive bodies quest for the White body, the heterotopic, gendered, and classed Whiteness that is like the orgasm that cannot be achieved.

To inculcate Whiteness, the Plantocrat director called upon the theme of "morally uplifting" the races. One can easily observe the repellent seriality with which Griffith approaches the same subjects (the sanctity of motherhood, the "virgin" woman confronted with threats of violence, the supposed "benevolence" of the patriarchy, the "legitimacy" of racism to uphold Victorian social values), just as the slave owners called upon religious sanctimoniousness and the greater social good while oppressing and martyrizing the "good slave" in the name of Christianity. Bernardi thus breaks down Griffith's output into three genres:

- stories of non-White servitude;
- stories of Colonial love, or turn-of-the century jungle fever; and
- stories of the divinity of the White woman. (112)

"Jungle pictures" such as *East of Borneo* (1931) and *She* (filmed in 1917, 1926, 1935, and 1965) may be viewed as captivity narratives, themselves appropriations of slave narratives. In *She* and *East of Borneo*, for example, the narratives are dependent upon upholding the primacy of the White woman and the White family, and thus Whiteness itself.

## GESTURES OF ABSENCE

One of the most striking elements of jungle pictures is the absence of Black, African, and/or African American women, coupled with another standard presence in jungle pictures: the White woman traveller and/or the White woman ruler of a lost civilization. This arguably constitutes a restaging and renarration of plantation sexual politics in the jungle picture. The absence of Black female sexuality also marks the denial and erasure of the history of Plantocratic sexual subjugation of African (American) women, and restages what Robyn Wiegman terms "slavery's commodified ungendering" (69). The slave woman's "sexual availability" to the master is often reflected in jungle melodramas by light-skinned substitutes, usually mulattos, Native Americans, Latinas, or Mid-Eastern women; women who often serve as sidekicks, potential sexual partners, slaves, or enticing bad girls; light-skinned projections of dark-continent threats of hypersexuality. Black women's sexuality is therefore renarrated through a gaze of Colonial empiricism, and remade to conform to a cinematically enforced zone of constructed "Whiteness."

But what of the racist construction of Black female hypersexuality? I would argue that the same myths of Black female "animality" that were introduced by such Colonialist campaigns as the capture of the Hottentot Venus are restaged in the jungle film. This erasure of Black African women is coupled with the infusion of White women rulers and virgins who are, in turn, suffused with sexuality. How else can we explain the denarration of the Black female body in films that usually take place in Africa or some phantom rerendering of an Othered place known simply as "The Jungle"? Jungle films take place metaphorically within the corpus of a mythic Black female body; they are projections of what Mary Ann Doane terms "the Dark Continent" (see Doane, 209–48), a murky suffusion of Africa, Blackness, and fear of female sexuality.

But anxieties around sexuality in the cinema are not confined to gender issues; instead, they are complicated by issues of Whiteness and masculinity, issues which arose in American Plantocracies and were never resolved, much less overtly addressed. The primary issues I'm addressing here include the myth of the Black male rapist and White fear of interracial sexuality. Ironically, both of these issues arise out of another glaring absence and erasure: that of the White male slave owner who routinely took advantage of the slave woman's sexuality, and the White female Plantocrat who was complicit in this patriarchal abuse of power. The end of slavery marked the beginnings of a wave of lynching, outcries against "miscegenation" (a central preoccupation of D. W. Griffith's), and attempts to resuscitate the eroticism and sexual license of White masculinity through tales of conquest in popular culture. As Robyn Wiegman notes, "the transformation of the image of the Black man from simple, docile Uncle Tom to sex offender characterizes the oppositional logic underwriting the representational structures of Black male images in the nineteenth- and twentieth-century U.S. culture" (96). This oppositional logic involves projection of such Colonial legacies as that of the "Black Beast" and the "White Goddess/adventuress" of popular jungle pictures. In addition, these films are marked by a culturally inscribed obsession with control over bodily fluids such as blood and semen. Fear of the mixture of raced blood is one of the primary reasons for the popularity of jungle pictures and the books upon which they were originally based.

## SHE WHO MUST BE OBEYED

The various film versions of *She*, from the H. Rider Haggard novel of 1887, for example, use oppositional logic to reverse the power structures of the Colonial Plantocracy. Here, White male adventures are at the mercy of "savage" Black male "beasts" who rule the jungle, but at the top of the inverted hierarchy reigns the "Aryan" White goddess "She, who must be obeyed." This twisted renarration of the Colonial legacy at once resuscitates the imperialist fantasies of conquest and capture of African bodies and African land, but at the same time works to reinscribe the Black male as slave to the hypersexualized White woman. The narrative of *She* involves a rapacious sexual predator who has been made immortal by bathing in a "Flame of Eternal Life," a mysterious chamber of fire, into which "She" steps. *She* thus invokes the sexual vampire discussed by Bram Dijkstra. Fear and fascination with the hypersexual White jungle goddess was also informed by the rise of theories of spermatology. Spermatology, the then popular belief in the transformative effects of ingesting semen, is another example of oppositional logic that stems from the postemancipation "literal and symbolic loss of the security of White patronym and an attendant displacement of the White male" (Wiegman, 92). Serge Voronoff and Havelock Ellis were among a number of scientists, gynecologists, and sociologists who recommended the practice of semenology, a phenomenon began at the turn of the century and was still being popularized in the 1930s. As Dijkstra recounts, Marie Stopes, ironically a champion of women's sexuality, was a proponent for semenology:

Marie Stopes, in the revised edition of her *Married Love* (1931), cited the sources Ellis had used to arrive at her conclusion that "it

FIGURE 12. Ursula Andress in the 1965 British production of *She*; hypersexualized images of British White Colonialist Imperial splendor. Courtesy Jerry Ohlinger Archives.

can confidently be stated that women do absorb and benefit from some ingredients of the masculine ejaculate." . . . To maintain their physical and mental health, women should not attempt to deprive themselves of "the seminal and prostatic secretions which they ought to have, and crave for unconsciously." (203)

Semen ingestion was also prescribed to "cure" female nymphomania and lesbian "perversion."

In resuscitating the Colonialist White male body as a source of bodily fluids associated with such transformative life-giving properties, these theories emphasized White women's sexual dependence upon men. These men, in turn, were increasingly threatened by the rise of the New Woman in popular culture, and jungle pictures of the 1930s reflect and coproduce these fears and fantasies. What better place to stage a comeback of the patriarchy than the Dark Continent itself, where the phantom Plantocrat, in the guise of Randolph Scott and Nigel Bruce, can metaphorically conquer both the Black Beast and the New Woman/Sexual Vampire? *She* represents the discipline and punishment of Black and female sexuality as much as it repatriarchalizes the White male body. All film versions of *She* involve the ritualized punishment of Black men; "Ayesha" orders them to be thrown into a fiery pit to their deaths, effectively invoking White female supremacy, and reinscribing memories of White women's complicity in the lynching of Black men falsely accused of raping White women. But each film version always ends with the self-punishment of "She," who dies because of her own "unnatural," "primitive," unlicensed hypersexuality. Ayesha steps one too many times into the Eternal Flame (metaphorically ingesting one too many prescriptions of semen) and dies as a consequence of her lust for power, youth, and eroticism. The 1965 version of *She*, in light of the "sexual revolution," seems particularly obsessed with punishing and disciplining sexuality and interracial bonding.

In the 1965 version of *She*, Ursula Andress as Ayesha murders her mulatto slavegirl Ustane (played by Rosenda Monteros) for becoming involved with her love interest (and the reincarnation of her lost love) Leo Vincey (played by John Richardson). When there is a slave rebellion, Ayesha gives the order to execute scores of African slaves, who are thrown into a pit of molten lava with such savage cruelty that the scene still evokes gasps from contemporary audiences, who are not traditionally affected by violence that doesn't involve the level of graphic sadism featured in films such as *Se7en, Kalifornia, Pulp Fiction,* and the seemingly endless number of current films that feature serial killers and graphic murders.

Probably the reason the scene from *She* surprises and outrages contemporary audiences is that they tend to believe in the myths of the sixties, which hold that racial and sexual equality were fully achieved during that period. A film like *She* brings the audience into a confrontation with her/his own scrutiny of the mythic legacy of equal opportunity and equal rights. *She* brings into sharp relief the remnants of Colonialism as nostalgia, inherent during the twilight of the empire, as British film companies desperately tried to repeat, or recreate, past visions of Imperial glory. Indeed, James Bernard's haunting score for the film is practically an elegy for Britain's slavemaster history, and despite the ghastly racism and empiric inequality presented by the film, *She*'s director, Robert Day, brings little self-reflexivity to the project. The result is a mixture of appalling self-assurance and arrogance which at once seduces and simultaneously repels the viewer.

*East of Borneo* (1931) features a "New Woman," Linda Randolph (played by Rose Hobart), who travels independently into the jungle to find and save her physician husband, Dr. Allan Clark (played by Charles Bickford), who has become a hopelessly cynical alcoholic in the palace of Prince Hashim (Georges Renavent). Directed by George Melford, *East of Borneo* champions the New Woman by locating her as an independent, strong-willed woman who is capable of taking on the elements of the Dark Continent to save her man; but from a feminist point of view, the film is certainly problematic. Though Hobart comes to stand for the strong New Woman, her agency is purchased at the expense of those around her, especially a mulatto woman Niela (played by Lupita Tovar, who also appeared in George Melford's Spanish version of *Dracula* [1931]), who has been involved in an interracial relationship with Alan Clark. While the interracial relationship itself is to some degree transgressive, the fact that the narrative ends with Clark leaving his faithful common-law wife Niela to return to Linda Randolph provides yet another exemplification of the cultural discipline of "miscegenation." The economy with which Niela is erased from the narrative is only matched by the inhumanity with which Ayesha treats her mulatto sexual opponent Ustane, whom Ayesha also condemns to be thrown into the pit of fire. Both Niela and Ustane are rapidly dispensed with in these Colonialist narratives; neither of them even get so much as a reaction shot or a musical cue when they are erased from the screen. The absence of African (or African American) Black women, coupled with the marked use and casual disregard for women of color, is thus a hallmark of the Imperialist jungle film.

These films exist primarily to construct *Whiteness*, not Blackness or any other ethnicity, though they do inform constructions of ethnicities which are, in turn, dependent upon the construction and resexualization of Whiteness. It is nevertheless worth noting the manner in which jungle pictures flirt with and even sometimes allow the onscreen representation of interracial sexuality, especially in a precode film such as *East of Borneo*. As Ella Shohat observes, Hollywood cinema observed what amounted to a filmic apartheid when it came to most interethnic (or mixed) love stories: "The possibilities of erotic interaction in films before the 1960s were severely limited by apartheid-style ethnic and racial codes" (233). This proscription was, however, much less rigidly enforced in precode Colonialist fantasies of lost jungle "empires."

## THE MARK OF THE PLURAL

Yet perhaps jungle pictures (and to some extent westerns) allowed for a loosening of these codes, particularly in a series of transgressive 1940s films starring Acquanetta, such as *Captive Wild Woman* (1943), *Jungle Woman* (1944), and *Jungle Captive* (1945). Acquanetta is probably the quintessential example of what Albert Memmi terms "the mark of the plural" (quoted in Shohat, 227). Though actually Native American, Acquanetta played Mexicans, mulattos, Latinas, and various ethnic types during her cinema career. The manner in which Acquanetta is called upon to represent many ethnicities by the Hollywood cinema is an example of the mark of the plural, wherein "various ethnic communities and nations are subject to homogenization" (Shohat, 227). Another "mark of the plural" can be found in Arthur Ripley's *Prisoner of Japan* (1942), in which an obviously European actor (Ernest Dorian) is forced to play the role of an Imperial Japanese secret agent, who holds an American scientist (Alan Baxter) in captivity on a remote Pacific island. In his portrayal of the nefarious Japanese agent, Dorian displays obvious discomfort in the role. Other 1940s actors, such as J. Carrol Naish, were routinely called upon to construct a variety of racist cinematic stereotypes, including a villainous Japanese secret agent in Lambert Hiller's serial of *Batman* (1943).

FIGURE 13. Ernest Dorian (left) and Alan Baxter (right) in *Prisoner of Japan*, race drag in service of the Empire. Courtesy Jerry Ohlinger Archives.

Taken as a whole, this system of racial displacement helps to construct Whiteness by diffusing and disarming ethnicities. In creating the "mark of the plural," Whites play African Americans in Blackface, Asians are interchangeably used as Chinese, Vietnamese, Koreans, Malaysians, and Japanese, and "nonoccidental" people play Arabs, Indians, and Native Americans, to cite just a few examples.

The politics and erasure of ethnicity around Native-Americans is well documented, but few instances seem more outrageous than the erasure of Acquanetta's Native American identity. She grew up in Wyoming on an Arapaho reservation and later became a fashion model. In New York, she drew the attention of gossip columnists such as Louis Sobol and Walter Winchell. However, studio bosses and talent agents told her that she needed a new identity. "Oh, nobody cares about Indians" (Weaver, 2), she was informed, as she recounted in an interview many years later:

> Roosevelt was president and the big South American Hands Across the Border policy was on, and it was decided that I was now going to be a South American. It was almost like Pygmalion—they fabricated for me this story that I came from Venezuela. I looked the part. I was dark and exotic, and I wore these big scarves and a big gardenia, flowered skirts, . . . (laughs) I became the "Venezuelan Volcano." (Weaver, 3)

Thus, Acquanetta's roles, indeed her performed persona as constructed by the patriarchal cinema, involved strong elements of interracial eroticism, as well as "the mark of the plural" in all her work.

In a series of three films, *Captive Wild Woman* (1943, dir. Edward Dmytryk), *Jungle Woman* (1944, dir. Reginald LeBorg), and *Jungle Captive* (1945, dir. Harold Young), Acquanetta played a woman who is transformed into a human being from an ape in a series of grisly experiments. This transformation reflects the deep-seated horror (and fantasy) of "miscegenation" or race mixing, as much as it marks a location of the filmic medical gaze and medical practices that often were called into practice upon the "dark" and/or female body. A scientist transforms an ape, the beast who harbors "The Soul of Satan," into a subjugated love slave who is bound by "The Flesh of Beauty," to quote the ad campaign for *Jungle Woman*. I'd suggest that these films mark another visitation to the site of the Plantocracy, particularly to the sexual subjugation of the African (American) female. The primate taken from the jungles of Africa in *Cap-*

*tive Wild Woman*, who is then artificially endowed with human characteristics, may be viewed as a racist stand-in for an African (or African American) female in 1940s Hollywood cinema.

John Carradine, as the doctor who medically transforms the ape into the gorgeous love object Acquanetta, restages Plantocratic fantasies (and realities) of the rape of the Black slave. In *Captive Wild Woman*, the subject is likened to an animal, with few possible means of agency. When she emerges from the experiments she is hopelessly in love with her White captor, and determined to destroy her sexual competitor, played by Evelyn Ankers, a stand-in for the reigning White slaveowner's wife (or love interest). The sexual and racial politics of such films can make them almost unwatchable, while the transreinscription of the Black female body as an ape is outrageous in its simultaneous erasure/replacement. Perhaps it should be remembered that this is just one more example of the making of gender and race in popular culture, a process described in detail by Londa Schiebinger in *Nature's Body*.

Schiebinger specifically locates the history of the study of the gendering of apes as female in the studies of "naturalists" from Aristotle to Linnaeus. Just as "scientists"of the Victorian era measured the labia and other sexual organs of the African female body, Africans of both genders were described as apes and studied like apes. Women in general were said to be sexually akin to apes. Female sexual organs somehow "proved" this kinship. As Schiebinger writes, "in some instances women's sexual organs were said to link her directly to apes" (89). The marked interest in the female clitoris and labia displays the naturalists' tendency to sexualize bodies across the spectrum of human and animal. The preoccupations of early naturalists, as in Linnaeus's question, "Do female apes have clitorises?," is demonstrably comparable to the fetishization of the African female body in the Acquanetta films and in other popular films of the period. Acquanetta, as ape and mulatto, replaces the absent African American woman who is *usually* seen on the screen solely in the sexually "safe" role of Mammy, maid, or mother.

The commercial display of Acquanetta in publicity shots that trade on S/M sexuality (Acquanetta bound in manacles, leg irons, and chains, or gazing seductively at the viewer in a posture of submission/defiance), coupled with her constructed hypersexuality, might be superficially viewed as yet another example of a White supremacist construction of an object without agency. Yet such a reading ignores a number of narrative suggestions of resistance within the films, along with Acquanetta's own interpre-

FIGURE 14. Acquanetta in chains: the "Third Eye" of the subaltern in 1940s dominant Hollywood cinema. Courtesy Jerry Ohlinger Archives.

tation of her work, which displays the star's considerable degree of ownership and control over of the production of her own iconographic status. Despite their racism and sexism, *Captive Wild Woman, Jungle Woman*, and *Jungle Captive* foreground "the Third Eye" or "the look back" of the subject in visual captivity. Acquanetta's countenance in all three films is suffused with a dangerous and uncontrollable power associated with her kinship with Nature. In several compelling sections of *Jungle Woman*, for example, Acquanetta uses her gaze to communicate with and/or control animals and people. In these wordless, hypervisual scenes of visual control, Acquanetta rules those around her with her wordless gaze.

The restaging of the Plantocratic rape of the Black female body, the eroticization of the mulatto supervixen, coupled with the elimination of the Jungle Woman in the narrative climaxes of all three films, suggests the lengths to which Colonial fantasies would go in order to tangentially address the unspeakable legacies of slavery, racism, and the discomfort with which the Colonial Plantocrat views the Black body, or the "racially mixed" body. Such bodies are, in presence or absence, reminders of the sexual politics of the Plantocracy, bodies that cannot ultimately be disciplined because they bear the power to disrupt through the gaze of the *femme vivante*.

Acquanetta herself describes in detail the ways in which she avoided becoming an iconic captive in the limiting roles that she was able to obtain, and how she turned those (often nonspeaking) roles into something of her own making. She states of her relationship with producer Walter Wanger, for example:

> I don't think of Walter Wanger as a friend, because he was more like someone who thought he could exert power over you. And when he couldn't, then he was vindictive! So, because I was not what he wanted me to be, he denied me roles that I could have had. It was not because they were unavailable, it was a simple matter of exchanging a role for what I was willing to give. I wasn't willing to do that, and I never will be willing to do that! I maintained my self-respect. I had it then and I have it now—that's a very important thing. It's not what other people feel about you, but what you know about yourself. (Weaver, 8)

Acquanetta *was* forced by studio economics and racial politics to accept roles that were limited, yet she was well aware of those limitations.

What she really wanted to play, she told Weaver, was "a *real* woman—a loving, sharing, caring person" (10). But even in the role of Ape Woman, Acquanetta became a legendary woman, and she cocreated that legend. With the popularity of the three jungle films, Acquanetta began to recognize her power as a coproducer of images: "They [the films and their producers] made money because Acquanetta was in [them]" she stated, noticeably referring to herself in the third person. "I came to realize that *I* [my emphasis] was the property, not the film" (Weaver, 10). When she found out that she would not speak in her role in *Captive Wild Woman*, Acquanetta devised a highly effective strategy for overcoming the limitations placed upon her. "I had to project more—because I had to do it with my body language, my eyes, my face. Every movement had to mean something!" (Weaver, 10). In the ultimate act of insubordination, Acquanetta eventually walked out on her contract with Universal. She recounts:

> People asked me, "You walked out on a contract, when they were ready to extend it?" and I said, "Not only that, but they offered me more money to stay." (Weaver, 13)

Though she did return to Hollywood for several more films, Acquanetta eventually settled in Arizona where she raised a family. Her story in some ways resembles that of Betty Page, the 1950s pin-up queen, who also walked away from the phantasmal image she coproduced.

The Plantocracy of images includes decades of icons of goddesses, most of whom are suffused with sadomasochistic sexual promise. From the blonde jungle goddess played by Edwina Booth in *Trader Horn* (1931), to the seductive and often captively bound Frances Gifford of the 1941 serial *Jungle Girl* (who is simultaneously billed as "mistress of an empire of savages and beasts," yet finds herself tied to a stake at the mercy of a spear-throwing machine), and films such as Sam Newfield's *Jungle Siren* (1942), produced at PRC, the infamous poverty-row studio, featuring the scantily clad Ann Corio luring men to their doom, to the various incarnations of the supervixen Sheena from Irish McCalla into the 1950s to Tanya Roberts in the 1984 television version, audiences have been confronted with a plethora of exotic constructions of the feared and yet desirable Other, as a phantom zone of racial and/or social reinscription and transgression.

FIGURE 15. "Mistress of an empire of savages and beasts!": the poster for the 15 chapter serial *Jungle Girl.* Courtesy Jerry Ohlinger Archives.

## CONSTRUCTING THE JUNGLE

The interchangeability of images of jungle pictures exists not just at the narrative level. When MGM assigned contract director W. S. Van Dyke to direct *Trader Horn* (1931), the enterprising director went to Africa to film most of the motion picture's key sequences. While there, Van Dyke shot literally miles of footage of tribal ceremonies, animals in their natural habitat, landscapes, and African people. Because Van Dyke completed his films so quickly (his nickname was "One Take Woody"), he completed filming on the "A" unit of *Trader Horn* (some pickups were later shot to complete the film) in record time, while his "B" (or second) unit was out shooting hours of background material. When *Trader Horn* was finally assembled, there were so many outtakes of indigenous people and wildlife that MGM was able to establish a stock footage library from Van Dyke's outtakes alone. At first MGM used these library shots exclusively in their own films (notably early entries in the long-running *Tarzan* series), but by the 1940s and 50s MGM was willing to sell the *Trader Horn* outtakes to any independent producer who wanted to use them. In this manner, Van Dyke's scenes of African life in the early 1930s were used and reused, in film after film, so that American audiences as late as the 1950s (in the *Jungle Jim* films, the *Bomba* films, or the teleseries *Ramar of the Jungle*) accepted these images as the authentic talisman of the African experience.

But "authenticity" was one of the least important aspects of the ethnographic lens of the Plantocracy of Hollywood, which fed off the simulacra of images that merely suggested the likeness of the phantom jungle. What mattered most to producers was that the directors of these jungle narratives delivered packageable exotic narratives to their audiences/consumers. Like package tours, audiences desired above all the familiar: to travel to exotic places which are virtually all the same, because you never have to leave the resort hotel once you get to the jungle. At a resort hotel one doesn't interact with the "natives." Instead, the "natives" stage constructed narratives of indigenous customs that have been coproduced by the Plantocratic imagination. In this way, the tourist industry and the tourism of images supports and maintains a steady stream of narratives that are simultaneously safe and yet provocative. But the faux performances of the "natives" are often marked by the Third Eye that reflects the realities of Colonial subjectivities. The real subject of the Plantocracy of images is always ultimately the Plantocrat, be it in the guise of the captive wild woman, the witch doctor, the lost White jungle

FIGURE 16. Edwina Booth in *Trader Horn*: White Jungle Goddess of the Colonial Domain. Courtesy Jerry Ohlinger Archives.

goddess, the sultry "mulatto," or the great White hunter. Where are the Africans in jungle films? They are outside the hotel, out of the range of the camera.

## CODE SWITCHING AND TROPES OF CAPTIVITY

The code-switching production of hybridization evident in White women's appropriation and renarration of slave/captivity narratives could ostensibly be seen as yet another racist commodification of female Black subjectivity, and indeed this would seem to be the larger metanarrative of this significant coopting. However, it should be kept in mind that White women, however complicit they have been in Colonialism and the practices of Plantocracies, have also been subject to oppositional contradictories that maintained and constructed "White woman" in all her overloaded essentialities. She is raced, sexed, classed, and subject to her own erasure in the complex representational contiguities of the troped body in forms of captivity seen in patriarchal body management systems. Her wish to escape narrative enclosure systems and captive alteric photomanagement erupts as a transgressive microfissure in the Foucaultian management of race and gender, displaying the limits of such a chronological and tropological reductionist theorem.

Early jungle pictures, like captivity narratives, derive their sexual potency from the heightened anxiety around the (created) need to protect the sanctity of White woman. That sanctity, coupled with its Janus-faced image of the jungle goddesses hypersexuality is largely, to borrow a phrase from Mary Ann Doane, "orchestrated by White male subjectivity—so much so that it is White female subjectivity which becomes the greatest textual stake" (221). In Doane's reading of Frantz Fanon's *Black Skin, White Masks*, for example, Doane notices an overpresence of the White woman at the expense of the disappearance of the Black woman in his appropriation of psychoanalytic readings of [White] woman's sexuality. Fanon writes: "When a woman lives the fantasy of rape by a Negro, it is in some way the fulfillment of a private dream, an inner wish. Accomplishing the phenomenon of turning against herself, it is the woman who rapes herself" (179).

Female Whiteness then is often as raced and sexualized as Black maleness. It is overdetermined *from without* and the White female is sometimes subject to Fanon's own phrase "skin/culture" (Bhabha, 75), as

outline in Homi Bhabha's analysis of Fanon in *The Location of Culture.*
Such a culture obsessed with skin color and, I would add, gendered sexualization, fetishizes the "White woman" in a manner not unlike that of the
albeit overdetermined category of "Black man." Skin/culture facilitates
stereotypes, and, as Bhabha writes: "The stereotype can also be seen as a
'fixated' form of the Colonial subject which *facilitates* Colonial relations,
and sets up a discursive form of racial and cultural oppositions in terms
of which Colonial power is exercised" (78).

Perhaps some White women recognized that they, like Fanon, were,
"overdetermined from without" (Fanon, 116). When they made films
they worked within the sphere of overdetermined markers and they
resisted these stereotypes as much as they coproduced them. Even in the
few jungle pictures White women directed, wrote, or otherwise coproduced, White women were clearly hyperaware of their captivity within
overdetermined stereotypes. In the case of Kathlyn Williams, who stars,
codirects, and writes Selig jungle pictures in the early teens, there is a
notably different approach to the genre. Kenneth M. Cameron notes that
Williams's film, "went against the received ideas of Dark Continent and
animal menace, and the corollary human domination through killing"
(127).

Kathlyn Williams's characters form a self-encoded stereotype, one
that evokes the New Woman who is cheerful, competent, neither hyper-
sexed nor undersexed, and is decidedly interested in animal rights. The
obvious parallel between the struggle for women's rights and animal rights
is set against the backdrop of the jungle of Colonialism, a significant
reminder of patriarchal ownership and management of raced bodies. This
is not to say that Williams's films, and films of other early White women
directors, are not highly problematic in their treatment of race, merely to
point out the interesting levels of political analysis that such films
demand. Often these narratives raised the issues of White privilege without ever even including narratives of people of color. Often White women
directors appear to appropriate the history of "images and acts" of various
forms of victimization, as Annalee Newitz states, "to reimagine themselves
as civilized and just" (139).

This is clearly the case in some of the work of early Canadian filmmaker Nell Shipman, whose first feature film (as actress) was *Back to God's
Country* (1919). Though nominally directed by David M. Hartford,
Shipman certainly cocreated the film. Shipman is indeed charming in her
scenes of interaction with various wildlife and it surely trades upon a

coopting of animal-rights issues in order to buttress the importance of an undernarrative supporting the equal rights of women. Though Shipman alone successfully evades the villain of the picture, and even rescues a male figure in the film *Back to God's Country* is extraordinarily racist and trades in the Colonialist rape fantasy involving a stereotypically drawn Chinese figure who serves as a backdrop to Shipman's virginal evocation of Whiteness. *Back to God's Country* is Canada's earliest extant feature motion picture and it strongly invokes the sentimentalization of the Great White North, a north besieged by "foreigners," "ethnic types," non-White Asians marked as rapists of the land, the flora and fauna of great Mother Canada and the virginal White jungle goddess.

This is not to say that all of Nell Shipman's films, either as actor or director, are as racist as *Back to God's Country*. It is merely to remind the reader that White women often reinscribed popular stereotypes of Colonial imagery. In their exemplifications of Whiteness, White women actors and directors often drew upon stereotypes of racial and sexual purity even as they sometimes worked against the ideologies upon which they were based. A simultaneous embrace of the Victorian pedestal of sexual purity and a desire to disrupt and hybridize that same moral pedestal informs many of the films of early women directors. These White women's images of autoethnography suggest that White women were highly aware of the possibility for meaning exchanges in the economy of the Plantocracy of images.

## HYBRIDIZED CAPTIVE NARRATIVITY

Reviewing early American women's cinema within the liminal landscape of Postcolonial demythologizing, such as that projected by Annette Kolodny ("Letting Go of Our Grand Obsessions"), I see an entirely new view of the hybridized forms and tropes of slave and captivity narratives in the films of Alice Guy, Lois Weber, Dorothy Davenport, Grace Cunard, Dorothy Arzner, and others. Such an imagistic recovery process displaces received notions about early women's films. Early women's films have often been derisively dismissed as unimportant, nonfeminist, melodramatic, or derivative, in a Colonialist display of voice suppression. However, the function of the narrative techniques employed by these filmmakers lies in a systematic substitution of narrative tropes, often using the forms and structures found in slave and captivity narratives.

The code-switching techniques of early American women filmmakers, like those employed by early American women writers, involve the adaptation and appropriation of the narrative techniques of Harriet Jacobs, Mary Prince, Mary Rowlandson, Harriet Beecher Stowe, and many other slave and captivity narrative writers. The troping of the bound body within the dominant White heterosexist family unit in early American women's cinema is reliant upon borrowings from the captivity narrative and slave narrative. Preoccupied with freedom of the body, ownership of place, identity in the cinematic marketplace, and disruption of the patrifocal marriage system, early women directors staked a unique claim in the engendered American landscape. Slavery, bondage, and captivity became trading sites in the dialogic discourse of the American wilderness, in many early women's films.

As in literary captivity/slave narratives, constructions of virtue, race, gender, and freedom are called into question by these and other films. The cultural work of the slave narrative and the captivity narrative is furthered beyond the bounds of literary discourse, and yet it is also hybridized by the demands of the cinematic medium. Thus, the figure of the woman in bondage (literal or figurative; "free" or within the bonds of slavery) in early American women's cinema is collapsed in the signifying frame of dominant historical discourse of patriarchal American cinema, and opens up a new set of configurations of the feminine corpus within the primitive cinematic captivity/slave narrative.

Though captivity narratives were used to maintain "racial as well as sexual boundaries" (Marchetti 31), they often exposed sexism and racism and were "susceptible to multiple and ambiguous readings" (Fitzpatrick 5). Female slave narratives adhered to the doctrine of Christian piety and submission, yet they represented bondage across the margins of race and gender. Mary Prince not only recounts her own bondage to slavery but notes that her master's wife was herself "much afraid" of her own husband (48). Harriet Jacobs's *Incidents in the Life of a Slave Girl* not only told of the monstrosities of slavery, but spoke in the rhetorical narrative of the suffragette: "The more my mind has become enlightened, the more difficult it [is] for me to consider myself an article of property" (205). She uses irony to move her White female audience, "Pity me, and pardon me, O virtuous reader! You never knew what it is to be a slave; to be entirely unprotected by law or custom; *to have the laws reduce you to the condition of chattel,* entirely subject to the will of another" (56). Similarly, Harriet Beecher Stowe showed us that even a privileged White senator's wife,

Mary Bird, was treated as a delicate object of chattel: "She ruled more by entreaty and persuasion than by command or arguments" (143). The cultural work of the female captivity and slave narrative included instruction of women in the nature of hegemonic power structures. They offered examples of women who used public speech to cause political change and they demonstrated political struggle for ownership of the female body. They reenvisioned public and private space in an effort to evoke a "philosophical freedom of place" (Harris 19). Early women filmmakers continued the cultural work of these narratives by seizing the objectifying gaze and inventing a female gaze which allowed women to gaze and yet not be a subject. When Harriet Jacobs, through Linda Brent, carves out three peepholes in a tiny crawl space in which she is hiding from her master, she uses the power of the female gaze to convert her limited physical space into an "empowering mental landscape" (19), according to Sharon Harris. Early women filmmakers too claimed a female landscape of power and desire as they reconfigured the early American landscape as a network of power relationships and their ownership and captivity of the female body.

In early women's films, the frequent portrayal of forced, or "arranged," marriages exemplify code switching of the captivity/slave narrative. Quite often these films center around an unmarried pregnant woman who is being forced to marry someone for the sake of propriety. Often the films imply that women are forced into sexual alliances with men out of economic captivity. Perhaps these narratives are reenactments of taboo plantocratic sexual relationships between White masters and Black women slaves. Like the plantation owners who disregard the responsibility, much less the existence of their offspring, the sexual predators of early women's melodramas often deny their responsibilities toward women and children. It is unfortunate that aside from a few African American women such as Eloice Gist, only White women had access to the tools of filmmaking during this period. Such pioneering male African American filmmakers as Oscar Micheaux and Spencer Williams would not come along until the 1920s and 1930s. White female film directors appropriated the slave narrative structure to create their own social commentaries, but the implicit racism of this early era of cinema practice effectively denies us any examples of African American, Native American, or women of color as cinema *auteurs*.

In Cleo Madison's *Her Bitter Cup* (1916), an early feminist melodrama, a factory owner forces an impoverished woman into a sexual relationship. In another Cleo Madison film, *Her Defiance* (1916), a young woman who has been seduced, undone, and abandoned is nearly forced by her father into marriage with a wealthy older man. The young woman does the unthinkable. She disrupts the wedding with emphatically defiant gestures and a speech out of defiance against her father. "You fool," she says in a title, as she flees the wedding. Cleo Madison encodes the film with a cleverly placed prop in the wedding scene of an oversized Bible on a table in the middle of the set. Thus the woman not only defies the Word of her Father, but the word of the father in the scene. In a scene comparable to that of Eliza's flight in *Uncle Tom's Cabin* (or any number of female escape scenes in slave and captivity narratives), the woman flees in her wedding dress in a stolen stagecoach, finding freedom in the landscape of the woman's text. In an interesting code switch, the captivity narrative then segues into a romantic narrative in which the woman finds her lover, forgives him, only on her terms, and lives happily ever after. The code switch from captivity to romance "validates the narrative renovation of female space—a space which not only shelters but constructs, then defines, the woman," Elizabeth L. Barnes notes (158).

Cleo Madison's early films are not unique or unprecedented in their feminist melodramatic themes. Another woman filmmaker, Ida May Park, made hundreds of films in the period of the suffragette/New Woman. Unfortunately, all of her films are lost. However, Park's films appear to have used similar narrative code switchings from captivity and slave narratives. Such films as *Bondage* (1917), *The Model's Confession* (1917), and *Risky Road* (1917) center around women who refuse to be victimized by forced sexual relationships or arranged marriages.

Though Ida May Park's films are lost, several domestic comedies of filmmaker Alice Guy-Blaché have survived. Blaché's films of this period also contain female heroines who outwit arranged marriages and other forms of domestic captivity. *His Double* (1913) and *Canned Harmony* (1912) rework almost the same exact plot. Both center around female trickster figures who outwit their father's plans for their arranged marriages. Both pass off their desired suitors as the men their father wishes them to marry by dressing up the men in false disguises until they are married. In *His Double*, for example, the female heroine is going to be forced to marry "Count Laking Coin." Through an elaborate ruse, she disguises her boyfriend as Count Laking Coin and marries him. In *Canned Harmony*, the female trickster also evades an arranged marriage. Her father is a music professor, and wishes her to marry an accomplished musician. The heroine is in love with a man who cannot play an instrument. He dresses up as a violinist and the heroine plays the Victrola as the imposter pretends to play the violin. The marriage ruse is pulled off and the couple is found out. Marriage, the ultimate captivity narrative, is duped in both films. The law of the father and the word of the father are called into question by the trickster heroine. The feminist humor in these films is comparable to that of the narrative of Harriet E. Wilson's *Our Nig*, whose central heroine, Frado, often plays the trickster to avoid punishment: "She was even at some sly prank . . . not unfrequently some outburst of merriment . . . she would venture far beyond propriety . . ." (38). The trickster heroine of the slave narrative and the woman's film narrative explores the freedom of the female body, ownership of place, and public speech and subjectivity.

The female trickster heroine is at the center of another important early women's film, *A House Divided* (1913), also directed by Alice Guy-Blaché. In the cramped set of the American home, a couple has a disagreement and decides not to speak to one another. They agree to communicate through written notes. Here the female heroine uses silence to liberate herself from an unequal domestic arrangement. She holds him hostage, in a sense, unable to communicate with her through the spoken word. Interestingly enough, the husband sees a (male) lawyer about the arrangement, seeking patriarchal legitimacy, while the wife seeks advice from a matriarchal figure, presumably her mother. The women laugh together at the men, looking through the notes together. The couple reunites when they think there is a burglar in the house. Reunited in a more equal relationship, the couple are almost split up again by the lawyer. However, they ignore him because their marriage is no longer one of captivity and inequality. It is code switched in the romantic comedy tradition into a female-centered arrangement of love. In all three of these Alice Guy-Blaché domestic comedies, the transformative female trickster heroine reenvisions the home as a female center of philosophical freedom. These films established early archetypes for the later domestic television comedies of Lucy Arnez (Lucille Ball), for example.

Women directors consistently used either serious or humorous melodrama to displace female objectification and powerlessness. Seduction and abandonment are played out in films by Dorothy Davenport Reid and Lois Webster. Reid's *The Red Kimona* (1925) is another narrative of a pregnant woman who is seduced and abandoned. Instead of accepting her fate, this transgressive heroine murders her exlover, and her actions are completely sanctioned by the director's handling of the material. The film has pronounced code switchings from the tradition of captivity and slave narratives. The first is the use of the opening direct address of the director herself. The stock device of direct appeal to the reader/viewer is an immediately recognizable feature borrowed from the slave/captivity narrative. The melodramatic direct appeal promotes audience identification with a transgressive female figure and disrupts the viewer/reader's passive position.

Another important code switching occurs when the heroine kills her exlover. The cinematic space of the bound woman becomes radically altered as a space of violent insurrection and justice. Reid sets this scene in a jewelry shop, where the Philistine male figure appears to be buying a ring to ensnare and enslave another woman. The jewels signify the plantocratic tradition of subjugation through manacles and promises. When the heroine shoots him she not only ends her own captivity but she insures that no other woman will become his slave. This radical departure from film practice frees the captive heroine from suffering and guilt. Reid places a signifying cross directly behind the woman in the scene of the killing. Another cross appears on the wall of the jail cell where the woman awaits her sentence. In an amazingly transformative code-switching narrative, the prison space is depicted as a safe female zone where the heroine is consoled by a sympathetic female prison warden. The transgressive heroine is absolved of guilt by the cross and by the series of glances from the female warden. The jail cell is transformed into a site of slippage between the signifiers of female friendship, female absolution, and male bondage. *The Red Kimona* renders the subjective female in a captivity/slave narrative that ends in the murder of the Plantocrat and envisions the liberation of the female outlaw.

The defiant trickster and the transgressive woman figure are combined in the central female heroine of Lois Weber's *A Japanese Idyll* (1912). *A Japanese Idyll* is a slave narrative of sorts in which a wealthy White merchant purchases a Japanese woman as a mail-order bride. Weber uses tinting to infuse the film with a distinctive moral indignation. In a red-tinted scene, a sinister looking "wealthy merchant" gazes lecherously at a postcard of Cherry Blossom, played by Weber herself in stereotypical "Japanese" race drag. He purchases her from an Asian couple involved in the slave trade. The red tint suggests evil incarnate and is underscored by a series of shots of cramped interiors that involve shady dealings. When Cherry Blossom and her boyfriend discover her fate, the scene is tinted blue to suggest moral good. The couple escape the sinister marriage merchants into a blue-tinted scene of the outdoors where they escape on a boat to freedom. The use of outside footage suggests freedom from the marriage of captivity and enslavement.

The heroine's ability to arrange her own escape in *A Japanese Idyll* is reminiscent of captivity narratives such as that of Mary Rowlandson, in which she arranges her own "sale" into freedom "that for twenty pounds I should be redeemed" (54). Similarly, Harriet Jacobs and Harriet Wilson recount their own ability to escape slavery in their slave narratives. Escape is the narrative center of scores of films by early serial queens such as Gene Gauntier, Ruth Stonehouse, Kathlyn Williams, Cleo Madison, and Grace Cunard, who starred and codirected *The Broken Coin* (1915), *The Purple Mask* (1916), *The Mysterious Leopard-Lady* (1914), and *Lady Raffles* (1914). Serial heroines reenacted captivity narratives and: "signalled the emergence of the New Woman. She wore less restrictive clothes, she was active, she went everywhere she wanted, and she was capable of resolving mysteries, solving problems, and escaping from danger" (Bowser 186). These strong action heroines signify an almost completely forgotten cultural moment in which women were portrayed as active, clever, and physically adroit warrior women who broke from captivity narratives, saved themselves, and even saved others. Grace Cunard's *The Purple Mask* featured a female Robin Hood who consistently outwitted the authorities on her trail. Gene Gauntier's early 1908–1909 production of *The Adventures of a Girl Spy* revolved around the adventures of a cross-dressing "girl spy" in an adventure action narrative set in the nineteenth century. Grace Cunard's *Last Man on Earth* (1929) inverted the captivity narrative's usual gender configuration. In this film Cunard plays a gangster who kidnaps and takes captive the last living man on Earth, and holds him for ransom from an all-woman government. The serial heroines marketed themselves as defiant trickster heroines who reveled in freedom of the body, public speech, freedom of action, and ownership of space in a manner that disappeared from the silver screen until the adventures of Ridley Scott's *Thelma and Louise* (1991) and other action heroines.

Heterosexual White women were not the only women filmmakers to appropriate and renarrate captivity/slave narratives into feminist tracts. Lesbian director Dorothy Arzner remade the confined all-girl environment in *The Wild Party* (1929) into a free zone of female friendship and lesbian sexuality. Arzner cleverly paints the outside "public" space as a threatening space of predatory heterosexual men who prey upon captive women. The girl's school is coded as a safe environment where female companionship and same-sex relationships may be allowed to flourish. The gazes between women, particularly Clara Bow and her close friend, are charged with sexuality. *The Wild Party* itself constitutes a reflection on the film industry, a patriarchally defined captivity narrative of the economy of desire as it is restricted by the heterocentricism of the "master" narrative of dominant cinema practice.

The films of Alice Guy-Blaché, Cleo Madison, Dorothy Davenport Reid, Grace Cunard, Lois Weber, Dorothy Arzner, and many other early White women directors remap the frontier of American cinema and women's narratives. They engage in hybridization of the tropes and codes of slave and captivity narratives in an effort to displace the objectified mute woman in bondage in the political discourse of early-American texts. They reinvent a Postcolonial landscape of desire where the captive woman escapes those "traps slyly laid by the vicious to ensnare her," as Wilson's Frado so resolutely avoids captivity (129). They demonstrate that, as author or auteur, women who use art in the form of rhetoric, by controlling the discourse, empower those who speak, write, and gaze.

# CHAPTER THREE

※

# *Captive Sexualities*

If pornography and sexploitation exploit the public's taste for erotica, mainstream narratives eroticize repressed images and render them perverse, thus erasing the boundaries of pornography and nonpornography. In perverting the perverse, obsessing over the obscene, and working to regulate desire and sexualities, narratives that insist that they are *not pornographic* actually call attention to themselves as "pornography." Defining the limits of pornography and the term *pornography* renders the critic (or the audience) a border patrol officer of pornography. I have no desire to redefine pornography or its limits, or to participate in the discipline of the body or the gaze, the heterotopic (or homotopic) Foucaultian discipline of gender order and its tyranny in the production of subjects, discourse, or knowledge. Instead, I suggest that the boundaries between pornography (or sexploitation) and mainstream narrative are a falsity, a "perversion" itself. Just as "art and perversion are similar in origin" (83), as Laura Kipnis notes, so the origins of porno/graphy and photo/graphy (and their correlatives ethno/graphy and cinemato/graphy) are contiguous and markedly alike. Just as Trinh T. Minh-ha sees no difference between documentary and narrative filmmaking, I would suggest that all forms of image-making processes are inherently pornographic. An insistence on the maintenance of the borders of porn would resuscitate and perpetuate Freudian, Lacanian, and Kleinian theories of the suppressed "libido" and the "perverse," and in turn sublimate the body and hold it hostage to "norms" of race, sexuality, class, and gender. As Lynn Hunt writes in *The Invention of Pornography*: "Pornography developed out of the messy, two-way, push and pull between the intention of authors, artists and engravers to test the boundaries of the 'decent' and the aim of the ecclesiastical and secular police to regulate it" (10).

If pornography is held hostage to the boundaries of Foucaultian policing and self-policing, narrative filmmaking is perhaps doubly bound by such disciplinary and discursive regulations and self-regulations. By the same token, narrative, "mainstream" films display a "push-pull" dichotomy between intentions and regulations of the boundaries of what is classified as "perversion."

## THE PORNOGRAPHY OF IMAGES

In fact, much visual evidence would suggest that the unregulated body (and its liberator) are winning the cinematic battle of transgressive figuration, when we consider the display of heterotopic (and/or bitopic and homotopic) bondage scenes in a film such as the ostensibly "mainstream" production *Step by Step* (1946). Here, the display of performative bodies in a tableaux vivant of sexually charged S/M pleasure is playfully rendered in a self-reflexive scene in which Lawrence Tierney and Anne Jeffreys perform the unregulated as regulated. What is captivating about this image is its banality and ordinariness, coupled with the actors' visual and aural cues. Both Jeffreys and Tierney are obviously aware that their performance invokes the prurient and the denied. Yet if the same scene were in a "pornographic" film, perhaps the spectacle of sadomasochistic interplay would not be as pleasurable. It would no doubt be underscored by the grubby, interchangeable "stock" music used in porn films, shot in the dismal, poorly lit style of porn films, subjected to the commercial limits for the production "values" of porn films, and the scene certainly would not be performed by Anne Jeffreys and Lawrence Tierney. Nor would it be surrounded by the fascinating plot of *Step by Step*'s metanarrative of a World War II veteran hunting and trapping Fascist agents. It wouldn't be directed by Phil Rosen, or evocatively lit and photographed by studio veteran Frank Redman. *It wouldn't be as pornographic an image in a porn film.*

This is one of the most fascinating exemplifications of the failure of the "border patrol" of modern spectacle. Like the image of Marlo Thomas bound and gagged, it supports Guy DeBord's thesis on the nature of spectacle:

Here we have the principle of commodity fetishism, the domination of society by things whose qualities are "at the same time perceptible and imperceptible by the senses." This principle is absolutely fulfilled in the spectacle, where the perceptible world is replaced by a set of images that are superior to that world yet at the same time impose themselves as *eminently* perceptible.

The world the spectacle holds up to view is at once *here* and *elsewhere*; it is the world of the commodity ruling over all lived experience. The commodity world is thus shown *as it really is*, for its logic is one with men's estrangement from one another and from the sum total of what they produce. (216)

The tyranny of perception and its critical apparatus works to estrange us from recognizing the true pornography that we produce. By rendering perverse images as both *perceptible and imperceptible*, it mimics psychoanalytic discourse that depends upon the binaries of conscious and unconscious perception. Furthermore, the current vogue for commodified spectacle (in such films as *Titanic, Batman Forever, The Fifth Element,* and other "blockbuster" films) heralds a rise in the production of perversions in all their ordinariness, banality, exoticism, and eroticism. As Guy DeBord would have it:

The spectacle is the bad dream of modern society in chains. . . . The fact that the practical power of modern society has detached itself from itself and established itself in the spectacle as an independent realm can only be explained by the self-cleavage and self-contradictoriness already present in that powerful practice. (18)

The pleasure of the spectacle of Anne Jeffreys bound and gagged by Lawrence Tierney, performs the perverse as sanctioned, sexuality *even as it operates in and renegotiates* the mechanics of pornography. Audiences and performers are not entirely the disciplined Foucaultian subjects that some cultural critics would have them be. Viewers are capable of registering, recognizing, and negotiating the pleasures of mainstream narrative pornotopias, just as they are capable of rescribing themselves across lines of gender, sexuality, race, and class. Nevertheless, audiences are also complicit as self-regulators who need to insist on the binaries of pornography and nonpornography. One might say that we want our perversions *perverted*, so that we can safely inscribe normalized images of ourselves into scenes of scopophiliac pleasure, without having to be regulated by the punitive systems that estrange us from our sexualities. The lengths to which we (as a culture) go to displace our complicity and coproduction of sexuality is remarkable, and here I should perhaps admit that I am speaking in terms of overdetermined, essentialized categories of audiences and subjects, not to mention scopophiliac pleasures and other categories of sexual pleasure.

In summoning such overdeterminisms, I seek only to open up a space to perform and engage in an ethnography of pornography that disrupts categories. To some degree I am responding to John Champagne's call to arms *against* the critical analysis of pornography, "Stop Reading Films!" (76–97). Champagne points out that the rise in serious analysis of pornography (especially homosexual porn) is subject to academic border patrolling:

> Given the role of the university in the maintenance and production of hegemonic forms of knowledge, and its collusion in the continued production of a (heterosexualized) subject prepared for the 'realities' of corporate capitalism, one cannot simply be sanguine about opening up formerly undisclosed territories to the academic gaze. There can be no guarantee, for example, that the analysis will not be used for homophobic ends and purposes. . . . If we consider seriously the claims made by poststructuralist thinkers such as Foucault, Derrida, and Gayatri Spivak, we in the academy in particular must acknowledge that we are not simply free to produce knowledge outside the constraints of a discipline or discourse. Our historical location as investigating subjects is unavoidable; our intellectual projects are necessarily structured by this location. . . . Possibly the best that we can hope for is what Luce Irigaray has termed a certain jamming of the theoretical machinery. (78).

I agree with Champagne on the problematics of the academic gaze, but if we are not free to produce knowledge outside the discipline of our disciplines, it would seem to me to be more important to open spaces of resistance within our disciplinarian sites of power/knowledge production. Let's look at porn, but let's reinvent and resist discursive boundaries of porn. Let's see porn in the mundane images of Disney's *Hercules* (1997), which features the title character as yet another beefcake retread "John" who embodies both homosexual and heterosexual fantasies of carnality: as a character, Hercules is displayed as a fetishization of Disney's empire, a prostitute who knows no limits, or, as Anthony Lane writes in *The New Yorker*, the star of a "picture [which] is distinguished only in its olympian money-grubbing—an unblushing will to sell itself and its spinoff products" (27). Let's reinvent what we mean by pornography. Doesn't *The English Patient* represent the pornography of Colonial violence, reinscribing the social normative values of the present across the reconstructed narrative of a 1940s War/jungle melodrama, that features "good" Nazi (Ralph Fiennes) in search of a lost White jungle goddess (Kristin Scott Thomas), who is, in turn, eroticized by her Whiteness and hypersexualized by her sexual conquest of a Sikh officer (played by Naveen Andrews)?

## THE EPISTEMOLOGY OF EXPERIENCE

In *The English Patient*, the eroticization of the exotic landscape marks a return to the pornographic pleasure of the Imperial Man and White Jungle Goddess of *She*. Only the genders are reversed here. Now, it is Ralph Fiennes as the Imperial Man who is consumed by the fires of sexual passion, just as Ayesha ultimately burns in the flames of eternal life in *She* as a punishment for her carnal desires and Colonialist pleasures. *The English Patient* is in fact a porn film: a jungle picture with a huge budget. Its levels of fetishistic pleasure seem to know no boundaries. The sexual acts represented on the screen are repetitive and banal, as in a low budget porn film, but the sexual longing for the lost continent of place, the exotic locale of the Colonial empire is suffused with an Orientalist desire for a return to the Dark Continent of repressed Colonial desire. The fetishism of the bandaged Nazi officer marks a pornographic image of the forbidden, and the film itself constitutes a perverse reinvention of the sexual and social politics of World War II. A jungle film that equates the victor with the victim, *The English Patient* is not unlike a Plantocratic American film such as *Birth of a Nation*. Both films are pornographic rerenderings of history that equate mastery with forbidden desire. The Nazi officer and the Klansman are troped as victims and saviors, protectors of the great White jungle goddess; both are seen as tragic martyred, yet ultimately triumphant figures of loss, desire, and pain.

In my estimation, these recombinant instances of double inversion constitute a pornography in that their resynthesization of narrative causality and rendering of the *mise-en-captif* provokes a rereading of the potentials for redefining pornography. We must resist the boundaries of discussion of the pornographic so that we may peer across the borders of narrative closure into the en/closure of the constructed (reconstructed) Colonial past. An examination of the mechanics of ethnography allows for a renegotiation of narrative filmic discourse. Such a discourse could profitably be applied across the spectrum of all generic filmmaking, including pornography and narrative feature filmmaking. As Bill Nichols writes, we can envision

> an experiential or perhaps physiological, repetitive, poetic form of filmic organization that would foster "haptic learning, learning by bodily identification" or would replace subject centered and linear models with ones "employing repetition, associative editing and nonnarrative structures. . . ."
> Efforts such as these would move away from attempts to speak from mind to mind, in the discourse of scientific sobriety, and toward a politics and epistemology of experience spoken from body to body. Hierarchical structures designed for the extraction of knowledge (the interview, the informant, the case study) might yield to more fully personal, participatory encounter that makes an expansion or diffusion of the personal into the social/political inevitable. Rather than "perforate" the surface of things to extract concepts and categories, falsifiable rules and generalizations, ethnographic film might respond to the call for evocation rather than representation. . . . Its production and interpretation requires both a poetics, and a phenomenology, to accompany, if not displace, the "production of knowledge." (73)

Performance theorists also emphasize the importance of physical corporeality and its significance in ways that emphasize the irreducible sites of meaning present in the performing body within cinematographic spectacle. Sondra Horton Fraleigh equates "lived-body theory" (13) with performative possibilities for agency at the level of the corporeal, phenomenological, and psychological. The haptic body of Betty Page as sex worker and coproducer of her own erotic image in "pornographic" films and photographs is a construct that decenters linear and heterotopic models of fetishistic pleasure, opening up spaces of agency, inquiry, and displacing the production of corporeal knowledge. Betty Page's autoethnographic pornographies celebrate the lived-body of denied and repressed fantasies, while simultaneously provoking a multiplicity of possibilities for gendered gazes and sexualities.

## THE BODY AS FETISH: BETTY PAGE

In reinventing the "prurient" images of pornography, Betty Page works to self-reflexively subvert the institutions that regulate and define the pornographic, while she transgressively invokes gender malleability, and displays a sexuality unmarked by the "prison-house of binary gender role assignment" (Kipnis, 86). As Laura Kipnis notes, "pornography's fantasy is also of gender malleability . . . it's possible that the women who are most offended by pornography are those most invested in the idea of femininity as something static and stable" (200). Page's dance performances, in particular, invite pluralistic decentralization of subjectivities and alterities. As female viewers, are we not haptic learners; participants in this ludic dance of the sex which is one? In her dance performances, Page invites lesbian and bisexual, heterosexual and transgendered identification and fetishistic pleasure. As dance theorist Judith Lynne Hanna writes, dance performances inherently evoke the transformative:

> The significance of a dance performance and its context can be reinvented through talking and writing about it . . . after the performance, when the dance remains etched in memory, the replay of the dancing surges forth in our thought to evoke the fire in a new transformation. (198)

The dance films of Betty Page, including *Betty's Clown Dance, Betty on High Heels*, and others (all filmed by Irving Klaw) seem to deliberately invoke bisexual pleasure and undeclared sexualities. As Hélène Cixous notes, "we are all bisexual. What have we done with our bisexuality?" (Cixous and Calle-Gruber, 50). In her dance performances, Betty Page constructs the most radical of sexualities, that of the undecided or undecidable:

> The factor of uncertainty, or what Derrida calls the *undecidable*, is indissociable from human life. This ought to oblige us to have an attitude that is at once rigorous and tolerant and doubly so on each side; all the more rigorous than open, all the more demanding since it must lead to openness, leave passage; all the more mobile and rapid as the ground will always give way, always. (Cixous and Calle-Gruber, 52)

Pornography, unlike most narrative cinema, deliberately invites audience agency on a remarkable number of simultaneous levels. Betty Page's performances invite, celebrate, and provoke audience/spectator participation in the pleasure of the perverse, rather than in the repressive act of perverting pleasure. Page thus operates in the zone of "free confrontation." As I have written elsewhere: "A free confrontational cinema is political by virtue of the fact that it is participatory. Rather than operating in the language of authoritative discourse, it encourages the viewer to act upon the material" (Foster, 89).

Betty Page's work is a haptic model of the performing female body that exists outside the regulation of desire and fantasy. The spectator, in turn, is unregulated, even if s/he is obliged to live by the rules that place pornography outside the borders of the "norm." Pornography's gaze is not necessarily disciplinary. As John Champagne notes, for example, gay men are not, in fact, disciplined by the gaze of pornography. I find particularly interesting Champagne's observation that gay men can "ignore the lines between heterosexual and homosexual imagery" (90). The same thing could be said of heterosexual/homosexual/bisexual or transgendered viewers of Betty Page film. Here, Champagne foregrounds the undisciplined consumer of gay porn:

> Clearly, my observations suggest that many public consumers of gay pornography do not seem to be watching the film with even the same intensity that one watches a commercial film. Some, in fact, do not seem to watch the film at all, except intermittently. The distracted spectator of television is perhaps an appropriate model for the consumer of pornography, but even this seems inadequate. Sections of the film may be watched with intense concentration; other sequences might not be seen at all, depending on the activity that accompanies viewing. With their undisciplined viewing habits, these spectators make it nearly impossible to provide an account of the textual reception of these films. (90).

Betty Page thus exemplifies the flipside to the image of the repressed American female of the 1950s. As Eric Schaefer writes, "The burlesque film undermined prevailing representations of female sexuality within American cinema during the 1950s as well as its very system of presentation" (50). Like Kipnis, Schaefer contends that erotic films projected "considerable ambiguity rooted in the variability of gender distinction and the polymorphous quality of desire conveyed by the films" (42). The girl-girl sexuality that is often foregrounded in Betty Page's photographs and films thus does not *automatically* imply a patriarchal capturing of the female body, lesbian sexuality, or bisexuality. On the contrary, the possibilities for active lesbian, gay, bisexual, and heterosexual interventions of subjectivity making by the spectator in the case of Betty Page's films seem almost unlimited. As Chris Straayer notes in "The Hypothetical Lesbian Heroine in Narrative Feature Film":

> Acknowledgment of the female-initiated active sexuality and sexualized activity of lesbians has the potential to reopen a space in which straight women [and I would add, bisexuals] as well as lesbians can exercise self-determined pleasure. (343)

Straayer's work suggests that compulsory heterosexuality has not been and cannot be effectively regulated. Perhaps it is in the arena of one of the harshest disciplinary regimes in the patrolling of bodies and gazes, the 1950s, that we can find instances of gender malleability and Queer looks most provocatively displayed. This would seem to be the case in the example of *The Dalton Girls* (1957), a film of extraordinary gender fluidity, and one that directly addresses the lesbian/bisexual/transgendered gaze.

## OUTLAW WESTERN GODDESSES

*The Dalton Girls*, directed by the expatriate Viennese filmmaker Reginald LeBorg features four gun-toting, cross-dressing outlaw women who ride across the American landscape, wreak havoc, rob banks, and hold men hostage. *The Dalton Girls* Queers the gender conventions of all-male family westerns, such as the numerous Dalton Gang and Wyatt Earp films. The Dalton women are a threat to the symbolic order which defines the female as a virtuous influence. These gangster women are anything but "civilized." They have no interest in taming men, nor are they interested in being tamed by men. They create their own codes of conduct, and act in self-defense when threatened. Thus, *The Dalton Girls* problematizes the rape-revenge film, in which "women are heroized and men vilified" (Clover 151), usually through the protection of a civilized "good guy" hero, such as Clint Eastwood or any number of male western heroes.

Male heroes are dispensed with in the *The Dalton Girls* and gender identity, indeed, identity itself is disrupted in this version of the west. In the film, four sisters of the Dalton clan band together after one of the sisters kills a man who attempts to rape her. Realizing that they will receive no help from the patriarchal law authorities, and have no chance at a fair trial, the women ride out together and initiate a series of "outlaw" acts to survive. The film depicts the plight of the White female with great sympathy, and reinscribes the female over the role traditionally assigned to White males in the western.

The presence of the figure of the White "woman with the gun" is a significant cultural rupture, in a move that anticipates such later works as *Thelma and Louise, Gun Crazy, Alien,* and *Blue Steel.* The female body acts as a performative disruption of the plantocratric order. *The Dalton Girls* exemplifies the phenomenologically unstable "act" of gender through the use of fetishization of the female body with an emphasis on guns, men's western clothing, and macho physical posturing. While the female may be read here in the context of psychoanalytic theory as "lack" which is "filled" with fetishistic phallic symbols, I wish to read the White female body as a site where, as Judith Butler describes, "gender is instituted through the stylization of the body and, hence, must be understood as the mundane way in which bodily gestures, movements, and enactments of various kinds constitute the illusion of an abiding gendered self" (1990b, 270).

From a psychoanalytic perspective, the film reperforms and recreates the feminine as a "phallic" woman. The cross dressing in the film would seem to "contain" the outlaw woman within the dominant gendered order. But *The Dalton Girls* operates on a number of different levels. It bespeaks a dialogic or dual language of signification of the performed self. On one level, *The Dalton Girls* seems to reinscribe the plantocratic order of the West; on another, the film may be read as a feminist text that seeks to problematize and overthrow the notion of the passive White female kept at "home on the range." From the perspective of performance theory, *The Dalton Girls* promotes slippage between binarist notions of gender and undermines the notion of fixed identity. The performed acts and utterances of the Dalton women also undermine the compulsory heterosexuality of the mythic western landscape routinely presented in Hollywood cinema.

*The Dalton Girls* is a pleasure to watch because it seems to invite an ontological investigation into the "realness" of identity and the mutability of gender. The frequent cross dressing of the central female figures supports Judith Butler's theory that "the body is only known through its gendered appearance" (1990b, 274). The pleasure of frequently viewing the women stripping off their dresses to reveal their cowboy clothing is heightened by the fact that we are "invited to share" in the disturbance of gender order. We are invited to revel in the fetishism and partake in an "act" of what has been culturally defined as "specifically masculine power" (Tasker 159). The scenes of cross-power-dressing in *The Dalton Girls* are pleasurable for female viewers, and comparable to butch/femme reconstructions in films such as *Thelma and Louise*. Sharon Willis feels: "One of the more compelling pleasures of [*Thelma and Louise*] is the radical change in women's body language—posture, gait, and gesture—a change that went along with the shift from dressy clothes to tee-shirts and jeans" (127).

The significance of body posturing is immediately apparent in the titles of *The Dalton Girls*, which open with a drawing of the "girls" outfitted as cowboys, posed in the swaggering gait of the typical male Western hero. Hands-on-hips, holsters and guns thrust toward the viewer, the women assume a threatening macho gesture which they often take up throughout the film. Though Holly is dressed in white, the picture of White female virtue and Republican womanhood; when she is brutally attacked and nearly raped, she takes up a dominant gait and protects herself by hitting the man over the head with a shovel. In an amazing gender reversal, Rose, the most "masculine" of the sisters, parodies sexual harassment against women, by sexually harassing men. In one of her performative acts of reinscription, she harasses a man by pulling at his facial hair and adopting a sexually dominant sadistic stance. "I'll bet you just tickle the girls to death with those whiskers" she taunts him, while holding a gun on him with one hand, and punching him in the stomach with the other.

This scene evokes memories of other western films, in which White women are threatened and molested, such as John Ford's *Stagecoach* (1939). In another scene, Marigold, dressed as a man, ropes and hog-ties a male figure as he begs for mercy. How many scenes have we endured in which women beg for mercy at the hands of men? The film causes the viewer to contemplate male violence that lies at the center of the supposedly Edenic paradise of the Western. Rose, like a swaggering gun-crazy male, is eager to kill the hog-tied man. "Killing him would give me a certain amount of pleasure," she says, reminding the viewer of countless incidents in films in which men take pleasure in violating the body of women.

Rose's cross-dressing is sometimes accompanied by a cross-dressing of body language. Rose sets up a bank robbery dressed in "feminine" clothing. Here, she assumes the "act" of femininity, the posture of the submissive White woman, by flirting with a bank manager to get into the vault. The minute he turns away from her to open the safe, Rose hikes up her petticoat to reveal her gun and begins performing as a tough butch again. Rose's penultimate cross-dressing scene, however, is her rendition of the theme song "A Gun Is My True Love." Dressed in the cowboy get-up, wearing the black hat and black jeans associated with the "bad" man in the typical Western, Rose reclines provocatively on a rock and directly sings to the viewer. The clear subtext of the song is primacy and constancy of female same-sex bonding. The song begins with the verse:

> Oh, you can't trust a man,
> Cause a man will lie.
> But a gun stays beside you,
> Till the day you die.

As Rose sings and plays with her gun, the film cuts to shots suggestive of butch/femme gazes and lesbian eroticism. One sister (more the femme type) plays the harmonica as she gazes with fondness at Rose and then another sister lays reclined with her head in the lap of her comforting sister, Holly. Every time the lyrics mention the unfaithful man, we view the two women caressing and consoling one another. In another astounding performance of Queer White resignification, Rose shoots her gun off, like a swaggering cocksure antihero, as she sings:

> Oh, the *man* is a cheater,
> with his trifling ways,
> But a *gun's* always faithful.
> Cause a gun never strays.

The actress who plays Rose seems to invite the viewer to read the song and the scene for multiple meanings. The most obvious reading of the gun, in a film of the fifties, a period rife with popular Freudian psychology, would locate the gun as a phallic symbol, but the intercutting of scenes suggestive of female same-sex love between cross-dressing women, subverts such a fixed reading. *The Dalton Girls* thus transgresses Freud's theory of women as "lack." It invites Irigaray's image of two lips which "prioritizes multiplicity and reflection and the gap between them" (Johnston 78); it seems obvious that *The Dalton Girls* was intended as a marker of the presence of Queer women within the White western landscape.

The unstable and multiple subject-object positions of the women in the film are markers of a phenomenological discourse of identity. As Gilles Deleuze suggests, in cinema, the representation of the body "forces us to think, and forces us to think what is concealed from thought, life" (189). Cinema forces us to contemplate the performativity of identity. "In film there can be no firm guarantees of identity and presence" (Shaviro 38). Identity is problematized in *The Dalton Girls* from the beginning of the film, when it is implied that being a "Dalton" is being an "Other."

The signifier "Dalton" is just as multivalent in meaning as the sign of the "gun." The man who tries to rape Holly Dalton says to her "Don't you think I know *who* you and your sisters are as well as *what* you are?" When Columbine, one of the girls, falls in love, her sisters remind her who she "is." "Have you told him who you are?" they ask. Being a "Dalton" means being an outlaw, Queer, a sexual outsider. At one point, the younger Dalton sister, Marigold, complains about her status as a Dalton. "Why can't we be like other families? Peaceful and polite?" The Dalton girls are referred to as "vengeful Amazons," and "female impersonators," yet they refer to themselves as "regular old *men* on a robbery" playfully slapping each other on the back after a holdup. Rose tells Columbine to quit trying to "be a 'lady' . . . stop dreaming, and face up to it. You're a Dalton. Whatever a Dalton is, it's not a 'lady'."

Narrative tension in the film revolves around the fluid gender identity of the Dalton girls. A befuddled male victim of the female bandits insists they are men, claiming, "I'd recognize a member of the fair sex when I see em!" But the viewer knows otherwise. *The Dalton Girls* forces us to think about the mutability of identity and the construction of sexuality in the cinematic frame. The performances of the women in the film are completely uncharacteristic of the roles assigned to women in most westerns, wherein "what matters is that [one must] be a man. That is the only side to be on" (Tompkins 18).

*The Dalton Girls* sidesteps the binaries that are hallmarks of the classic western film. The film opens with a White woman's protection of herself, decentering the rape-revenge narrative. The narrative is denied the privilege of easily read good-versus-bad male cowboys. The Daltons are neither good nor bad, neither masculine nor feminine, neither civilized nor civilizing. Consequently, Mr. Grey seems like a good choice of name for the gambler who is drawn to the Dalton girls. Mr. Grey makes statements designed to mirror the fragmented moral universe of *The Dalton Girls.* When Columbine informs him that she isn't a virtuous civilized lady ("you know what I am"), he responds with surprising understanding and explains his heterotopic moral philosophy of equality between the sexes: "You and three other women held up a stagecoach, so what? You had to make your way out on the frontier. It's more honorable than some others. . . . I won't hold myself above you, or you me."

Mr. Grey stands in as a signifier between Plantocratic referents of good and evil. He is the grey area between, where gendered notions of virtue are flattened, binaries of race are called into question, and Queerness is a distinct possibility. He dwells in a failed heterotopia of Plantocratic gender politics. His big mistake, within the context of the symbolic order of the film, is trying to help and court the Dalton women. By trying to help the women, he imposes on their outlaw status. Though his intentions are "good," Grey seems to want to enforce his symbolic order upon the women. Regardless of his desire for sexual equality, Grey is actually more comfortable with the convention of the helpless female body. He is ultimately an Imperial male who wishes to go back to the ways of the Plantocratic order.

The helpless White female body is a commodified body within conventional westerns. This trope is overturned in the beginning of the film, before the near-rape scene. Mr. Grey offers Rose and Holly Dalton his "help" in handling the burial of the Dalton brothers. "There's bound to be a certain prejudice, miss. You and your sisters might need help," he says. "If we need any help, Mr. Grey, you'd be the last man I'd ask," Holly states flatly. In the next scene, male "help" is exposed as a form of disempowerment. "I could do a lot of things for you" is the sleazy proposition put to Holly by the undertaker, who implies he could defray the expenses of the burial in return for sexual favors. Holly kills Grey in self-defense, effectively killing the trope of the helpless White female on a symbolic level.

Mr. Grey's "help" constitutes a disruption within the world of the Dalton girls. This culminates in a failed heterotopic romantic happy ending, thus subverting the requirement of the genre. The actions of Mr. Grey neither save the women nor provide a happy ending. The film ends with a brutal showdown in which three of the sisters are shot. The music is decidedly downbeat, as Mr. Grey carries away the body of Marigold, his wounded love interest. Queerness would seem to be contained by this narrative even as it is staged and foregrounded.

However, the film lacks the narrative closure afforded by a typical western, a closure often marked by marriage. According to the rules of compulsory White heterosexuality, marriage signifies the "return to order," a basic requirement of the conventional western. The somewhat ambiguous ending of *The Dalton Girls* suggests that the body of "outlaw" woman brings disorder, rather than harmony to the landscape. The Daltons dislodge the order of sexuality and the order of White corporeality. It isn't even certain which girls survive, and which are dead. Is it a tragic happy ending, or a happy tragic ending?

The unfixed identity of the Daltons causes on-screen anxiety, but off-screen pleasure. The pleasure is in witnessing the exposure of the banished abject playing with the masquerade of stability. The Daltons' transgression within the repressed nineteen fifties is underscored by the fact that the viewer knows that off-screen "social stability depended crucially on people staying just as they were (identity), where they were (location), and doing what they always had done (calling)" (Dollimore 291). The Daltons are constantly moving around the landscape; they "range" from Texas to Colorado. They freely range through the landscape of gender identity, as well, frequently changing clothing from cumbersome bustiers into leather cowboy garb, and then into frilly "ladylike" dresses.

Through their actions, The Dalton women "remark" the boundaries of the White female with a fluidity of posture from "butch" defiance to "femme" submission in an outrageous performance worthy of Madonna. They are as impossible to identify as they are to locate; their only "calling" in life is to survive and transport themselves above the containment of the phallocentric order of the west. They murder, rope, rob, and hogtie, yet they sing of a lost female-centered home on the range. These crossdressing, cross-identifying, cross-locating women could only erupt across the screen of a low-budget film in the era of the nineteen-fifties, precisely because of the conventions the film contravenes.

As Linda Williams notes, even today "It is left to the cheaper movies to explore more fully a woman's view" (1993, 111). Singing cowboy/girl, Rose and her six-gun challenge "the destruction between appearance and reality that structures a good deal of popular thinking about gender identity" (Butler, 1990b, 278). She invites us to read her as a figure of cultural rupture. In so doing, she reaches across the cinematic apparatus, the screening space and rewrites herself, in a reperformance of the White female body, which, in Cixous's words "has been confiscated from her, which has been turned into the uncanny stranger on display" (879).

Rose cannot be read as a passive victim, and she won't let herself be read from a passive spectatorial position. Destabilizing and multiplying the effects of subjectivity, *The Dalton Girls* compares favorably to such films as Katt Shea's *Poison Ivy* (1992), which is noted for the postmodern manner in which it "plays with and questions power relations in the same way that it plays with and perverts the constraints of low-budget filmmaking: not by distancing us from these manifestations of power, but precisely by actualizing them in the most extreme way possible" (Shaviro 263).

Like *Blue Steel*, *The Dalton Girls* is thoroughly immersed in fetishism, whether it be that of guns, whips, jeans, or petticoats, and it revels in appeals to voyeuristic pleasure of scopophilia. As viewers, we take pleasure from the fetishistic display of the cross-dressing female corpus. Our gaze is ruptured by frequent gunfights and violence, often committed by women. The gunplay of women in *The Dalton Girls* erodes the myth of a comfortable passive "male gaze." Onscreen identity is so mutable and sexually charged that off-screen identification becomes problematic, if not impossible for the viewer; unless she or he is able to embrace the fluid abjectivity of the Dalton order.

The landscape of the conventional western cannot "contain" the outlaw woman of *The Dalton Girls*. Perhaps that is why the film is a cult classic. Dorothy Allison's *Bastard Out of Carolina* includes a scene in which the female narrator recalls how she "played" the game of the "Dalton Girls," even though she hadn't seen the movie. "All of us girls loved the idea of the gang of sisters who robbed banks" (211). Merely the "idea" of the outlaw woman was apparently enough to appeal to the budding young Queer Southern novelist. Even though the film is obscure and hard to "locate," it seems as if the Dalton girls have stepped off the screen into hypereal phantasms of Queer White desire filling a "lack" in popular culture of White badgirl imagery.

The idea of the feminist western film continues to be disruptive and controversial. Recently, director Tamra Davis was fired after several weeks filming of the 1994 western *Bad Girls*, and replaced by male director Jonathan Kaplan, a veteran of the Roger Corman school of exploitation filmmaking. *Bad Girls* chronicles the story of four White women who set out on their own, after one of the group members kills a man in justifiable self-defense. As with *The Dalton Girls*, the women are convinced that no one within the patriarchal society of the Old West will believe them, and see their only hope of survival as outlaws, continually on the run.

For all women's advancement in other areas of cinema, women still display a disturbing lack of artistic control within the world of the western genre film, where they are portrayed predominantly from the heterosexual White male point of view, as objectified sex toys, "rewards" for successful male protagonists, or as victims in need of rescue. In an interview, Tamra Davis spoke out against the mistreatment by the producers of *Bad Girls*, and the continued artistic interference she had to endure during what little filming she was able to accomplish. And yet Davis was understandably reluctant to go *too* public with her complaints; after all, she still has to work in Hollywood, within the rules of the economic and generic games played in that town. "I don't want to say anything bad, but I also don't want to be another woman director who keeps quiet when something bad happens" (Garey and Hruska 74). Davis was going for a more realistic, less frilly approach, with little or no makeup, low-light photography, and a gritty, documentary look to the visuals, something like Clint Eastwood did in *The Unforgiven*. But instead of being a transgressive feminist western film, the completed version of *Bad Girls* was accurately described by Henry Cabot Beck as "a western less arty than tarty" (62).

In comparison to *The Dalton Girls*, *Bad Girls* is thus a step backwards in terms of feminist politics and self-actualization. *Even Cowgirls Get the Blues* and *The Ballad of Little Jo* are much more in keeping with the spirit of *The Dalton Girls*, but these films remain isolated instances of generic disruption. *Even Cowgirls Get the Blues* features an ecofeminist group of women who seize control of a corrupt dude ranch, and thus, by extension, the land of the west itself. "There's never been a movie about cowgirls," one of the film's central characters notes at one point, and for the most part (except for a few unusual westerns with Barbara Stanwyck, such as the 1954 film *Cattle Queen of Montana*), the statement is distressingly true. *The Ballad of Little Jo* follows the adventures of Jo Monaghan, a woman who dressed as a man in order to survive within the hostile western landscape. Perhaps some future westerns will live up to the standard set by *The Dalton Girls*, and follow in the disruptive footsteps of *Little Jo* and *Cowgirls*. But for the moment, the central factor behind the current lack of feminist westerns is best described by B. Ruby Rich: "the basic dilemma facing anyone intent on fashioning a mainstream version of the female western is obvious: how to find a way to give women as much power as men" (22). This construction of an alternative figure of feminist agency is in direct contradiction to relationships between women as configured in more traditional forms of the western, such as Fred Zinnemann's *High Noon* (1952).


## THE ABYSS OF REPRESENTATION

Classical Hollywood westerns usually exemplify the homogenizing practices of White supremacist values, particularly as these values are applied to the marginalized "others" of American patriarchy, women, people of diverse sexual orientations, and all people of color. As Vivian Sobchack has noted, this tendency has left the modern critic a major task; that is to locate the place from which the Other has been "elided or marginalized within the homogenizing rhetoric of culturally dominant discourses" (147). Fred Zinnemann's *High Noon* illustrates a site in which a seemingly classic western narrative of the White male heroic quest is seemingly subverted by the inclusion of a metanarrative of the Other. This surprising element of the movie, which has been overwhelmingly praised as a male quest narrative, is that it is ultimately a complex split narrative that elucidates the struggle of a White Quaker woman and a Mexican American woman, who, in turn, fully represent the struggle of the difference of the Other in a heroic struggle that is in many ways far more interesting than that of the central hero, Will Kane, played by Gary Cooper.

In many ways, the women in *High Noon* overturn the codified, expected gendered and radically troped behavior of the Hollywood western. Katy Jurado, who plays Helen Ramirez, a Mexican American businesswoman, shares the metanarrative with Grace Kelly, who plays Amy Fowler Kane, a woman who is Othered by religion; her Quaker pacifism clearly places her oppositionally in face of a violent, brutal patriarchal White power structure. Both women surprise the viewer with their ability to survive in the narrative. Both are mature women with principles, and neither fit the binaristic mold of the classical good-girl, bad-girl scenario. In fact, Zinnemann plays off these clichés, female Western archetypes that commonly support the order of the Plantocracy of images.

While Amy is introduced into the narrative in the classically White female submissive posture expected of a wedding sequence, she subsequently disrupts our expectations, and continually threatens to leave her good man, as well as the narrative. She argues aggressively with her partner, rather than passively listening, yet she does not adopt the mother role

FIGURE 17. Katy Jurado (Helen Ramirez) and Grace Kelly (Amy Fowler); the metanarrative of difference in *High Noon.* Courtesy Jerry Ohlinger Archives.

of guidance and temperance. Instead, she forms a bond with Helen Ramirez, from whom she learns to question White male supremacy. Though Helen Ramirez is dressed in the classical bad-girl garb, dark haired and Black bodiced, and Amy Fowler is dutifully White skinned, White bonneted, and classically beautiful, neither character corresponds with the codified behavior of the dichotomized female of the highly raced and gendered Hollywood western.

The viewer might expect to learn that the Mexican woman, Helen Ramirez, is a prostitute bent on the destruction of the good girl who takes her man. Instead, Ramirez is a business woman, we learn, who must protect her investment when the town is disrupted by evil forces. Amy Fowler and Helen Ramirez, one might expect, would become polarized by the skin color and by the fact that they are both emotionally involved with the hero. Instead of the expected interracial cat fights, Zinnemann evokes female bonding across racial lines. In a few key scenes, which the women share, Zinnemann's women criticize the patriarchal and Plantocratic systems. They recognize their racial difference, even as they find common ground for speaking to one another as feministas.

In addition, both women take action in the narrative and power over their bodies, and neither is sacrificed in the film. Zinnemann does not take the usual route of killing off the non-White Other as a sacrificial tribute to her inacceptability in hegemonic discourse, nor does he pander to audience expectations with a lengthy heroic rescue scene of the White woman by her White man. Instead, Amy Fowler tries to scratch out the eyes of the antihero, and only after freeing herself does Zinnemann allow the hero to shoot Frank Miller.

*High Noon* is significant as an example of a film that includes a dual positional narrative of male and female perspective. Vivian Sobchack has identified films that share such a "paranoia of split vision," in which the filmmaker desires "not only to describe the structure of cinematic signification but also to critique the hegemony of classical cinematic practice" (262). *High Noon* engages in a multilayered narrative in order to criticize cinema, White societal codes, and gendered expectations from a safe perspective. *High Noon* fulfills the requirements of the heroic narrative on the most basic level—by offering a White male quest narrative—but this narrative is decentered by the metanarratives of the women in the film.

But as Dana Polan has demonstrated, some westerns stray from the monologic form and follow a "two-part structure," in which "there is no longer a place for the individual western spirit" (1986, 265). These westerns schizophrenically attach pastoral values to spaces that "represent the unproductive places left behind in modernity's expansion" (1986, 267). *High Noon* fits a pattern of the western of dystopia. The White hero's quest is viewed as futile, and the quest of the Other is marked as that of the women characters within Zinnemann's narrative.

*High Noon*, as many critics have noted, is centrally consumed with the cynicism of the postwar years. Zinnemann anticipates the modern narrative of the repressed and the disenfranchised. The question is why he weaves his White hero's quest into the metanarrative of the female Other, or, as Mary Ann Doane puts it, "why must the woman always carry the burden of philosophical demonstration, why must she be the one to figure truth, dissimulation, untruth, the abyss, etc. . . ." (74)? The answer is to be found in an analysis of Zinnemann's women as representations of difference, rather than gender. "Because the female is the repressed it is, in this fabric of understanding, the silenced, the unexpressable" (93).

Thus, Helen Ramirez and Amy Fowler speak of the repressed anger of the Other in American postwar society. Amy Fowler's line of dialogue "I don't understand any of this," in response to her husband Will Kane, who feels he must go back to face his opponent, is the voice of pacifist America who still refuses to "understand" acts of war. The comment may be taken as stereotypically White female, as a woman who can't understand a White man's world, but within the metanarrative of the repressed it is calculatedly a rupture of the discourse of warmongering and blind patriotism. This is a fine example of Zinnemann's articulation of a fifties' "paranoia of split vision," as used by Sobchack.

The inherent multivalency of Amy's measured response is later revealed in a scene in which Amy Fowler discusses with Helen Ramirez how she came to become a pacifist. Amy explains that she watched her nineteen-year-old brother and father die from bullet wounds. Helen Ramirez's reaction to Amy Fowler's tale is to bond with her and to explain why she must leave town: "I hate this town. I've always hated it. To be a Mexican woman in a town like this . . ."

Amy Fowler responds "I understand," as if a White woman can easily come to grips with racial hatred as a compound to gender-based discrimination. Surprisingly, Helen responds, "You do? That's good. *I don't understand you.*" In this moment, it seems that the two women will not be able to overcome their racial Otherness. But Zinnemann allows for the *difference* to exist between the women's world views, and Helen and Amy form a union which is continually visually reinforced through the inscription of shots of the women together, watching and waiting, until the climactic male killing spree is over.

Zinnemann's inclusion of such a strong Xicana character as Helen Ramirez in the metanarrative may be an early example of a "deflection" of the suffering of the Other, as defined by bell hooks (1992, 25), in which the dominant culture is continually "reenacting and reritualizing in different ways the imperialist, colonizing journey as narrative fantasy of power and desire," but Zinnemann does not choose the characteristically racist route of "seduction by the Other" (25), typical of the scenario painted by hooks. Helen Ramirez as a character subverts this expectation; she seduces neither the hero Will Kane nor the criminal Frank Miller.

Edward Said notes that imperialist American culture often evokes a centrality that works in "preventing counter-narratives from emerging" (1993, 324). *High Noon* is a Hollywood western that seeks to disrupt centrality, both in the White male heroic narrative, which one character, played by Lon Chaney, Jr., describes as "All for nothin'," and in the counternarrative of the women as others. The reading of the interracial female metanarrative is certainly against the grain of criticism that perpetuates the centrality of the heroic male narrative in *High Noon.*

But, as Judith Mayne reminds us, it is by "reading against the grain" (1990, 98), that we can begin to see how "traditional cinematic representations of women [can demonstrate] how they can be read in ways that contradict or otherwise problematize their function within male-centered discourse" (1990, 98). Zinnemann's choice of interweaving an early feminist and socially conscious metanarrative through the voice of the female is subtly effective precisely because women are, as Lois McNay notes, "engendered across a vast number of subject positions" (67), and are therefore more capable of fully articulating the gaps, ruptures, and silences enforced upon a culture of domination, such as the one in which Zinnemann was immersed.

Rereading *High Noon* with an eye open to the possibilities of racially charged narratives and multiple female subject positions allows for a fuller dialogic reading of the carefully woven texts critical of postwar America, of war, of gender expectations for both White and Mexican women, of racism in America, of McCarthyism, of commercialism, of hero worship, and of the mentality of the Hollywood movie machine itself. Ironically, the film's theme incessantly recurring song "High Noon," written by Dimitri Tiomkin and Ned Washington and sung by Tex Ritter, only adds to the criticisms of the multifaceted narrative. The lyrics are heard so many times throughout the film that they become almost humorous:

Do not forsake me, oh my darlin'
You màde that promise when we wed.
Do not forsake me, oh my darlin'
Although you're grieving.
I can't be leavin'
Until I shoot Frank Miller dead.

The song would seem to suggest that Will Kane's quest in *High Noon* is the stereotypical desire to please and then possess the White female within the narrative. But in fact, the song foreshadows that it is the White men in the film, the hero's best friends, who will forsake him, and not Amy Kane. It is his supposed comrades and constituents who will refuse to help him in his "heroic" quest. Some lines in the song specifically raise the issue of the idiocy of masculine hero role playing:

If I'm a man I must be brave.
And I must face that deadly killer . . .
or I'll lie a coward in my grave.

Zinnemann interweaves a subtle attack on these gender expectations throughout both narratives. As these words are sung, an old, presumably wise, Native American woman who has no other place in the film, is shown crossing herself as she looks upon the three bad White men who ride into town. The figure of the old woman foreshadows the senseless violence in a grave manner, but in other sites in the film, Zinnemann includes women of color laughing at the stupidity of White male stereotypical roles.

Helen Ramirez, in particular, ridicules the masculine domain of senseless brutality. As a Mexican Other, she apparently owns the privileged subject position of being able to see and know the foolishness of the violence of patriarchal White western culture. When Ramirez's boyfriend makes fun of the Kane's initial flight from town, away from the oncoming violence, Helen regards him with a look of revulsion which turns into a grave laugh. Kane himself makes an utterance that establishes a strong undercurrent against hero worship and expectations of White men: "If you think I like this, you're crazy," he says to Amy, even as he is compelled into turning around to return to town to fight his enemy.

But the most revealing criticisms are offered by Helen Ramirez, who voices a strong subtext against male power and violence against women.

Not only does Zinnemann create, in Helen, a strong central Xicana character of profound significance within the narrative of *High Noon*, Zinnemann allows Helen to speak on equal terms with Will Kane, Amy Kane, and others within the narrative, and in her world-weary presence, Helen embodies the violent and reductive truth of the location they all share more than any other single character within the film. In a pivotal scene, Kane suggests that Ramirez leave town because of the impending return of Frank Miller. "You know how he is," says Kane.

Helen gazes at him for a moment, then responds wearily, "I know how he is." That Zinnemann would include such allusions to White male violence against Mexican/Chicana women, especially in a recognition across gendered lines in the western, is atypical. That he would contextualize a criticism against it is remarkable. In a later scene, in which Helen explains why she must leave her boyfriend, Helen Ramirez restates her revulsion to White male violence and power over her body: "I'm all alone in the world. . . . I have to make a living . . . and as for you . . . I don't like anybody to put his hands on me unless I want him to, and I don't like you to, anymore."

As if to totally reverse our gender expectations, Helen delivers these lines and immediately slaps her White boyfriend out of the frame as a seeming answer to White male violence. The possibility of male violence against women is continually if subtly referred to throughout the film. In the church meeting hall scene, for example, an older woman gets up in defense of Kane and says, "Don't you remember when it wasn't safe for women and children?"

Metaphorically, Zinnemann adds touches that remind us of the omnipresence of brutal violence in American western society. One sequence, for example, highlights the villains carefully oiling and cleaning their phallic weaponry in anticipation of the upcoming violence. Another scene suggests the probability of the rape of women in the future, if Kane does not succeed in eliminating the violent male figures. In this scene, one of the men breaks a window, steals a bonnet, and attaches it to his belt, in a metaphoric equivalent of rape. Seeing this action, another member of the gang comments, "can't you wait?"

The violence itself erupts methodically when it finally erupts in *High Noon*, after a montage sequence. The montage sequence foregrounds the faces of the women, Amy Fowler and Helen Ramirez, who are seen in tighter close-ups as the tension builds. In this way, Zinnemann plays up the importance of the female interracial metanarrative. Zinnemann firmly establishes the bond between the women with several shots of them riding in a wagon together.

With a final look over her shoulder, Helen Ramirez leaves the film's narrative, as if to remind the viewer that this is, after all, a White struggle. In the final shootout, Amy Fowler Kane is the central viewer of the White male violence. Surprisingly for the period, Zinnemann then turns the White female narrative into the central narrative. The White woman is the silent but omniscient presence that carries the filmmaker's social criticism to the end of the film. When Amy views a slain man in the street, we identify with her quest for nonviolence and pacifism, instead of the machismo of the conventional male hero.

Rather than foregrounding the traditionally inviolate nature of the stereotypical White western hero, Zinnemann shows us a marked change in Will Kane's humanity, as well as the pain he bears as the standard bearer of "justice" within a patriarchal society. As critic Stuart Kaminsky notes in his essay on the narrative structure of *High Noon*,

> At one point Kane, alone in his office, puts his head down on his desk, possibly to weep, and then wearily pulls himself up again. In the final confrontation with Miller and his gang, Kane does stand alone until the last moment, when Amy saves his life by shooting down Frank Miller. (in Thomas, 387)

The White woman is unable to free herself from *High Noon*'s patriarchal violence, and in fact is positioned within the narrative at the center of this superscribing aggression. Because the violence documented in *High Noon* occurs in order to protect the sanctity of White women, the White woman is not able to completely step aside from it. Amy is forced instead to accept it and deal with it, despite her revulsion to it, as part of the then-existing societal system. Because Helen Ramirez has left the narrative, the possibility for consistent sisterhood across racial lines is highly problematized. Amy Fowler must ultimately stay and fight for her own life, as well as the life of Will Kane. As Joanna Rapf notes, the script for *High Noon* went even further in its description of the unusual character of Amy Kane than the finished film articulates. Rapf writes that "the unique, indeed revolutionary position of the two main women in *High Noon*, and in particular, of the seemingly conventional Amy, is supported not only by character descriptions in the script, but by a significant piece of dialogue that, unfortunately, was cut from the final film. In Amy's conversation with Helen just before the two of them leave for the train station at noon [Amy says in the script, but *not* in the finished film], 'Back home they think I'm very strange. I'm a feminist. You know, women's rights—things like that . . . (Script 95)" (78). The burden of representation of feminism falls to Helen, an early filmic exemplification of the Mexican feminista who exhibits what Ana Castillo terms "Xicanisma" (40).

Thus Zinnemann's intent throughout the film is clear; he wishes to foreground the voices of Helen and Amy within the cinema/text of the film, and this sequence in the script makes the centrality of this intent unquestionable. Rapf suggests the lines were cut because "to have included them would have been anachronistic" (78). Perhaps this is true, but whatever the reason for the deletion of these lines of dialogue, the other textual evidence grounded within the work is more than sufficient to support a feminist Postcolonial interpretation of the film.

In the final analysis, Fred Zinnemann's women in *High Noon* are presented to the viewer in a charitable progression towards reclamation of the White female body, and the inscription of a strong Mexican woman who rides off in the sunset as a transgressive heroine of Otherdome. Amy Fowler's final act of attempting to tear the eyes out of Frank Miller can be compared with Fred Zinnemann's ability as a filmmaker to tear the eyes out of the passive onlooker, and make him/her work on the material of this problematic Plantocratic western landscape. Set as it was in the 1950s, what surprises us in retrospect is how much the film questions of the values that make up the White supremacist fabric of American society, a fabric that can be ripped asunder with unsettling ease.

Zinnemann presents us with a paranoid and dual set of narratives which, in the end, deny the viewer the comfort and distance of a passive spectatorial gaze. The well-developed female characters, who display the disenfranchisement of America, the Mexican American worker and the pacifist White Quaker woman, disrupt the expectations and limitations of classical Hollywood western stereotypes. Their action speaks as loudly as their words. These mature women introduce dangerously regarded subject matter into what may have been wrongly regarded as a hegemonic monologic, patriarchal discourse.

In addition, Zinnemann further subverts Hollywood generic convention by continuing his dystopic vision into a reversal of the wedding trope. Instead of ending with a happy wedding, the film begins with a wedding, and from there the trouble begins. In this way Zinnemann displaces the notion of the White female as commodity, a usually sacrosanct notion in Hollywood filmmaking, particularly in the forties and fifties. Though the White couple does ride off into the sunset, it is less with a sense of jubilation than grave acceptance of the current state of White supremacist American values, and of the false lip-service these values are given within society. It seems that Zinnemann is saying that no one will be emancipated from this thoroughly corrupt and valueless system unless White women and Xicana women, along with men, are willing to work together to bring about effective change. One coefficient of this change in representations of the male and female body in the cinema is the absence of the figure of the unclothed and thus commodified and captive male phallus.

## DESIRE AND IDENTIFICATION

The lack of full male frontal nudity in mainstream Hollywood cinema continues to be an enigmatic, but strictly enforced, code that denies demystification of the penis and substitutes for fetishization of the male body the fetishization of weaponry and clothing. At the same time, the female body continues to be freely used as the symbol to inscribe the power/knowledge relationships between the sexes. Films increasingly expose the female frontally; whether in sexual repose, activity, passivity, or danger and dismemberment, yet the penis remains visually masked by taboo, and by tradition, in films directed by men or women. One film that has broken this taboo, *Bad Lieutenant* (1992; written by Zoe Lund and directed by Abel Ferrara), is the welcome aberration. Meanwhile, male and female audience members alike continue to be denied the pleasures of spectatorship of the male body.

The phenomenon is acute and demonstrable. Male actors are not only prudish about exposing their genitalia, but they vocalize their discomfort with exposing their backsides as well. There are exceptions to this general rule, as in *The Crying Game* (1993), but this highly successful British import is no way representative of Hollywood studio cinema. On the other hand, female actresses routinely find themselves expected to disrobe on screen. Full female frontal nudity, while still somewhat taboo, is increasingly becoming de rigeur in Hollywood cinema, with the obvious example of Sharon Stone exhibiting her *mons veneris* in *Basic Instinct.* With more and more films in the 1990s being directed by women, one would expect this disparity between the full representation of the male and female body to be somewhat closed, but perhaps the underlying cultural reasons for this disparity itself is more complex than our assumptions have led us to believe.

Conventional psychoanalytic film criticism stresses the importance of locating the female body in film as a "raw material for the active gaze of man" (Mulvey 208). Though some feminist criticism has argued that woman can represent something other than a signifier of castration, a voyeuristic or fetishistic pleasure fulfiller (or denier), much film criticism continues to analyze the female body from the point of view of the male gaze. I don't wish to argue with this strain of criticism, but instead wish to build upon it, in a reversal strategy, by questioning why Hollywood cinema, and to some extent film criticism, continues to repress the possibility of female, lesbian, bisexual, or transgendered fetishization of the male body. Female fetishism, while sometimes regarded as a nonexistent, improbable, or unwanted attribution, has been relegated to the ranks of supposed nonexistence through the literature of psychoanalysis.

As Naomi Schor has accurately demonstrated, "traditional psychoanalytic literature on the subject states over and over again that there are no female fetishists; female fetishism is, in the rhetoric of psychoanalysis, an oxymoron" (365). Freud, according to Schor, effectively masculinized fetishism, yet Schor and others have identified female fetishism in the writings of George Sand and other women writers (see Emily Apter's *Feminizing the Fetish* for a more comprehensive view of female fetishism). Psychoanalytic approaches are also responsible, to a large degree, for marking fetishism and voyeurism as perversions. Thus female directors who wish to cross the borderlines of acceptable cultural limitations of the troping of the male body do so at risk of defining their female audiences as "perverts" or "deviants."

Jonathan Dollimore's analysis of sexual deviance contradicts the Freudian account of "perversion." Drawing on the writings of Michel Foucault, Dollimore locates the societally allowed "perversion" as a power construct, highlighting "Foucault's insistence that perversion is not an innate desire which is socially repressed, but an identity and a category which is socially produced to enable power to gain a purchase within, and through, the realm of the psychosexual" (226–27). Dollimore reminds us of the costs of "perversity" in society: "death, mutilation, and incarceration have been, and remain, the fate of those who are deemed to have perverted nature" (230). Dollimore's remarks are ironic when we consider that underground male homosexual filmmaking has been one area of relatively safe display, reverence, and fetishization of the phallus. The films of Andy Warhol and Derek Jarman are sites in which societally termed "deviant" or supposedly "perverted" gazes are allowed to act upon desire. In noting the paucity of images of the phallus in mainstream Hollywood cinema, we must remember the validity of Dollimore's remarks regarding repression in society:

> The symbolic harnessing of the deviant is rarely creative, regenerative, or benign, it involves a violence open to any authority which wants a witch-hunt/scapegoat. . . . At the very least we should recognize that the process being described is usually more destructive than regenerative. (221)

It is certainly hard to calculate the ramifications of culturally silencing around the fetishization of the male body. It is equally difficult to understand the underlying presumptions about societal codes of masculinity as they would conceivably be disrupted by the introduction of female erotic desire, fetishization, or even misandry. Fetishism itself has been established by nineteenth-century discourse, as a masculine occupation. "As defined by the early psychoanalysts, [such as Krafft-Ebing and Havelock Ellis] fetishism was the fantastic creation of a male erotic imagination: a fin-de siècle imagination spurred by castration anxiety or repressed homosexuality," writes Emily Apter (102). Even the phrase "female fetishism" is one "coined primarily by feminist thinkers as part of a general revisionist critique of gender stereotypes and phallocentric psychoanalytic presumptions," as Apter notes (168). Even in the study of pornography, there is less discussion of naked male bodies than naked female bodies. As Laura Kipnis writes:

> Why has there been such reticence about dealing with the issues raised by pornography in which the bodies depicted are bodies possessing penises? Perhaps it's because doing so throws any certainty about what pornography is and does into question. (65)

Of those feminist thinkers who have "attempted to rescue female spectatorship" (6), Mariam Hansen has introduced the possibility of female fetishism at work in audiences viewing the films of actor Rudolph Valentino. Hansen documents the eroticism of the body of Valentino as a sort of safe harbor for the female gaze at work in America in the nineteen twenties. Nevertheless, Hansen notes that Valentino films cloaked the feminine gaze in an "emphasis on costumes, disguises, on rituals of dressing and undressing, [which] undermines in tendency, the voyeuristic structure of spectatorship" (17). Men were routinely fitted with clothing and props as early as the first primitive films, as demonstrated by Linda Williams. Williams's analysis of the Edweard Muybridge studies of *The Human Figure in Motion* (1901) notes the disparity between the "gratuitous fantasization and iconization of bodies of women that have no parallel in the representation of the male" (511). The "studies" of men tended to portray men in activity with props such as "dumbbells, boulders, baseballs, the equipment of various combat sports . . ." (512). Already, in the earliest cinematic recordings of the human body, gendered tropings of the body of considerable importance were marking the boundaries of cinematic discourse of the White male body.

The Muybridge projections would influence future representations of the male and female body to the degree that the phallus is routinely suggested or replaced by props in Hollywood filmmaking, with the penultimate example of Arnold Schwarzenegger's display of a grotesquely overabundant super-gun in *The Last Action Hero* (1993). Perhaps mainstream Hollywood cinema will be forced by the marketplace to eventually begin to display full frontal male nudity. The waning vogue of the techno film might suggest that audiences may soon tire of inflated phallic weaponry, and demand to see the male human penis. Mass-marketing forces have already responded to the needs of a female-gazing audience with the rise, of course, of male strip clubs, but women enjoy these activities only in female dominant situations, not in mixed audiences. Only when women are finally considered as sexually mature and erotically active will women fully have access to the power/knowledge relationship of repressed sexuality, including fetishism and voyeurism.

An active female sexuality disrupts the very basis of gender identification. Since the eighteenth century, as Thomas Laqueur demonstrates, women were identified as the "passionless" sex (150). Early physicians used women's bodies as a "battleground for redefining the ancient, intimate, fundamental social relation: that of woman to man" (150). The "discovery" of the female reproductive organs defined female sexuality and denied the importance of orgasm, much less any other sexual characteristic. In the nineteenth century, as Michel Foucault notes, sexuality was "rigorously subjugated" (1908, 8). Hollywood filmmaking in the twentieth century would continue to operate in a gender-based paradigm identified by Richard Dyer as the "Playboy philosophy" (1988a, 76), wherein [male] "sex drives" operate supposedly on a "biological mandate" seeking "release" (1988a, 76). An important attribute of sex icon Marilyn Monroe, according to Dyer, was her projection of "guiltlessness" (1988a, 76). Though Monroe would subvert the ideals of the "guiltless" sexually active female, she certainly had no male counterpart. Dyer locates the body of Marilyn Monroe at the center of the pleasure-seeking gaze of the male within the culturally approved Playboy philosophy. If Monroe was of the current era, she would of course be expected to do scenes with frontal female nudity, and her male costars would only be obliged to perhaps show a fleeting glimpse of their hindquarters for the titillation of the female audience members.

In the past, objectification of the female body in Hollywood film has been easily traced to the lack of women in the film industry as filmmakers or producers. As Debra Fried explains, "Film refuses to record men because they are all the time choosing that it shall not record them; because they control the camera, the continuance of their absence from the picture pervasively attests to their presence as its recorders" (49). Fried's remarks are in reference to classic Hollywood cinema, before the current explosion of a new wave of women directors. Women directors such as Chantal Akerman, in her film *Night and Day* (1992), explore the arena of a liberated female who fully acts out her erotic desires. In *Night and Day*, the central female character, Julie, sexually desires two different men, who fulfill her desires throughout the movie; one by day and one by night. Interestingly enough, Akerman only briefly allows the viewer to gaze at the bodies of the fetishized male characters. Instead, Akerman's camera treats the audience to equally languorous displays of both male and female bodies. A number of mainstream women directors have had similarly ample opportunity to display the male body in detail (for one example, in Kristine Peterson's *Body Chemistry* [1991]), and yet they overwhelmingly choose not to include frontal male nudity in their films. Perhaps this policy is partially dictated by the front office, but it also seems to be a matter of individual choice.

The taboo of frontal male nudity is only equalled by the pictorial prohibition against anal and oral sex among men, which is rarely depicted in mainstream films directed by men or women. The regulation of subversive representations of the body are invested with a power that is thought to be dangerous and is thus marginalized. At the margins, in independent gay cinema, for example, the male body is freely represented in bodily activities unsanctioned by mass culture. These margins, and those that would operate on the desire of an active female gaze of fetishization of the male body, are considered equally dangerous. As Judith Butler concludes, "If the body is synecdochal for the social system per se or a site in which open systems converge, then any kind of unregulated permeability constitutes a site of pollution and endangerment" (1990a, 132). The representation of the male body for the scopophilic gaze of the female or the homosexual male is unconsciously recognized as a dangerous trope of unregulated desire, one that is rarely broken by Hollywood cinema.

The ease with which society allows representation of full frontal female nudity is unsurprising when one considers the semiological signifying abilities of the female body on Western culture. As Teresa de Lauretis comments, "women contribute to the wealth of a culture both as objects of exchange and as persons, as both signs and generators of signs" (1984, 19). The female body has long had the dubious distinction of being a veritable metaphor hanger for centuries in mass culture. It is surprising, however, to note that in early medieval culture, the male body, the phallus itself, was a common signifier of humanity, particularly in the depictions of the body of Christ and the body of the Christ child.

Before the medicalization of the human body of the eighteenth and nineteenth centuries, notions of gendered body were considerably different, allowing for the frequent display of male genitalia, within complete accordance with Christian orthodoxy. As Carolyn Walker Bynum notes, the body was probably seen more as "generative" than "sexual" (117). Bynum submits that female devotional writers and artists "did not either equate body with sexuality or reject body as evil" (116). Medieval women mystics wrote freely of their physical union with the body of Christ. Bynum sees the eroticism of the body of Christ in the work of these female mystics as less fetishistic or erotic as a modern reader might expect. Even Bynum doesn't entirely dismiss the more than remote possibility that writers such as Hadewijch, whom Bynum describes as "embracing Christ feeling him penetrate deep within her and losing herself to ecstasy" (86), are actively involved in the fetishization of the body of Christ, in an early display of the female gaze. The ample evidence of medieval and Renaissance artwork which depicts the penis of the infant and adult Christ and the instances of devotional writing describing the physical body of Christ in what looks to be an erotic display, at least from a modern perspective, provides an illuminating backdrop on which to juxtapose a discussion of the representation of the male body in twentieth-century films. The striking direct incidence of frontal male nudity in *Bad Lieutenant* is, appropriately enough, located in the discourse of a religious theme. In the film, Harvey Keitel is the embodiment of grotesque physicality and evil, yet he seeks redemption. It is provocative that this redemption includes a scene in which Keitel is shown in a fairly long take in which he silently begs forgiveness from God, in a full-figure nude shot that recalls the crucifixion of Christ. Frontal male nudity, it would seem, is only sanctioned in a religious embrace of the male body, yet it suggests the possibility of an active Queer male or heterosexualized female gaze. *Damage* (1993) ostensibly seems to be one example of this. The frontal male nudity in the film is infamous, and was cut considerably from American prints of the film, Yet the sexuality of the couple in *Damage* is seen as aberrationally excessive, and the frontal male nudity is in keeping here with a view of sensuality as base and "perverse." The majority of Hollywood male icons of heterotopic "healthy" sexuality, from *Batman* (1989) to Michael Douglas, are prudishly tucked away from the examining or fetishizational female or Queer gaze.

A good example of this phenomenon is the film *Sliver* (1993), which was originally shot with a great deal of male frontal nudity of actor Alec Baldwin, none of which survived in the final cut of the film. However, the film seldom missed an opportunity to present the nude body of Sharon Stone. In addition, an entire metaphoric subplot of the film comparing the hero's penis to a volcanic sculpture prominently displayed on his coffee table was dropped from the film as being too risqué, and with it, a final sequence depicting Baldwin and Stone descending into the crater of a live volcano, again with direct metaphoric intent.

Hollywood's maintenance of a strict code against male nudity reveals more, perhaps, about White male heterotopic spectatorship of the female body than the reverse. Mary Ann Doane's analysis of the "clinical eye" in the woman's film of the 1940s locates the female body as a site of spectacle operated upon by the "doctors look," which Doane places within the boundaries of "what Foucault describes as the medical glance rather than the gaze" (1986, 158). According to Doane, even the female spectator of these films is encouraged "to repudiate the feminine pole and to ally herself with the one who diagnoses, the one with the medical gaze" (1986, 171). If a tradition of women's films encourages the female to oscillate between male and female modes of looking, the tendency to deprivilege and desexualize the female as fetishist is a fervent display of a denial of female power over the male or female body. Perhaps it is a subtle recognition of the power of the Queer male or female gaze as a clinical force that acts as a social mechanism to continue the mystification and veiling of the penis?

Bette London's rereading of Mary Shelley's *Frankenstein* undermines previous critical readings of the novel that have ignored "its fixation on masculine spectacle," and the manner in which the novel "opened up the possibilities of female spectatorship" (264). Indeed, Mary Shelley's clinical eye was quite capable of an "insistent articulation of the male body [which] would seem to challenge the pieties of masculinity" (261), as London charges. Perhaps one day a film version of *Frankenstein* will be able to capture some of Mary Shelley's original intentions in this vein: sadly, Kenneth Branagh's 1994 film *Mary Shelley's Frankenstein* does not, despite its title, qualify in this regard. For now we will have to content ourselves with fully dressed or sexually neutered male monsters who objectify female bodies. Or perhaps we may read *Bad Lieutenant* as a postmodern version of *Frankenstein*, in which the monstrous Harvey Keitel is displayed as a criticism of the expectations of White masculinity in America?

A larger question remains. If cinema is the apparatus of fetishist pleasure, if cinema truly "brings about a state of regression and narcissism in the spectator" (Williams, 1986, 508), then why are women denied the state of regression? When women attend male strip-tease acts, it is viewed as harmless fun, yet some unspoken rule persists in denying them the pleasure of the clinical eye. Even when a female writer has offered us an example of female fetishism of the male body, as in the case of Mary Shelley or George Eliot, it takes a century for critics to recognize it as such. Perhaps one of the reasons women filmmakers haven't allowed themselves to wallow in regressive states of pleasure and narcissism is that women have had the more pressing task of telling narratives of liberation.

If the male organs displayed in early texts are "contingent certificates of status" (140), as suggested by Thomas Laqueur, the lack of male organs in Hollywood cinema is equally a certificate of status. The male body on the screen is fetishized and mechanized to the point of absurdity, as in the case of *Robocop* (1987), but presumably with the White male viewer in mind. The fusion of the White male body with the machine in the *Robocop* and *Terminator* movies may be read as a desperate attempt to mystify the phallus, and more generally, the outmoded ideals of Imperialist masculinity. The tradition of these Robo-male movies is longer than one might think, extending back to nineteenth-century obsessions for medical control of the body. As Linda Williams points out, pioneer filmmaker Georges Méliès "was already engaged in an obsessive pursuit of mastery over the human body" (1986, 523). Before becoming a filmmaker, as Williams has discovered, Méliès constructed robots in the late 1880s. Méliès's fascination with robots would be demonstrated in his early films, such as *Extraordinary Illusions* (1903). As Williams demonstrates, many of these films are thematically drawn around "dismemberment and reintegration of both male and female bodies" (1986, 526). This description could easily apply to films such as *Robocop* and especially *Terminator 2: Judgment Day* (1991), in which male dismemberment and reintegration suggests phallic infallibility and mastery.

The scores of mainstream Hollywood features that are narratives of body exchange extend the reintegration hypothesis, suggesting the probability that modern society depicts the male body as regenerative, rather than sexual. The possibility of a space for female fetishism and Queer male fetishism within this paradigm seems remote, even in the hands of female directors. While *Playgirl* and other mass entertainment vehicles allow some degree of female master over the male body, mainstream Hollywood cinema continues to offer the gaze of White mastery to the predominately White male audience. However, because Hollywood is a box-office-driven business, the demands of the marketplace, rather than aesthetic choice, may change all this considerably in the future. Perhaps male icons will someday be forced to bare their penis in order to maintain their blockbuster appeal. Perhaps nowhere is the issue of sexuality problematized more concretely than in the deconstructive films of Barbara Hammer. What is even more unrepresentable than the male phallus in mainstream White cinema are images of lesbian sex between older women, a challenge which Hammer confronts directly in her work. An examination of two of Hammer's key films, *Tender Fictions* (1995) and *Nitrate Kisses* (1992), brings the exclusionary tactics of contemporary commercial cinematic discourse into sharp focus.

## THE INVENTION OF LESBIAN AUTOBIOGRAPHY

Barbara Hammer has made over seventy-seven films and videos, and is one of the most inventive and prominent Lesbian experimental filmmakers. In *Nitrate Kisses*, Hammer began the cultural work of rediscovering and reconstructing Lesbian and Gay histories. In many ways, *Tender Fictions* continues that work. *Tender Fictions* is about the constructedness of biography, autobiography, and the self. In this film Barbara Hammer constructs her own biography before one is constructed for her. She introduces performative selves and performativity as a means to self-construction. This film destabilizes the notion of an integrated self that is constituted through the manifestation of the cult of the individual. *Tender Fictions* works towards the construction and reconstruction of lesbian autobiography and invents a postmodern self that can be experienced across multiple subjectivities. It is both a playful and provocative film and in the tradition of the greatest postmodern works, it is a self-reflexive film. In a way, all become facets of the multiplicity of selves of Barbara Hammer.

*Tender Fictions* and *Nitrate Kisses* thus work to re/construct lesbian autobiographies and histories. Both are highly experimental feature films that interweave archival footage with personal documentary "evidence" of lost and found lesbian history, combining evocative and the performative in a haunting blend of images and sound that is uniquely her own. In all of her works, Hammer is most interested in the creation of lesbian biography and autobiography, and it is these questions she addresses in her first feature films. At once sexy, erotic, and confrontational, Hammer's work operates at the margins between truth and fiction, memory and history, opening up a web of discourse for a new conceptualization of lesbian auto/biography. In the spring of 1997, I spoke with Barbara Hammer about her work.

GWENDOLYN FOSTER: In *Tender Fictions* you create new ways of looking at truth and its constructedness in autobiography and biography, yet you are careful to point out that history and biography are important political tools; that for example, when you looked back through your mothers, so to speak, you saw no lesbians. You underscore this point with a very touching and playful use of sound and voice. When we hear you singing a fragment, "looking for lesbians," it strikes me as a stunning use of humor for an important political statement. This might be a good place to begin talking about your use of humor and strategies of opposites to make the viewer/listener want to look again. In my interview with Trinh T. Minh-ha, she talked about how some audiences did not seem to be able to approach her films with a sense of humor. I wonder if that happens with your films and I wonder what you think about using humor as a performative political strategy.

BARBARA HAMMER: Humor in a film leads to instant gratification for the filmmaker when she is sitting in the audience. No one has talked about "receptivity theory" in regards to the *maker* as audience member in an audience community. When I hear laughter or giggles or murmurs at junctures in *Tender Fictions* and other films that I enjoyed, laughed out loud at while editing, I am rewarded, pleased, feel connected to the community that is my audience. Similarly, when the film falls flat, and I am greeted with silence, I feel anxious, not sure that the film has been read with the intention with which it was made. Humor is a great way to make a point. I like to pleasure myself while working, so it was with great surprise and joy that I found the over thirty-year-old, black and white, super 8 roll of a kitten playing with my exhusband's penis. Yes, it was directed! Filmmaking can be such hard work. When you work as an independent using your own resources or limited grant monies, you are spending time that is your life. I want to enjoy myself as much as possible within the limited time and resources I have, even with a life expectancy of eighty-four. If I am working on a subject that is not humorous, I want to feel deeply.

G.F.: I'm interested in your theories about performative gestures between lesbian couples, and how lesbian couples develop a complimentary set of movements and gestures.

B.H.: I thought that was so funny, to notice the carefully precise back and forth movement in the footage I found of Sally Cloninger and Marilyn Frasca in their motorboat on the Puget Sound. I noticed that within my own relationship I was sensitive to the nuances of body gestures of my partner and myself; nuances that I didn't have with my friends. I imagine if someone were filming Florrie Burke and myself today they would find in the footage the same careful acuity of sensitivity to emotional/intellectual variations of each of us to the other. This borders on the phenomenon of couples picking up each others' habits, ways of wording phrases, even laughter patterns. And, of course, the ultimate is finishing your partner's sentences. "Till death do us part," but it may be sooner, if sentence completion sets in!

G.F.: Another section in which you cut together a performance of your cross dressing with a voice-over describing an entirely different, if related, scene strikes me as an enactment of the slippage in biography itself, between the referent and the signifier. You also embed the notion of multiplicity in the voice-overs, which are sometimes read by two or more people of different genders. You have, in post-production, changed the pitch of your voices so that we can no longer "read" gender and we are confronted with our own participation in what Kate Bornstein calls "the cult of gender." You move across subjectivities here and elsewhere. Aren't you, in a way, enacting the call for politicization of location in the words of, for example, Barbara Smith, whom you quote as saying, "White feminists and lesbians should render their own histories, subjectivities, and writing complex by attending to their various implications in overlapping social discursive divisions and their histories"?

B.H.: The voice is my own, but the frequencies are changed. I first used this technique (of course, Laurie Anderson used it long ago) myself in a performance at The Women and Technology Conference in April, 1994 at the Yerba Buena Gardens in San Francisco. In a live performance I noted in my script arrows going up or down (up for feminist theorists, down for male cultural analysts, and normal for my "I stories") and I gave it to the sound person with instructions to lower or raise the frequency according to my directions. This was so successful with the audience (laughter, again), that I incorporated the technique throughout the film as a way of using theory and poking fun at it at the same time.

When I repeat the story of driving around the world on a motorcycle and use a different pronoun with every telling, I am suggesting the patriarchal incorporation of power and words. I heard that the "she" pronoun carried less significance in the story than the "he," and that when I used the first-person singular "I," there was a greater suggestion of truth-telling. All these attached conditions interest me. This is the cultural baggage, be it a pronoun or a moustache.

G.F.: I wrestled with the question of the role of biographer as I was writing an encyclopedia of women directors. I must admit I reexperienced a sinking feeling when you talked about biographers telling other/s stories in *Tender Fictions*. I was highly aware of constructing selves, highlighting one thing over another, putting things in a positive or negative light, trying to write women directors into a history which has traditionally excluded them. These women had extraordinarily complex lives, as we all do, but I had to look at them primarily as filmmakers.

To some extent I see a parallel in your story of your selves. You include a section on your father and another on your mother. I'm sure you were thinking about the politics of telling another's story and you do fascinating and moving things with their stories. In the section on your father, who is remembered as being many things, including suicidal, you demonstrate the constructedness of truth and biography by having his photograph framed and reframed with mattes that a hand moves in the frame. In the sections on your mother, you capture the elusiveness of the truth or truths of her existence. According to the film's multivalent planes, she was either a product of her times, which demanded women to act in horribly confined ways, and/or she was a woman who controlled her own destiny and her own self. Your work with the dualities of constructions of selfhood here is profound; between the culturally defined self of the televisual and fashion culture and the self-defined person. Are you working toward a self that can be experienced across subjectivities and therefore a different way to look at the familial construct?

B.H.: Definitely, and the placement of the individual within the community is important here. I see myself as defined and defining myself alongside and sometimes within the burgeoning feminist movement of the late 1960s and early 1970s. These were formative years for me as an artist as well as a political woman. If the rising surge of lesbian/feminism hadn't been happening at that time, I don't think I could have identified myself as one (a lesbian/feminist) without the community. I have always read that a biographer needs to look at the context of an individual's life; but looking back on mine it seems even more profound. More like a tribal context, something we read about in some African cultures where the individual (as such) isn't even a construction. He or she is there only as part of a long tradition that includes ancestry, tribal rites, and histories, etc. In many ways, I can see those of us participating in the early culture making of women who were self-defining, as part of a tribe/community. That's the new family. The "old" family, the "natural born killers," is to be understood, then left.

G.F.: In *Tender Fictions*, you utilize several quotes having to do with postmodern experiences of truth, memory, and subjectivity. You have a voice-over from Hélène Cixous: "Her speech, even when theoretical or political is never simple or linear. She draws her story into history." You include another voice-over from Roland Barthes, stating "The one who speaks is not the one who writes and the one who writes is not the one who is." One of the most profound quotes, however, is from Barbara Hammer: "I is a lesbian couple." Can you place this in the context of your developing theories and experiences as a postmodern filmmaker?

B.H.: As a developing postmodern filmmaker, I must give credit to the many, many literary sources as well as my own lived experience that prompted the statement "I is a lesbian couple." The statement that continues to make me uneasy and confirms my emotional ambivalence to, perhaps, any definition. The chapter "A Signature of Autobiography: 'Gertrice/Altrude'," by Leigh Gilmore in *Autobiography and Questions of Gender*, as well as Biddy Martin's "Lesbian Identity and Autobiographical Difference(s)," in *The Lesbian and Gay Studies Reader*, were especially important to me. In all my research, these were the only two essays on lesbian autobiography I could find.

So "I is a lesbian couple" addresses the dilemma of self-naming and polarities. Since taking a class at UCLA in my undergraduate years on Ethics, I have been perplexed by the idea that one cannot understand freedom without constraint. Similarly, if one accepts the genital definition of lesbian (Tee Corinne), rather than the intellectual definition (T. Grace Atkinson), one knows one's lesbian self in relationships. There are a whole lot of selves, however, that are unknown in relationships and continue to be important functioning, creative, artistic, and other parts of play that exist outside of the couple. This has yet to be addressed in essay literary form, but I address it in my film with all the material, and image/sound conjunctions, that come before the introduction of "the couple."

G.F.: Let's talk about your preheterosexual identity.

B.H.: I call my preheterosexual identity the years up until thirteen, or more like fifteen, when I became acutely aware of my interests in the adventures of having boyfriends. Of course, the heterosexist training and cultural conditioning started with my name and from day one, I'm sure. However, what I'm talking about is the time when a girl thrives on just being herself in all her fullness with imagination galore, fear unknown, and turning a blind eye to prescriptive behavior. That was my life from until fourteen or fifteen. I lived without a mind to "femininity," restrictive clothing, ideas on what a girl should or shouldn't do. Even when I became interested in "boys," I chose the ones who were rebels, older than me, and sometimes out of school. During high school and college there is such pressure to date, to attract men, that I can imagine even the hardiest of girls in the fifties trying to conform to some precast mold of docility, etc. So, when I became a dyke, at the ripe old age of thirty, I felt like I was back inside the "old" me of thirteen and now I could keep on growing. It felt like a continuum that had been broken was restored. It felt absolutely great and still does.

G.F.: I am especially drawn to the beginning of *Nitrate Kisses* in which you perform an active and living biographization of Willa Cather. What I am struck by is how you make her history alive again. I'm interested in the way that you bring out the visual evidence—what should be quite obvious evidence, photographs of her cross dressing as a young girl, calling herself Will, the testimony of her lifelong lesbian relationship—but instead of simply stating these things as fact you reenact them in a way, onscreen. How did you arrive at the strategy of exposing the uncovery/recovery process?

B.H.: Traditional cinema uses a story line of ever-changing events to keep audience interest. This is boring because it is so programmed and predictable. Experimental cinema presents film in a new and changing light either through content, formal concerns, or exhibition practices and awakens me to myself, stimulates my ability to perceive, gives me pleasure of process and imagination. That's why I like to watch it and why I like to make it. I don't have to be a historian, or an expert on Cather, to let the film give the viewer the distinct experience of what it is like to investigate, to look for traces, to uncover and find forgotten or misleading paths. I try to make an experimental cinema of investigation. The viewing audience become the archeologists, the historians, piecing together the fragments, feeling the emptiness of blurred and over-exposed film, seeing through the scratches of dated emulsion, and finding the memories to recover their own history. For if one history is lost, all of us are less rich than before.

124

FIGURE 18. A scene from *Nitrate Kisses* by Barbara Hammer; costumes and gender play in a world of fabrics and fleshtones. Courtesy Barbara Hammer.

G.F.: Both *Nitrate Kisses* and *Tender Fictions* feature the use of multiple narrators. One sequence that struck me as particularly self-reflexive and performative was the section in which we hear a female voice-over intercut with what I assume is the male voice from a recording that one would hear at the Willa Cather home. This authoritarian voice gives us the "official" biography of Willa Cather and she is treated almost as an ethnographic subject. Naturally, the official version tells us nothing about Willa/Will that has to do with her sexuality. In this sequence, I get a sense that you are asking the viewer to participate in the regenerative process of the recovery of lesbian history, no?

B.H.: The tour guide's voice that you hear with the photos of Willa Cather's home in Red Bank is even further removed than you think! The guide's voice is piped in from a prerecording and as visitors walk through the house a different sequence is played. It was very funny. The feminist author who visited Willa's home herself and who wrote a book on midwestern women, Sandy Boucher, is the other voice you hear telling the story that hasn't been told. I believe we need multiple voices to present multiple viewpoints. As light can neither be defined by particle or wave theory, it seems to me varying phenomena need different approaches. There is no reason we can't hold several "truths" to be self-evident.

G.F.: What are the political implications of someone, like myself, who, though bisexual or heterosexual, is not of the lesbian community; how do you feel about nonlesbians working in the field of recovery and regeneration of lesbian history?

B.H.: A person who describes her/himself as a nonlesbian would have difficulty in understanding and interpreting cultural innuendoes, just as lesbians from different generations can easily make errors of interpretation by not knowing the coding, the subtleties, the distinctions that are generational differences. Anyone can be a lesbian, but I still agree with identity politics, in that difference is best illuminated by those members of the self-inscribed group.

One of the more challenging ideas that has come from the internet is the possibility and practice of assumed identities. These "masked" selves can be heroes, personify inanimate objects, project sexualities. Anyone can be a virtual lesbian in cyberspace. This is so different from the seventies, when we limited our identity to particular women who wore particular clothes and hairstyles and who practiced a particular type of sexuality. There is such strength and sureness now in identity practices around sexuality that the door can be opened, the reins loosened, that the sexual horse can canter into the field without fences. If everyone can be a virtual lesbian than there are no nonlesbians and everyone can work in the recovery of marginalized peoples, their history as well as their contemporary contributions to late twentieth century politics, economics, and culture.

G.F.: I found the images of decay and loss equally compelling in *Nitrate Kisses*. For example, I wanted to discuss the black and white images of rubble that are reminiscent of World War II documentaries. The tracking shots along the rubble reminded me of the loss of the history of sexualities as well as the constant war our society wages against sexuality, especially Lesbian/Gay/ Bisexual /Transgendered people and practices. I was struck by the element of performativity in these strong images. You lay them as a bed under the voices of women and men who talk openly about their coming out and living in the world as Lesbians and Gays. It has a transformative effect. Do you generally preplan this sort of idea, or do you do this more intuitively in postproduction?

B.H.: I was living in a home in the Oakland Hills that was nearly destroyed by the catastrophic Berkeley-Oakland fire in October, 1991. Many people lost their lives or their life work in this fire. When I drove through the rubble a few days after the fire, I felt a terrible loss. A loss that could have been my own loss of work.

I think a distinguishing characteristic of my films is that they all come from deeply felt personal experience. An image will have personal resonance for me and I will use it. I trust that there will be enough of a collective reading of the emotional text in the image to be useful, to propel the forward movement of the film. In the editing as well, there are many personal meanings that I hope are understood. For example, in the older woman section, a dyke historian, Frances Doughty, is commenting on how people will inscribe history if there is a blank background. The image is of a naked older woman's back without clothing. To me that is the background onto which we viewers inscribe meaning: the lesbian body. This work is not preplanned. I find meaning through the process of making. I use intuition to guide the research, filming, and editing of picture and sound. In these films I did not use a script, and only wrote the script afterwards from the completed film so that translations for subtitling could be made in Germany, France, Japan, and Taiwan.

G.F.: I would like to ask you to discuss the importance of the sequence in *Nitrate Kisses* dealing with the Motion Picture Production Code of 1930. In the film you run the text of the code as a crawl title over anal interracial sex. This strikes me as a performance of transgressive activism which works on a number of important levels. Not only is this funny and politically and sexually charged, but it has a visceral effect on the viewer that takes me back to what we were talking about earlier: the unnameable. The text is scored with an opera, and there are again multiple voices speaking about how the code itself was designed to work against "The Mixing of the Races" and a host of other social taboos, including homosexuality. This sequence has elements of the performative documentary, it reads like a postmodern opera, erotica with commentary, a poem. How would you describe this sequence?

B.H.: In selecting the four separate couples who would have explicit sexual relations in the film, I searched for couples that historically or contemporary lesbian, gay, bisexual, and transgendered communities might censor. We have our own issues about acceptability and presentability. No community is without its own censoring phenomenon. I chose old women, an S/M leather couple, two tattooed and pierced women of color, and the Black and White gay male couple to represent some areas of experience the gay community, itself, might censor.

The most exciting element in the gay male scene was the beautiful shape of the rounded butts of different color, almost an abstract shot that went on and on. The Motion Picture Code completely forbid representation of "mixed races" on the screen for twenty-five years. I was making this film with NEA monies and trying very hard to not self-censor in the conservative time when the agency was under attack. The sequence became a perfect metaphor. The scripted code rolls up the screen and makes the viewer choose between looking at the beautiful sexuality or read the fascinating "no-no"s in the code. The code acts as a jailer to the image; we must see the underrepresented, the disallowed, through the bars of censorship. I, as a filmmaker, must make the invisible, visible.

## QUEERING IMPERIALISM

Thomas Waugh argues that "Since the invention of photography, the Queer nation has had a privileged relationship with image technology" (166). Just as the Colonial Male cultivated and coproduced images of lost utopias, lost jungles suffused with forbidden pleasures, and White jungle goddesses, Queer utopian desire was often imagined and captured by gay and bisexual writers, photographers, and filmmakers. Waugh notes that utopian gay male desire was subject to Colonial conquest and as "an imagined community" it was "unidirectional and knit by blunt economic and political power" (153). I quote Waugh at length here to demonstrate a tip of the iceberg of Queer Colonialists and Colonialisms:

> The dividing line between individual erotic fantasy and collective sexual utopias is seldom clear. Alongside the erotic fantasies of the exotic homosocial Other, Queer collective histories have always invested ideologically in imagined homelands situated elsewhere in time and space. Slightly more historically minded than Proust or Harry Hay but equally in search of the justifications of Elsewhere, our 19th century intellectual ancestors made it through the Victorian era with scholarly and not-so-scholarly constructions of classical Athens (John Addington Symonds), the South Seas (Edward Carpenter), and the sensuous 'Sotadic' zones of the 'Orient' (Sir Richard Burton). Our awakening twentieth century Queer consciousness continued in a similar vein with its series of cultural and geographical meccas: Edwardian and Georgian Bloomsbury, Weimar Berlin, Greenwich Village of the 1950s, Copenhagen of the 60s, San Francisco of the 70s, Amsterdam of the 80s. In the cultural sphere, Elsewhere provided a continuous stream of havens for the gay male artist and intellectual: Herman Melville and Somerset Maugham went to Polynesia, Pierre Loti went to Turkey, E. M. Forster and J. R. Ackerley to India; the thirties saw F. W. Murnau in Tahiti, S. M. Eisenstein in Mexico, Sam Steward to Paris, Christopher Isherwood in Berlin, W. H. Auden and Federico Garcia Lorca in Manhattan, Herbert List in Greece, Charles Henri Ford in Italy, Norman McLaren in . . . Ottawa; after the War, Paul Bowles, William Burroughs, Allen Ginsberg, Claude Jutra, Joe Orton, Roland Barthes and Rainer Werner Fassbinder all came to North Africa, James Baldwin, Ned Rorem, Dirk Bogarde and Kenneth

Anger to France; Pasolini took his restless camera through Palestine, Morocco, Turkey, India, Tanzania, Yemen, Eritrea, Iran, Nepal and the Middle Ages; Tobias Schneebaum found himself on the Amazon, Noel Coward in Jamaica, Michel Foucault in San Francisco, and Robert Mapplethorpe in the internal third worlds of New York City. *Cultivated colonies indeed* (emphasis mine, 153)

Waugh discusses the complex power negotiations of cultivated homosocial Colonial subjects, and elaborates on the increasing problematization of "masochistic fantasies of the occidental bottom" (157), for example. But, as Waugh notes, "Silenced for generations, the Other increasingly talks back and looks back at the looker in the Postcolonial era" (157). *Looking for Langston* (1989), Isaac Julien's first feature film is a case in point. *Looking for Langston* not only comments on White supremacy in the 1930s and its impact on homosexuality, but it does this through a transgressive reinscription of the metapoetics of Langston Hughes, the revolutionary gay African-American poet. Drawing on David MacDougall's theories on ethnographic films, one can envision Julien as an insider-informant and autoethnographer of raced homosexuality from the 1920s to the present.

## LOOKING FOR LANGSTON

*Looking for Langston* draws upon imagery that evokes *signs of resemblance, absence, and memory* as they are defined by MacDougall. In one example, Julien stages moving tableaux vivants charged with erotic glances between and among Black men, White men, and men of all colors. These gazes stage the ethnographic third eye in a strikingly postmodern sensibility. Here everyone is "Other," so the look back of the Other is at once dangerous and inviting, comforting and acknowledging. In this context, *Looking for Langston* operates in the arena of signs of absence:

Signs of absence often make ironic use of objects and testimony, positioning the audience uncomfortably by asking them to make judgments and comparisons, to search for and interject meanings. Here the sign for a lost object becomes not its surrogate but what has displaced it. These signs define memory by its true opposite, an embodied absence. An empty factory thus represents a fully operating one. (MacDougall, 264)

As a film of memory, *Looking for Langston* is not only an autoethnography for and of Isaac Julien, but also a polyglossic recontextualization of the many-voicedness of Black and White gay culture, both that which is lost and absent, and that which is reclaimed through the voices of writers Essex Hamphill, Bruce Nugent, and James Baldwin. The self-reflexive use of multiple speakers connotes signs of survival viewed through the gaze of pansexual looking, onscreen and off. Signs of survival in ethnographic films often include physical objects, but Julien foregrounds the lost Queer gazes, as well as the iconicity of the male body, as the major testimony of the film. MacDougall's description of signs of survival is aptly used in this context:

> *Signs of survival* are images of objects which have a physical link with the remembered past. These memorabilia serve half as symbols of experiences, half as physical proof that they occurred, and like Kane's "Rosebud" they often turn up amidst a clutter of other, less familiar objects. They are "astonishing" and precious not so much for their visual resemblance to remembered objects as for the fact that they are perceived, like Proust's handful of dried lime blossoms, as the "very same" objects. (262)

*Looking for Langston* allows for a multiplicity of readings and polyambiguities. Yet the film is also a nostalgic fantasy of Queer Colonialism set in a postmodern world, one in which Postcolonial subjects are highly aware of the sexual politics of Imperialist nostalgia. *Looking for Langston* thus emerges skillfully as a manipulative film that announces its many transmutations of imagery and subject matter. For example, in the film's ironic use of thirties blues music juxtaposed with steamy bebop of the forties and fifties, Julien calls to attention the suturing of images and ideas across an unlimited range of reclaimed historical moments and junctures. As MacDougall notes, "among signs of resemblance, music is the analogue *par excellence . . .* musical styles 'date' and are culturally specific [; making] ideal aural icons" (263). Other signs of survival and reconstruction in *Looking for Langston* include refilmed newsreels, archival film clips, and exquisitely lit homoerotic sequences that both revel in and move beyond the Master/Subject model.

The Master/Subject model works to "suppress gender subtext" (Fraser, 173), and I'd add that it also reduces and defines subjectivity and sexual pleasure to roles defined by political power. *Looking for Langston* conjures a netherplace of intersubjectivity, a space described as a "glove" in the work of Merleau-Ponty:

> It suffices that from one side I see the wrong side of the glove that is applied to the right side, that I touch the one *through* the other (double "representation" of a point or plane of the field) the chiasm is that reversibility . . .
> It is through it alone that there is passage from the "For itself" to the For the Other—In reality there is neither me nor the other as positive, positive subjectivities. There are two caverns, two open-nesses, two stages where something will take place—and which both belong to the same world, to the stage of Being. (263)

The notion of subjectivity as "glove" permits a renegotiation of the power mechanics of the cinematographic operator, the keeper of the "recording zone." Instead of viewing the photographer as captor (or "stalker," in the words of Sontag), we can begin to see that the cine-matographer is as much captured by the act of recording as is the subject being photographed. In the case of *Looking for Langston*, the film's subject is Isaac Julien as much as it is Langston Hughes. The performative bod-ies of the film thus mimetically function within the omnisubjectivity of the "glove." The sex scenes invite the viewer to coproduce the intersub-jective space of the "glove," for, as Marco Demarinis remarks:

> Action and *the simulation of action* combine and corroborate each other . . . performance always provokes *effects of the real* as well as *theatrical effects* . . . in the sense of its real production of meanings, kinds of awareness, events, and lived experiences. (157)

## BOMBA'S LOST LOVE

It is interesting to contextualize *Looking for Langston* against the backdrop of a highly homoerotic jungle film of 1949, *Bomba, the Jungle Boy*, which starred Johnny Sheffield as Bomba, a boy who grew up in the jungle. There were ten films made about Bomba: low-budget films that were based upon Roy Rockwood's series of popular boys books from the 1920s. *Bomba, the Jungle Boy* is so undeniably homoerotic that it seems amazing that the film

132

FIGURE 19. Bomba as figure of homoerotic desire in *Bomba, The Jungle Boy*. Courtesy Jerry Ohlinger Archives.

was even released as a mainstream heterotopic narrative film. In the *Bomba* films, boy-love is set against an artificial construct of "nature," and thus homosocial bonds are constructed through a backdrop of Roussouian longings for that which is lost and irrecoverable; in this case, lost male children's sexuality. Since the Victorian era, we have insisted as a society that children have no sexuality, but the ruptures and fissures signified by the *Bomba* films demonstrate otherwise. In *Pleasures Taken*, Carol Mavor describes the connections between the eroticization of children, the Colonial search for utopia, and the rejection of children's sexuality:

> For the Victorians, the charm of buying childhood grew out of an active imagination that envisioned one's early years as a lost utopia: a bower to retreat to, a secret garden that every middle-class person could enter through children's books and other child-centered products. The material culture of Victorian childhood produced souvenirs of a time and place that never was—a true Neverland. The evolving commodity culture, fecund with useful and not-so-useful, pretty and bizarre things was also providing a kind of vulgarity that the middle class took pleasure in shunning. Of course, they often shunned it by purchasing even more of its vulgar products and promoting a myth of historical decline or even degeneracy to shadow the often flickering official optimism of an undimmed future. (2–3)

*Bomba*, however, marks yet another manifestation of the Plantocratic imagination, a nature boy who fights off Colonial imperialist forces. In Ford Beebe's *The Lost Volcano* (1950), for example, Bomba fights off greedy African Colonialists who attempt to steal and sell buried treasure. Bomba takes on ivory poachers in Beebe's *Bomba and the Elephant Stampede* (1951), and effectively ends their regime of commercial exploitation. But what stands out most in *The Lost Volcano* is the powerful on-screen homoerotic relationship between the characters played by Johnny Sheffield and Tommy Ivo. The boys play together, tie one another up, and generally display disdain for anyone who attempts to separate them. Sheffield's body within the film is highly eroticized, as is that of Ivo. Both are viewed in seductive sadomasochistic poses that appropriate their form from beefcake pornography. Oddly enough, by the late 1950s, Tommy Ivo's on-screen fascination with Bomba would be transferred to the fetishization of Ivo's real-life custom built hot rod, lovingly described by Ivo (now playing himself) in William Hole's *The Ghost of Drag Strip Hollow* (1959), prefiguring Kenneth Auger's love affair with motorcyclists and their machines in the intensely homoerotic *Scorpio Rising* (1963) by almost a half-decade. In the *Bomba* films, it is the human corpus itself which is fetishized, dressed, stripped, and then adorned with new accoutrements, just as in the later films the hot-rod and/or the chopped-down Harley serve as a new site of ritual reconfiguration of the sexual self.

Looking for lesbian, bisexual, and transgendered Queer Colonialist imagery is always problematic because, as Judith Roof notes in *Come as You Are*:

Heteronarrative informs the choice and deployment of political strategies, particularly those linked to identity, identification and invisibility. While these processes belong to the registers of the imaginary and the visible, they are also completely bound up with narrative . . . and inflected by narrative heteroideology. (145)

Regardless of the boundaries of narrative heteroideology, Queer Colonialist imagery surfaces frequently in mainstream cinema, as in Roy Ward Baker's *The Fiction Makers* (1966), a feature-length film based on the long-running television series *The Saint*, co-starring Sylvia Syms, Roger Moore, and Justine Lord. The main narrative exists in the fetid vacuum of heterotopia, as The Saint (Roger Moore) is hired to protect a young White female author (Sylvia Syms) who has been kidnapped by a twisted White criminal mastermind. But *The Fiction Makers* also offers us the spectacle of yet another resuscitation of the Imperial Man suffused by the interplay of latent lesbian imagery, as Sylvia Syms and Justine Lord engage in a prolonged sequence of light bondage, "Slave/Master" role playing. That a hot sadomasochistic lesbian metanarrative of difference should surface within (and despite) the master narrative of 1960s British heterodoxy should perhaps come as no surprise. The dualisms of gender and the cult of heterosexism are perpetually and inherently challenged by the healthy threat of Queer, bi, and transgendered sexualities, especially in British films and television of the fifties and sixties.

## QUEER HOSTAGES, QUEER AGENTS

Dirk Bogarde films of this era single-handedly managed to threaten the binarisms of hetero and homosexualities in such films as Joseph Losey's *The Servant* (1963), Basil Dearden's *Victim* (1961), as well as Losey's *Modesty Blaise* (1966) and *Accident* (1967). Often Dirk Bogarde's characters in

FIGURE 20. Dirk Bogarde in *Modesty Blaise*: the Queer gaze in early 1960s British transgendered cinema. Courtesy Jerry Ohlinger Archives.

these films were sadomasochistic bisexuals and/or homosexuals, and Bogarde's bisexuality challenged the dualisms of the cult of gender, as well as the cult of heterosexuality. Another example of the challenge of bisexuality surfaces in *Performance* (1970) which centers around the relationships of a series of pansexual, androgynous characters played by Mick Jagger, James Fox, and Anita Pallenberg. *Accident* foregrounded the bisexuality of characters played by Dirk Bogarde, Michael York, and Jacqueline Sassard. Because these films did not offer "positive images" of homosexuality or bisexuality, they have not generally been embraced in Queer film theory. I suggest, however, that we quit looking for "positive" images of Queer and bisexual practice, and do the cultural work of reclaiming "perversion" as a tool that operates to open nomadic celluloid zones, and encourages gender fluidity.

As transgendered theorist Leslie Feinberg reminds us, it is "*passing* that is a product of oppression" (89). In the case of *The Fiction Makers*, we can locate a film that passes itself off as yet another narrative of the Imperial sleuth, but the visual evidence sports a strongly suggestive metanarrative of lesbian eroticism. Certainly many critics would insist that such images are contained by an overdetermined White heterosexual male gaze and thus subject to the discipline of heteroideology. While this argument has validity, as performative entities, Sylvia Syms and Justine Lord create within the film a scene of lesbian desire that is so overloaded with sexuality that it is used to hold together not only the fragmenting heterotopic order, but also the narrative of the film itself, thus doubly betraying the failure of the filmic cult of gender and sexuality. Heterosexuality is thus revealed as another construct, and lesbian and bisexual women perform Queer identities. As Kristin G. Esterberg notes, "When lesbians and bisexual women present themselves to each other and the world, they are, in effect, performing. . . . Lesbian identity is constructed *in* and *through* such performances. In this way, women signal to themselves and others the nature of their desire for women" (81). Lesbian and bisexual desire, along with other forms of Queer Colonialisms and Postcolonialisms, simply cannot be contained by filmic narratives that seem to support Imperialist claims of heterotopia and compulsory heterosexuality. In short, these films fail to take into account resistant viewers, and the hostage takeover of a transgendered gaze. Such a reading across the grain is commonly invoked in interpretive ethnography. Anthropologist Dan Sperber, for example, asks:

FIGURE 21. James Fox and Mick Jagger in *Performance,* Queering the Imperial Male. Courtesy Jerry Ohlinger Archives.

Why not say, one might query, that an interpretation has *two* objects: a set of mediatory representations, which is the primary object, and the object of these representations themselves, which is the secondary (and often the most important) object of the interpretation? (21)

Films don't simply contain knowledge, they offer a performative vehicle to explore the spaces in which one may transgress against normative values spaces. As Michel de Certeau notes, "Stories about space exhibit on the contrary the operations that allow it, within a constraining and non-'proper' place" (121), a place that allows for enunciative acts of transgressive reinscription. A superb example of such a filmic space is conjured in the lesbian vampire film *Blood and Roses* (1961, Dir. Roger Vadim), a film that invites the transexualized gaze, especially the lesbian and bisexual gaze.

## THE VAMPIRE'S KISS

Adapted from Sheridan LeFanu's novel *Carmilla, Blood and Roses* stars Annette Vadim as a reincarnated vampire who is marked by lesbian desire for Elsa Martinelli. Though the film passes off the main plot as routinely heterosexualized (Carmilla [Annette Vadim] seeks to be reunited with her dead male lover), the metanarrative effectively opens a location for performing lesbian desire. In one particularly memorable scene, Carmilla seduces Elsa Martinelli in order to fulfill her vampiric (read lesbian) desires. Indeed, one might argue that Carmilla merely *performs* heterosexuality to quench her eternal thirst for blood. In this reading, Carmilla is actually a centuries-old lesbian, who takes over the body of Carmilla so that she may wed nobleman Mel Ferrer and finally emerge as a young woman vampire, the symbol of lesbian and bisexual desire. The success of *Blood and Roses* inspired a series of related films, including Roy Ward Baker's *The Vampire Lovers* (1971), and Vincente Aranda's *The Blood-Spattered Bride* (1969). This conflation of lesbian desire with bloodlust also reappears in Abel Ferrara's *The Addiction* (1996), and remains potent material for future generic use.

Lesbian and bisexual desire is also often invoked in various women's prison movies. An early example of this phenomena is Edgar G. Ulmer's *Girls in Chains* (1943). Such prison films seek to encode lesbian desire as

FIGURE 22. Elsa Martinelli, Mel Ferrer and Annette Vadim in *Blood and Roses*; the lesbian vampire as figure of agency and power. Courtesy Jerry Ohlinger Archives.

FIGURE 23. The urgency of lesbian desire in *The Vampire Lovers*. Courtesy Jerry Ohlinger Archives.

the monstrous Other, but behind every scenario of perversion stands an insistent fantasy of lesbian reinscription. *Girls in Chains* offers images of "homovestism," described by Laura Kipnis as a process whereby "gender impersonation of the same-sex person [is] a way of acting out gender conflicts through dressing in exaggerated or ritualized versions of same-sex clothing" (80). Kipnis cites the photographic autoethnographic performances of Cindy Sherman as an example of homovestism, where "female perversions reside in behaviors that exaggerate femininity" (80). Thus the beskirted imprisoned women in *Girls in Chains* "stage" perversion in their transvesticism (women as women) constructed heterotopic in the same the way various versions of Ayesha in *She* can be viewed as a drag act of constructed, heterotopic femininity. This leaves one with two final questions: Are all White jungle goddesses drag acts of the heterosexualized female? Don't they all invite the Queer gaze across the spectrum of race, class, ethnicity, and gender?

# CHAPTER FOUR

—————— ✗ ——————

# Doubly Bound:
# The Postcolonial Resistant Body

## FILMS OF RESISTANCE

Despite the overwhelming supremacy of the Plantocratic gaze within the corpus of the conventional Hollywood narrative cinema, there is a strong movement of artists, filmmakers, and writers who are working to decolonize discursive norms, often through the hybrid form of autoethnography. *Rouch in Reverse* (1995), written and directed by Manthia Diawara, constitutes the quintessential example of autoethnography. Here Diawara employs an active Third Eye turned against the ethnographic (and narrative) regime of cultural repression. The subject is ostensibly Jean Rouch, a French documentary filmmaker who seemingly broke with "traditional" ethnographic practices with his early films known as exemplifications of "cruel cinema," such as *Jaguar* (1955), *Les Maitres Fous* (1957), *Lion Hunters* (1965), and *Six in Paris* (1965). Visiting Rouch in Paris, Diawara subjects Rouch to the same sort of "objective" ethnographic treatment Rouch afforded his African subjects. Rouch thus predictably emerges as a quixotic "Other," full of caprices, whims, and cultural eccentricities. But Diawara is also the subject of *Rouch in Reverse*, as "performative documentary, like reflexive documentary, does not propose a primary object of study beyond itself but instead gives priority to the affective dimensions struck up between ourselves and the text" (Nichols, 102).

Bill Nichols cites other examples of resistant, performative documentaries such as *Tongues Untied* (Marlon Riggs, 1989), *Sari Red* (Pratibha Parmar, 1988), *Who Killed Vincent Chin?* (Renee Tajima and Chris Choy, 1988), as well as the films of Trinh T. Minh-ha, Chris Marker, and Su Friedrich. There are many examples of performative autoethnographers, but one of the most audacious of these is video artist Sadie Benning, who picked up a Fisher-Price toy Pixelvision camera and began making a series of autoethnographic black-and-white videos that were originally filmed primarily in the privacy of her bedroom. Benning revolutionized a Queer self-mastering gaze that looks out from her camera-eye, often in distorted micro closeups, as she documented the thoughts, feelings, and embodied subjectivity of an emerging lesbian teenager. Her videos include the signs of presence of her embodiment: toy cars that imaginatively take us on a lesbian cross-country spree of romantic longings and sexual master, in *It Wasn't Love* (1992), coupled with scrawled diary entries and her gently sardonic voice-over narration. Benning is one of those remarkable examples of artists who use whatever equipment they have, in this case a toy camera that would be immediately limiting to others, to produce transgressive self-reinscriptions such as *Me and Rubyfruit* (1989), *Living Inside* (1989), *If Every Girl Had a Diary* (1990), *Jollies* (1990), and *Girlpower* (1992). Along the way, she discovers her sexuality on camera, playfully cross dressing and kissing the camera itself. Benning's deeply personal and politically charged autoethnographic practices not only celebrate Queer alterity, but also capture that stage of inbetweenness, when young people have not yet been entirely circumscribed by the systematic regulation of desire, race, class, and sexuality.

## THE BISEXUAL GAZE

Benning's films put me in touch with my own bisexuality. I had become accustomed to viewing myself as heterosexual because I am involved in a long-term relationship with a member of the opposite sex. I had been bisexual in college, but, following the rules of the doubly bound (the pressure of the binarisms of [hetero] and [homo]sexuality), I wrote off my desire as a period of experimentation; many bisexuals do this. Though I am not entirely happy to adopt yet another label, bisexuality accurately describes my sexual desires, even as I challenge the bi-phobic-centered world around me. As Susie Bright, who describes herself as a lesbian sex expert and a bisexual, notes:

Behavioral scientists know that human sexuality spans a spectrum from very homo to very hetero, and most folks fall down some weird crack in the middle. Accused of being "infantile," or "fence-sitters," described as "traitors" by the gay world and "perverts" by the straight one, bisexual activists have told the status quo on both sides of the argument to grow up and get real. (150–51)

Bisexuality is neither popular with the "straight community," nor the "Queer community"; in fact, it challenges the notion of community as much as it challenges the dualisms of sexuality (male versus female, heterosexual versus homosexual). As Kristin G. Esterberg suggests, bisexuality lacks institutionalization. It also lacks "fixed and determinate labels" (169), and thus it actually "may be freeing" for the individual seeking a sexual identity (169). For the present, it seems, bisexuality remains both free and doubly bound. Though the term is now included in the oft-repeated phrase "Gay/Lesbian/Bisexual/Transgendered," it is still shrouded in silence, even though most people are probably bisexual. Ellis Hanson, in "The Telephone and Its Queerness," describes the telephone as "a bisexual symbol in that it possesses both a receiving and a sending apparatus" (38). Though the concept is theoretically innovative, in light of the fact that there is so little written about bisexuality, it is perhaps easier to describe it through a metaphoric mechanical apparatus. I agree with Esterberg when she writes that, "as long as Queer theory remains at the level of texts, it cannot help us understand the very real concerns of lesbians and bisexual women, most of whom have never heard of a floating signifier, let alone considered it had anything to do with their sexuality" (29).

I ultimately agree with the views expressed by many younger men and women who now often term themselves "undecided." This is perhaps even more threatening as a label because it really *is* a floating signifier. Younger people who are studying and living in an era that celebrates (and argues) the "alternative lifestyles" of Queerdom instinctively see that "it's preposterous to ask sexual beings to stuff ourselves into the rapidly imploding social categories of straight, gay or bi, as if we could plot our sexual behavior on a conscientious, predictable curve" (Bright, 152). In the spirit of combining theoretical writing with personal experience, I include here an autoethnography of my experience as a performance artist when I was an "undecided."

## THE CELIBATE SLUTS

Some people think little girls should be seen and not
heard/But I think, "Oh, bondage, up yours!"
—Poly Styrene and X-Ray Spex, 1980

I saw a performance of Poly Styrene and X-Ray Spex in New York about
seventeen years ago. As a college punk feminist, I was thrilled to hear and
see this leather-clad outlaw Black woman perform the transgressive reinscription of a female body. I attended a women's college (Douglass College), and I was a peripheral member of an all-woman performance group
called The Celibate Sluts, whose principal figures were Vanessa Cole and
Tina Maschi. We not only attended concerts by such punk feminist acts
such as the Slits, The Bush Tetras, ESG, the Raincoats, The Delta Five,
and Nina Hagen, but we emulated them through our acting out in performance.

Sappho might well be considered to be the first feminist performance artist, and one might equate her public speech with our public
outbursts. Against the backdrop of the history of rhetoric, feminist performance art, like personal writing in the classroom, conjures the personal
and political woman, the becoming-woman of Deleuze and Guattari. The
performative body of Poly Styrene signifies the gap between personal and
public discourse, between objectivity and subjectivity. As Kate Ronald
notes, "Writers who 'take it personally' operate somewhere between cer-
tainty and speculation, and their authority resides in the tension between
objectivity and subjectivity" (1990, 36). Poly Styrene is a resistant Post-
colonized and decolonized answer to the objectified "seen and not heard"
captive Colonialized Black female body.

Our group, The Celibate Sluts, took its name as a reclamation of
sexual ownership and self-inscription; obviously we meant to play up the
tension between notion of public/private women's sexuality. We actively
worked to disrupt norms of sexuality, we wielded dildos as we sang songs
such as "Fuck Me? . . . Fuck you!" and we encouraged public display of
affection in lesbian, bisexual, and interracial couplings. We were dubbed
a pop-porn feminist band, and it wasn't too long before were were banned
from many of the local venues. In the late eighties, performance artist
Karen Finley rocked New York with her "pornographic" feminist performance art. The fact that her gestures and utterances are found shocking
locates a cultural discomfort with women who disobey the rules of sexu-

ally prohibited and public behavior. The regulation of the female body is a history of restraint. It is this restraint to which female performance artists responds: "Oh bondage, up yours!"

Nineteenth-century codes of female behavior exhibit the cultural history of Foucaultian restraint of the female body. In *Our Deportment*, young ladies read that, "the girl who has so educated and regulated her intellect, her tastes, her emotions, and her moral sense as to be able to discern the true from the false, will be ready for the faithful performance of whatever work in life is allotted to her" (Young, 239). While it may seem obvious that regulation of the body is a prerequisite for female deportment, a rereading of the history of gesture in rhetorical literature provides a glimpse into the phenomenological corseting of the female body in Eurocentric discourse.

One of the first levels of corseting that is "unbuttoned" in women's performance art is the notion of a binaristic split between public and private. Jeanie Forte observes that in the public performance, it is a "position of intimacy [that] is one of the most noteworthy characteristics of women's performance, and one of the primary appeals of the genre for women" (257). Women performance artists capitalize on "rhetoric as the elaboration of ambiguity" (Covino, 2) and return to a utopic rhetoric that perhaps once operated outside the binaries of gender, race, sexuality, and class.

The regulation of the body has been the subject of many cultural critics, but few have emphasized the importance of the history of gesture and the rise of *sprezzatura* (feigned naturalness) in the Renaissance as an important cultural moment in the discipline of the female body. The binaristic splits between "natural" and "artificial" stances, particularly as they have been applied to the performances of women, can be connected with the relationship of gesture to ethos in public performance art.

## THE RHETORIC OF GESTURE

It has become popular to accept a universalizing approach to the modern body as a mechanized being, to evoke a "problem of the body in machine culture" (Seltzer, 21), for example. But the history of the body is irreducible. The commodification and mechanization of the nineteenth- and twentieth-century body is familiar terrain, but looking back at our early notions of the body problematizes the mechanics of gesture.

The classical rhetoricians worked from a culturally defined body that does not easily fit into our twentieth-century notions of rhetoric and gesture.

Fritz Graf's rereading of Quintilian warns us of the temptation to see the system of Roman *gestus* through our own system of gesture. As Graf notes, Quintilian emphasizes that "the body signs of the orator demonstrate his own emotions which in turn excite similar emotions in the audience" (40). Gestures were not always separated from an audience, nor were they always devalued as empty "acts." Plato recognized the use of gesture in the "winning of men's souls" (Graf, 40), though he is suspicious of an over-abundance of gesture, or empty body motions meant to solely appear to emotion. L. Marin sees a "harmonious correspondence" (176) in the body of the ideal Quintilian orator, one whose "voice, mimicry and pantomime must be, along with the tropes of discourse the object of an exercise . . . with the content of the words and the nature of the thoughts" (176).

Feminist performance artists work to reclaim classical rhetoricians' definitions of gesture. This involves the whole speaking public-private body of embodied knowledge and sexualities. Karen Finley's gesturings include the "method of art of healing," not unlike that defined as rhetoric in Plato's *Phaedrus* (Bizzell and Herzberg, 137). The rules of gesture in oration move increasingly away from excess and toward moderation with the rise of scholasticism. As Jean-Claude Schmitt notes in "The Ethics of Gesture," the medieval redefinition of the body and its gestures is dominated by a concern for the Christian conception of ethos. In this tradition, "gestures are good or bad in light of universal values which, depending on the period, may be human reason or the game of God" (131). Thus the body is captive to the constraints of religion as well as the Imperialism of patriarchal order.

Moderation and control are directly connected with gesture in this period, but in a distinctly different way than in classical forms of rhetoric. Schmitt describes a cultural equation of *honestum* or "moral goodness" with *modestia*, or "moderation" (130–31). In the rhetorical literature of the middle ages, Schmitt locates a "distrust of the body as the occasion and site of sin" (134). The Ciceronian public man who united eloquence with goodness in his gesture and speech is later, Bizzell and Herzberg note, replaced by a new public man, reconfigured as "the Renaissance courtier" [468]). The "notion of self as performance" radically altered the conception of the body as an objectified location, in a "political world governed not by virtue but by force" (Bizzell and Herzberg, 468). Twentieth-century conceptions of the body are not only informed by a religious dogma of distrust for our natural body but also informed by the Renaissance embrace of *sprezzatura*.

*Spezzatura*, feigned naturalness, is defined by Bizzell and Herzberg as a process whereby "the talented and humanistically learned person should make his or her accomplishments appear to be the outcome of unstudied nature, not art (468). As a woman, I am quite familiar with the art of *sprezzatura*, having been acculturated to value feigned naturalness. My mother's handbook on beauty tells me, "the more natural you look after making up, the better job you've done (Hart, 212). My mother's etiquette book tells me that "the clever woman who through the right uses of her body keeps it merely the instrument of her personality, will discover that she has become a delightful *concept* in other people's minds" (Wilson, 20). American females are quite used to the ideology of *sprezzatura* as it applies to the production of an artificial "natural" self.

In his study of human kinesics, Ray Birdwhistle noted as early as 1970, that

> American females, when sending gender signals and/or as a reciprocal to male gender signals bring their legs together, at times to the point that the upper legs cross, either in a full leg cross with feet still together, the lateral aspects of the two feet parallel to each other, or in standing knee over knee. (44)

The "effortlessness" of *sprezzatura* comes into play in every bodily act of the culturally conceived female. Gesture and rhetoric underwent a cultural reduction to the realm of style and taste with Peter Ramus's Renaissance tract *Arguments in Rhetoric against Quintilian* and later with Hugh Blair's influential Enlightenment text, *Lectures on Rhetoric and Belles Lettres*. Perhaps it is because I am such a dedicated "slave of style" that I'm fascinated by *sprezzatura*?

The classical rhetoric of gesture which embraces the passions of the body is largely lost with the Renaissance dominance of *sprezzatura*. Performance theorist Joseph R. Roach calls for a return to Quintilian's definition of the performing body. Rather than an empty gesture, Quintilian, argues Roach, insisted on feeling the emotions that the actor or speaker embodies:

His [Quintilian's] advice that a speaker "excite the appropriate feeling" in himself, one that "cannot be distinguished from the truth," concludes paradoxically that true emotion should be deeply felt by the person who is faking it. (26)

The rhetoric of gesture has had a profound effect on female body experience. The dominance of *sprezzatura* as a behavioral model for women in conduct literature, the strict enforcement of modestia upon the female body in modern film, and the many ideologies designed to silence women have an immeasurable effect on women's ability to become "rhetors," or performers.

It has become commonplace to regard rhetoric as an empty gesture, and even the word *gesture* conjures a notion of emptiness, quite possibly informed by the rise of *sprezzatura*. But the history of gesture is ideologically important in a feminist reclamation of the becoming-woman. As Herbert Blau makes plain, "rhetoric makes a difference, and *so does its abuse* [as] one of the surest ways for the colonized to lose their voice" (193).

In a sense, gesture itself has been colonized; shorn of its original meaning, displaced from the offices of classical rhetoric in which it was indelibly inscribed. This dialogic/dialectic organism originated under delivery, which was only one portion of rhetoric. Cicero's *Rhetorica ad Herennium* and *De Inventione* placed gesture alongside voice and costume under the office of delivery; but delivery was not split off from invention, arrangement, style, and memory. The classical rhetors could not actively conceive of a model in which the speaker is disconnected from her own gesturing body, much less her audience. Plato distrusted *sprezzatura* for its cookery and flattery; its distrust of audience of self.

## FEMALE BODY EXPERIENCE

As women, we are bombarded with rules of behavior. Every gesture, every nuance, every speech-act we make is policed by a social system designed to control us as colonized subjects. Though I have made a case for a feminist reexamination of classical rhetorical discourse, the same period is rife with examples of the silencing of women. Though Plato and other classical rhetoricians offer prayers to the Goddesses, they give little of the floor over to female philosophers and orators. Recent scholarship (Snyder, for example) proves that women were gesturing, performing, and involved in public speech since the Oracles at Delphi. Sappho may be seen as one of the first women performance artists, in a long line of gesturing women. But these women have always had to work in social environments designed to control them, to "seize their bodies," to coin Cixous's famous phrase (1976). Performing the body on a private level is not unlike performing the body at a public level in terms of enactment. "Enactment," as performance theory would have it, "occurs as the performer seeks to become, as much as one can, an other, to experience, as if for the first time, whatever the text's speaker experiences" (Long, 111). Women performing their bodies experience enactment of embodiment and self-actualization. But women as performers of everyday life undergo severe restrictions and continual pressures that displace them from bodily enactments.

Performance artists such as Karen Finley enact the unspoken, the things not self-actualized by women. Finley's antietiquette manual, *Enough Is Enough: Weekly Meditations on Living Dysfunctionally*, encourages readers to enact "Being a Bitch" (n.p.) and "Make a Scene in Public" (n.p.). Finley would have made Emily Post cringe at the thought of her "disgraceful" manners. In 1945, Post carped, "The young girl who can walk across a room with grace is rare" (139). Grace is equivalent to restraint in the rhetoric of etiquette. Self-control of outward gesture is equated with virtue and politeness in the "rhetiquette" of American women. "To conceal feelings meant to discipline them, and etiquette manuals praised such discipline as fundamental to politeness" (Kasson, 148). The "rhetiquette" of sexuality, even as late as 1970, taught women that "being able to sit very still is sexy" (Brown, 81).

Iris Marion Young, a socialist feminist and philosopher, notes the connection between disciplining the female body and the objectification of the female, in a study of the phenomenology of feminine body comportment. I want to place her findings next to my study of gesture and feminist performance art. The feminist performative outbursts of Karen Finley, seen in the context of female body experience, forms a connection between the history of gesture and the silencing of women. Woman lives her body "as object and subject" (155), and thus as private and public. In a return to the roots of classical rhetoric feminist performance artists reclaim the margin between these falsely contrived definitions of modality. Young notes:

One of the sources of the modalities of feminine bodily existence is too obvious to dwell upon at length. For the most part, girls and women are not given the opportunity to use their full bodily capacities in free and open engagement with the world, nor are they encouraged as much as boys are to develop specific bodily skills. . . . The modalities of feminine bodily existence are not merely privative, however, and thus their source is not merely in lack of practice, though this is certainly an important element. There is a specific positive style of feminine body comportment and movement, which is learned as the girl comes to understand that she is a girl. The young girl acquires many subtle habits of feminine body comportment—walking like a girl, tilting her head like a girl, standing and sitting like a girl, gesturing like a girl, and so on. (154–55)

The disruly speaking woman is increasingly disciplined in popular culture and its rhetoric. Look no further than the mass media's continual scrutiny of the utterances of Hilary Rodham Clinton for an attempt to hamper the gesturing-talking-woman. Susan Jarratt accurately describes the perception of the public female performer as a "cross dresser" (2). Hilary Rodham Clinton is a cross dresser, in a sense, for not only does she speak publicly, but she obviously speaks privately to the president about "public" issues. In her public utterances, she is being punished for her cross dressing across gendered spaces. As Judith Butler explains:

Performing one's gender wrong *initiates* a set of punishments both obvious and indirect, and performing it well provides the reassurance that there is an essentialism of gender identity after all. That this reassurance is so easily displaced by anxiety, that culture so readily punishes or marginalizes those who fail to perform the illusion of gender essentialism should be sign enough that on some level there is social knowledge that the truth or falsity of gender is only socially compelled and in no sense ontologically necessitated. (1990, 279)

The body of the president's wife is like the body of every woman. It is corseted and "caught in a web of categories dominated by moral expectations" (Vigarello, 156) and gender expectations, but it continues to resist such corseting and tight lacing. Performance artists unleash the female body in gesture and performance. They give "diverse renderings of eros, impregnation, pregnancy, giving birth, midwifery, and paideia as metaphors for philosophical inquiry, discourse, and truth-seeking" (Swearingen, 118).

## ACTING OUT: RENEGADE WOMEN

Shedding the many subtle habits of feminine body comportment is as important to feminist performance artists as is the reclamation of female metaphors. In 1979, the all-woman British group of performance artists The Slits captured attention with the album *Cut,* which featured a song entitled "Typical Girls." Our group saw them perform live at the Mudd Club in New York in 1980. In "Typical Girls," The Slits deconstructed the performed constructedness of femininity:

> Typical girls,
> Buy magazines.
> Typical girls,
> Worry about spots of fat.
> Typical girls,
> Feel like Hell.
> Typical girls.
>     (Chorus)
> Who invented the typical girl?

The audience consisted of mainly women, straight, bi, and gay. The performance claimed space for an arena of public community of renegade women who refused to conform to societal codes of gender. In the second act The Slits enacted a spiritual performance, including the audience in the experience. They sang of the earth when there was only rhythm (in the song "In the Beginning There Was Rhythm"), a prepatriarchal time of matrifocality. We were asked to join hands in celebration of female spirits. The Slits reared from angry questioning to earth-centered, rebirthing metaphors in the same performance. We took our experience home and continued to perform as the Celibate Sluts.

People on campus heard about our performances because of our increasingly outrageous gestures, performances, lyrics, and sexuality. We were a multiracial group of women. We were gay, straight, bisexual, and undecided. We dressed in a punk cacophony, designed to subvert gendered and Colonialist conventions. Our drummer, an African American, wore men's African clothing. Our guitarist, a White femme/butch, wore bizarre mixes of men's and women's clothing. The lead singer, Vanessa (aka Venom), wore extremely suggestive femme clothing. She appropriated and constructed a Black drag Marilyn Monroe look, and frequently sported a dildo as she screamed and writhed around the stage singing such songs as "My Barbie Doll Masturbates." Our common ethos was a firm belief in the ability of women to reclaim their body and their sexuality. I called myself Doris Dayglo and did a drag version of this 1950s emblem of repressed female sexuality. Though I didn't now it then, our behavior that exaggerated and burlesqued femininity as drag was a perversion strategy, one that Louise Kaplan would identify in *Female Perversions*. As Kipnis observes, such homovestisms are a "way of acting out gender conflicts" (80).

We liked to play on the boundaries of feminine metaphors and conduct. Our identity intentionally shifted between "butch" and "femme" behavior. We instinctively reconstructed ourselves in a way, by rejecting *sprezzatura*, or feigned naturalness, instead we reveled in our drag. We overdid our makeup to expose it as an attempt to look artificially "natural." We sought out locations such as laundromats for our performances that were usually reserved for the silencing of women. Our most infamous performance was on the front lawn of the Douglass College Student Center as a wedding was being performed in opposition to women's submission to male authority and ritual. The police stopped our performance, but not before we had our audience dancing and screaming "Gidget was Queer. Moondoggie was a girl." Identity was always an issue we argued and sang about. We were particularly interested in women's sexual freedom, regardless of sexual preference. We demanded hot sex with "Fuck Me While I'm Standing Up" and we attacked domestic violence with "I'm Nutsy Over You, Please Don't Hurt Me." We attacked homophobia with "Don't Touch Me, I'm a Les-BEAN!," a song which satirized homophobia as much as it celebrated lesbian and bi sexualities. "You're so Fucking Obvious" was a song that we wrote about the obviousness of White supremacy. "Fuck Me? . . . Fuck You!" attacked the routine complacency with which fraternity members would assume sexual license over our bodies as we walked by their frat houses during "Take Back the Night" marches.

Like Poly Styrene of X-Ray Specs, we were interested primarily in the politics of identity. Poly Styrene and her group, X-ray Spex, would enter the stage in a set of artificial test tubes. Poly Styrene problematized the issue of subjective identity in the song "Identity:"

> Identity
> Is the crises
> Can't you see
> Identity Inventing

When you look in the mirror
Do you see yourself
Do you see yourself
on the TV screen
Do you see yourself
In the Magazine!

The performances of the Celibate Sluts and Poly Styrene and X-Ray Spex question the notion of a body constituted by *sprezzatura*. In so doing, X-Ray Spex and The Celibate Sluts questioned the notion of a received feminist ethos. As Nedra Reynolds explains, "The idea of *ethos* as a social construction, in which subjects are formed by habits of their culture belies the change that *ethos* can be 'faked' or manipulated" (328). The ethos of these performance artists takes part in a community on the margins. In our acknowledgment of *differences*, we responded to feminist theorists who insisted on the politics of location.

Feminist performance artists have a history of marking a variety of heterogenous communal *ethos* inextricably bound by audience and orator/performer. Carolyn Marks, a Berkeley-based performance artist, creates a "Wall for Peace" (Orenstein, 127), in which 1,350 people commune to share an *ethos* based on world peace. In another, more ritualistic performance piece, Marks builds Goddess sculptures (of Aphrodite, Isis, and Hathor) into a ritualized rebirth of the Goddess (Orenstein, 127). This Goddess ritual ends with the burning of the sculptures. I did not witness Marks's performed rituals, though I did see Karen Finley perform "We Keep Our Victims Ready," one of her most accomplished work.

I read reviews of Karen Finley's performances, yet these accounts gave me no clue to Finley's in-person *ethos*. I'd read that Finley appeared on stage and performed "unladylike" acts such as stuffing yams and peaches in her vagina as she screamed about the history of women. Mainstream media accounts of Finley's performances tended to dissect her behavior from any notion of the ethos of her performance, but when I finally witnessed a performance of "We Keep Our Victims Ready," the experience was an altogether different affair from the image that had been so persuasively engineered by the dominant media. Using a minimum of props, Finley appeared on the stage and performed a monologue that covered subjects as diverse as alcoholism, AIDS, abortion, and dysfunctional families. Finley stripped, smeared chocolate on herself ritualistically, and smeared it on as she talked about the degradation of women:

You know why I only feel comfortable around the
collapsed, the broken, the inebriated, the helpless and the
poor—'CAUSE THEY LOOK LIKE WHAT I FEEL INSIDE!
You see, I WAS NOT EXPECTED TO BE TALENTED.
And when I see you.
After you degrade me
After you beat me
After you stand on top of me
in some god-awful museum
You say to me,
There are no great women artists!
There are no great women artists!
There are no great women artists . . .
They are trying to take abortion away and freedom of speech . . .
When our own citizens' stomachs are burning with hunger,
When people with AIDS are burning with fever.
(1990, 107–10)

As Finley went on gesturing and speaking the body, it became clear to
me that she was enacting an *ethos* of location. She was forcing the audience
to confront their own *ethos*. As she did this she recreated the feminine body.
At one point in Finley's performance piece she begins speaking as a man,
from a decidedly feminist perspective. Her rhetoric clearly shows an understanding of the socially constructed corsets that men are expected to wear:

'Cause I'm a man—a man doesn't have friends like a woman does.
We don't tell our feelings like women do.
We don't show our feelings like women do.
The only feelings we show are no feelings at all.
'Ain't got no friend, but I got a drinking partner,
'Ain't got a confidante, but I got a hunting buddy,
'Ain't got a shoulder to cry on, but I got a shoulder to carry my gun.'
(1990, 120)

By the end of "We Keep Our Victims Ready," Karen Finley moves the
audience into an engagement with her performed body. She transcends an
individually constructed *ethos* into an *ethos* of something of a performed
community. After a painful monologue about a friend dying of AIDS,
and a paean to all the "Black sheep of the family," Finley speaks directly
to the audience, engaging in the "look back":

But tonight we love each other
That is why we're here—
to be around others like ourselves—
In our world, our temple of difference. (142)

Karen Finley's rhetoric thus works on the border zones of the performed construction of selves. She knows the sound of her audience and she loves them and moves them. She takes a place in a postmodern revision of the history of gesture and rhetoric in her recognition of difference.

In the history of rhetoric, classical modes of gesture were replaced by the concept of *sprezzatura*. *Sprezzatura* implies a feigned naturalness, which necessitates a sublimation of *ethos*. In feminist performance art, women artists, such as X ray Specs and Finley, challenge the notion of feigned naturalness, and thus the concept of "natural." The Slits, The Celibate Sluts, Karen Finley, and other women artists actively reclaim classical notions of gesture as an office of a rhetoric that once valued *ethos* over *sprezzatura*; in so doing they problematize the postmodern notion that gender is simply a constructed act.


## HIDE AND SEEK

*Hide and Seek* (Su Friedrich, 1996) is a performative autoethnographic inquiry into the construction and realities of Gay/Lesbian/Bisexual and Transgendered identity. *Hide and Seek* mixes recreations, staged footage, interviews, and clips from instructional films from the 1950s to create a multiply voiced portrayal of lesbian childhood storytelling and coming of age. Unveiling the fantasies of young lesbians, the film is about remembering an age when sexual feelings are still unformed. The fictional narrative tells the story of Lou, a twelve-year-old "tomboy" living in Brooklyn in the mid 1960s, coming to terms with her lesbian sexuality. Her point of view is skillfully juxtaposed with contemporary interviews. She begins visiting animals at the zoo. In her search for an identity that makes sense, she looks for clues from society. This film recounts the struggle of so many young women and men who found their sexual identities were at odds with societal standards, yet managed to stake out a site of Queerness in a world that is maintained by an unspoken celebration of compulsory heterosexuality.

*Hide and Seek* also includes more than one hundred photographs of lesbians when they were young girls, and archival footage from educational films and home movies. It shows that the childhood experiences of a lesbian are often quite innocent but can be seen in retrospect to have a significant bearing on her adult life. The film is remarkably funny at times, especially when one woman recounts her same-sex kissing with associations with The Monkees. She remembers, as a little girl, pretending to be The Monkees and kissing her friend passionately. At times, the film demonstrates the frustrations and problems of coming of age as a lesbian. One of the moments of testimony I am drawn to is the problematization of the current gene theory that is being used to "explain" homosexuality. As several women state, lesbians and bisexuals have problems with the "scientific" explaining away of their sexuality; most reject it as yet another cultural devaluation of Queer subjectivity.

## JUNGLE CAPTIVES

*Hide and Seek* includes footage from Osa and Martin Johnson's *Simba, King of the Wild Beasts* (1928), linking social construction of race with those of sexualities as they were practiced in the ethnographic films of the Johnsons. Osa and Martin Johnson became famous in the early twentieth century for the "documentaries" they filmed on location in Africa, including *Cannibals of the South Seas* (1912), *Jungle Adventures* (1921), *Head Hunters of the South Seas* (1922), and *Trailing African Wild Animals* (1923). Like the repressive instructional "sex-ed" films of the fifties, the Johnsons' films signified Black Africanicity as exotic and uncontrollable. In this way, Friedrich notes the similarity of approaches to "perverse" and unregulatable desire, and the "primitive" unregulatable inhabitants of the "Dark Continent." The Johnson's films exemplify the legacies of Colonialist ethnographic practice and White women's complicity in such practices.

Passing themselves off as objective documents to a public who seemingly coproduced them as "truths" that supposedly represented real African bodies and customs, the films of Osa and Martin Johnson actually demonstrate the exploitational narrative techniques of "nature" filmmakers who traveled to "the jungle" and rather than recording reality, staged a series of violent tableaux vivants. These repeatedly reproduced narratives center around the safety of Osa Johnson, White adventuress, who is always in danger, always being "attacked" by wild animals, and who is almost always saved by Martin Johnson, Great White Hunter and

Ethnographer. The "stagedness" of these films is hard to miss: shots don't cut together, film grains don't match, animals are shoved into the frame only to be brutally murdered. Africans are not portrayed as humans, but as minions of the Colonial Empire who exist to serve and protect Osa and Martin Johnson, a White heterotopic couple who inscribe across the constructed cinematic landscape they inhabit a variety of codes of dominant mastery in terms of color, gender, and sexuality. Black bodies are filmed as if their tribes are interchangeable, like the performing bodies in pornography. The sight of Osa Johnson leveling her weapon at a defensive offscreen beast (killed in offscreen space) serves to demonstrate (within the context of the film) that White women can "protect" themselves in the jungle from the "beasts" around her, be they animal or human.

## THE WATERMELON WOMAN

While it is tempting to overdetermine the link between the regulation of sexuality and the regulation of race, both bear the social mark of dis/ease. These dis/eases are effectively scrutinized in Cheryl Dunye's *The Watermelon Woman*, the first narrative feature film made by an "out" African American lesbian director. The release of the film was met with a congressional hearing on the already embattled National Endowment of the Arts. Representative Peter Hoekstra, head of the House Education and Workforce Committee's Subcommittee on Oversight and Investigations, questioned the "decency" of federally supported artworks. In particular, Hoekstra, according to Judith Miller of *The New York Times*, "strongly objected to taxpayer support for a film described in one review as the 'hottest' lesbian sex scene 'ever recorded on celluloid' [in Cheryl Dunye's *Watermelon Woman*]" (2). Hoekstra singled out for particular censure two major independent film distributors, Women Make Movies (whom he incorrectly assumed was the distributor of *Watermelon Woman*) and Canyon Cinema. David Sherman, director of Canyon Cinema, responded to the attack by saying that, "as an alternative voice to Hollywood, we deserve support" (Miller, 2), and Debra Zimmerman, director of Women Make Movies, noted that "it was 'outrageous' that Mr. Hoekstra was using them as a 'pretext for shutting down the Endowment'" (Miller, 2).

The crackdown on *The Watermelon Woman* and independent cinema in general demonstrates once again that we live in an era of New Victorianism, which is perhaps even more repressive than that of the late nineteenth century. The repressive cultural practices of our legislators are equally matched by current disciplinary practices, which seek to invent new taxonomies of sexuality under the rubric of the supposed "discovery" of "new" sexual diseases, such as sex addiction and "cutting" (self-mutilation). As Janice M. Irvine notes:

> In the second half of the twentieth century, the invention of new sexual diseases has been central in the regulation of sexuality. In our culture, diseases, like sex, are not simple organic entities, but rather serve as expanded paradigms imbued with diverse meanings. Diseases are artifacts with social history and social practice. In the area of sexuality, the discursive practices of medicine since the nineteenth century have spawned what Foucault terms a "proliferation of sexualities," most of which carry the stamp of perversion reborn as disease. (207)

Irvine emphatically states that it is *not* that she doesn't believe these conditions exist. Like me, she is suspicious of the medical and psychoanalytical industry's tendency toward taxonomizing bodily desires as perversions and disorders. Irvine's work enters around the "discovery" of sex addiction and inhibits sexual desire, but an article in *The New York Times* charts the "discovery" that teens commonly use "cutting" or self-mutilation to cope with emotional distresses. As Jennifer Egan writes, self-mutilation "is finally being properly identified and better understood" (21). As an example of this phenomenon, *Female Perversions* (1997) is a filmed account of psychiatrist Louise Kaplan's book of the same name. The film pathologizes "female perversions" such as shoplifting and self-mutilation, but its metanarrative suggests that it is society's fault that women are threatened by new sexual disorders, because society does not allow women to express their sexuality. While I agree with Kaplan, I wondered if the film version of her work actually reinscribes the female body as a site of perversion, much in the same way that I feel an ambivalence toward "Venus," the play about Venus the Hottentot. But, as Janice Irvine points out, the creation of "new" sexual disorders also provides a site of resistance. This space of resistance is, not surprisingly, marked by a high degree of ambivalence:

> The creation of new sexual disorders reinscribes traditional sex/gender relations while possibly providing a site for resistance, however

minimal. Central to this resistance, however, is a consistent and sharp awareness of how these new diseases, as signifiers of social relations and anxieties, are generally supportive of dominant political interests and social structures. This is especially true in an era when, as medical experts are asserting guidelines about "safer" and hence "appropriate" sex, many individuals feel more vulnerable and therefore susceptible to medical definition, intervention, and control. (222)

Ambivalence is perhaps the best intermediary zone in which to begin to decolonize our minds in terms of race, class, gender, and sexuality. *The Watermelon Woman* is a film that veers toward ambiguity in its appropriation and renarration of offensive images of African American women. Cheryl Dunye plays an aspiring filmmaker who becomes obsessed with the imaginary figure of Lisa Marie Bronson, a fictional actress known in the thirties as "the Watermelon Woman." Dunye transgressively reinscribes the offensive imagery of Bronson as Civil War mammy with her spirited cry, "Girlfriend has got it going on!" The archival footage is faked magnificently by Dunye and cinematographer Michelle Crenshaw, calling into question the "authenticity" of narrative and ethnographic practice, and inverting the power/knowledge paradigmatics of Osa and Martin Johnson's staged ethnographics of faux Negritude. In its playful interaction between real and unreal, fiction and memory, race and reinscription, Dunye's *The Watermelon Woman* offers a substantive site of resistance in contemporary cinematic discourse.

## TRANSGENDERED CINEMA

Other gay/lesbian/transgendered films of note include *Shinjuku Boys* (1995), written and directed by Kim Longinotto and Jano Williams, *Jodie* (1996), directed by Pratibha Parmar, and *Naomi's Legacy* (1994), directed by Wendy Levy. In *Shinjuku Boys*, Kim Longinotto and Jano Williams take the viewer to the world of Japanese female to male transvestites. We visit the New Marilyn Club in Tokyo—where the "hosts" are women cross dressing as men, and the "clients" are women—and take an extraordinary look at gender and sexuality in Japan. *Shinjuku Boys* introduces Tatsu, Gaish, and Kazuku, three *annabes* who work as hosts at the New Marilyn Club. *Annabe* are women who live as men and have girlfriends, although they don't always identify as lesbians. The film displays a neorealist flavor and the filmmakers avoid objectification of their subject by using extensive on-camera interviews in which these s/he's tell their stories. *Shinjuku Boys* alternates gender-bending interviews with handheld sequences shot inside the Club, where the suave *annabes* drink beer in their natty threads and turn the heads of the wannabe girlfriends. The film is a fine example of cross-cultural contextualization of gender issues.

*Jodie*, produced and directed by Pratibha Parmar, demonstrates how and why Jodie Foster has become an international icon for many lesbians, confirming Jodie Foster's place within the world of lesbian desire. Parmar looks at the phenomenon of Jodie Foster as an icon for lesbians whose status has been shaped as much by her authentic and strong screen personas as by the rumor mill of the media, which constantly speculate about her sexuality. The film combines interviews with short film clips from favorite scenes from Foster's films that demonstrate the manner in which Foster may be read as a hypothetical lesbian heroine and a feminist figure.

Lesbian critics Claire Whatling and Terry Brown discuss many of the key iconic moments in Foster's films in relation to lesbian viewers. For instance, Whatling examines the on-screen lesbian relationship between Natassja Kinski and Foster in the film *The Hotel New Hampshire* (1984)—especially the steamy looks between the actresses. Another clip from an underground cult favorite, *Carny* (1980), shows Foster at her peak of sexuality as she flirts with two women. Lesbians continue to see Foster as lesbian icon fueled by the gossip mill around Foster's sexuality and perhaps supported by the rumors about a relationship between Foster and Kelly McGillis or the 1991 "outing" campaign in New York where the streets were plastered with the "Absolutely Queer" posters of Jodie's image. Parmar also features footage from the Jodie Foster look-alike contest in San Francisco, and Professor Mary Cardenas, a Foster fan who built the incredibly popular Jodie web page on the internet. *Jodie* is a fun yet compelling look at the different ways in which Foster is admired, adored, and celebrated as an international icon by lesbians. Whether or not Foster is a lesbian herself is no longer the issue; *Jodie* demonstrates the power of Queer iconicity.

*Naomi's Legacy*, directed by Wendy Levy, is an autoethnographic film that is in some ways reminiscent of Su Friedrich's masterful film *The Ties That Bind*. *Naomi's Legacy* is a film about three generations of women in Levi's Jewish family. Like *The Ties That Bind*, it incorporates text and image, testimony and evidence in ways that are both inviting and distancing to the viewer. In the film, Levy examines shared memories and family secrets and presents them as a young lesbian's legacy. She questions the veracity of the film image by repeatedly showing home movie footage that features a happy-looking family with the testimony of loss, alcoholism, domestic abuse, and, perhaps most importantly, the suppression of these uncomforting family stories. Levy examines the nature of identity and self as it is exhibited through the stories passed on among women. It is a cinematic history of an assimilated Jewish family's struggle. But it is not a film of easy resolutions or easy endings, in fact one of the most significant things about the film is its seeming use of multiple endings. Each time the viewer thinks that the film is about to announce a closure of emotion or an easy answer, the film picks up again to review the three-tiered legacy. One of the most intriguing references is to a leather jacket brought home for Naomi, a jacket meant for a boy, and the metaphoric connection that Naomi makes with a similar black leather jacket. *Naomi's Legacy* springs from the need to tell a woman's story as it unfolds through multiple voices and multiple generations. It is a story of women raising each other despite formidable obstacles such as domestic abuse, immigrant exile status, language barriers, and the complexities of mother-daughter relationships. Levy acts as witness for several generations and comes to terms with a past so often silenced. The intends to give voice to a contemporary Jewish woman's struggle to reckon with the men and women in her past, the inherited pain, the unspoken cycle of unuttered truths.

Other transgressive re-visions of the feminine in cinema include Wendy Levy's 1996 film, *"Swim, Swim . . .": Talking to Sperm and Other Desperate Acts*. The film gives a whole new twist to the infertility roller coaster ride shared by couples all over the world, as it details one woman's two-year odyssey with the emotional highs and lows of not getting pregnant, month after month. By intercutting Levy's running commentary with images from health education documentaries, popular culture, and Hollywood movies, *"Swim, Swim . . ."* is a performative vision of the personal transformation of a feminist heterosexual who is locked in the seemingly Sisyphian cycle of fertility and pregnancy. A strikingly different videotape of images of visual resistance is *Conversations Across the Bosphorous*, a 1995 work directed by Jeanne C. Finley, which intertwines the narratives of two Muslim women from Istanbul: Gokcen and Miné. Gokcen, from an orthodox Islamic family, tells her story of taking off the veil after years of struggle. Miné, who immigrated to San Francisco ten years ago, describes the discovery of her faith in a series of letters to the filmmaker living in Istanbul. Through a series of images and sensuous aural constructs, the two women describe how their relationship to their faith shaped and determined their personal lives.

Set on the banks of the Bosphorous, the narrow waterway that divides the Asian and European continents, *Conversations Across the Bosphorous* suggests that the relation of personal faith to cultural and political structures is one of the most critical issues in both the Islamic and Christian worlds. Gokcen immigrated with her devout family to Istanbul from an Anatolian village. She reveals in this videotape how her personal life reflects the larger cultural dilemma of a city being torn apart in a struggle to maintain its secular government against the rapid growth of Islamic fundamental power. Miné, from an old Istanbul family of many generations, writes from San Francisco of her memories of growing up in a city that since her departure has gone through a radical transformation in political structure, unprecedented population growth, and environmental destruction. In conjunction with evocative visual imagery, sound, and lively debate, these narratives question the possibility of continued peaceful coexistence between groups of opposing ideologies in a relentless urban landscape.

Yvonne Welbon's 1995 film *Remembering Wei Yi-fang, Remembering Myself* is an autobiographical documentary about the director's experiences as an African American woman living in Taiwan for six years (1984–1990). Using a narrative created through dialogue in English and Chinese between the director and her Chinese persona, along with stories of Taiwan told by the director's grandmother, the documentary examines Welbon's discoveries in a country free of American racism. Recreations, presented through memories, historical documents, photographs, and video and film footage move from Welbon's family's ancestral home in Honduras to Chicago to Taiwan, creating intersections between Latin American, African American, and Chinese cultures.

In *A Tajik Woman*, a 1994 videotape by Mehrnaz Saeed-Vafa, the director creates a documentary reflecting on the issues of exile and cultural conflicts of Muslim women from Afghanistan and Iran in the United States. A picture of an unknown Tajik woman found in a Russian book on Tajikistan brings out memories of the filmmaker's past, and encourages her to visit a mosque and interview four women, including her own mother. These women form the first and second generations of Muslim immigrant women from Afghanistan and Iran. Most of them have experienced war and revolution and have endured many hardships, including the loss of their homeland and the conflict with Western culture juxtaposed with their own fundamentalist Islamic values. The video is structured by the filmmaker's voice talking about her own stories and thoughts, using the image of a Tajik woman. Thus main, centering thematic image is complemented by the aforementioned interviews with four other women, footage of the 1979 Iranian revolution shot by Mehrnaz Saeed-Vafa when she visited Iran, the saying of prayers in a mosque in Chicago, pictures of women refugees from the Iran-Iraq war (1980–1989), and pictures of the filmmaker herself during her stay in Iran.

Another major postmodern cinema/artist is African American/Native American Alison Saar, whose work was displayed at the Brooklyn Museum in October, 1996. Saar uses found objects associated with the ambiguous desire surrounded by fetishized fragments of Colonialism. Saar's artwork evokes ambiguity and discomfort as much as it provokes controversy and discussion. "Stone Souls," which was constructed for the Grand Lobby of the Brooklyn Museum, evoke allusions to African and Caribbean cultural legends. They stand as huge egglike objects that refer to fertility rites and female sexuality. "Tree Souls" are more clearly representational forms, but Saar leaves evidence of chain-saw carvings on the raw and unfinished copper. Saar's work brings to mind nineteenth-century slave narratives and the history of African American people who escaped slavery and fled through the jungles of Florida. Saar uses found objects in the way Dunye invents found footage. In an interview with Judith Wilson, Saar explains:

> I liked the fact that found metals and found pieces of wood have a history. It was almost a fetishism. So I liked that about these materials—that they had had another function at one time and that ghost is still hanging around. (1990, 41)

## THE RESISTANT CINEMA OF TRINH T. MINH-HA

The autoethnographic impulse to reclaim and reinscribe the fetish object is at the center of Trinh T. Minh-ha and Jean-Paul Bourdier's *A Tale of Love* (1995). Trinh/Bourdier take on the ambiguity with which the female body is inscribed as a fetish object in conventional cinematographic discourse. *A Tale of Love* thus reimagines and regrounds eroticism within the boundaries of subjective knowing, in a feminist reclamation of the repressed female body as spectator/voyeur. At the same time, Trinh/Bourdier expose the link between male voyeurism/scopophillia, and the virtual decapitation of women in romance and sexuality. The film is experimental, and so its narrative contains a considerable degree of resistance. The film centers on Kieu, a quest-heroine who supports herself as a sex worker (model) and is also studying a famous nineteenth-century Vietnamese poem, "The Tale of Kieu." Trinh/Bourdier renarrate the poem through a performative act of postmodern, autoethnographic practice. The narrative itself deconstructs and metapoetically reperforms the sexual gazing and the politics of "looked-at-ness." Indeed, the film requires a great deal of mediation and discussion to fully explicate the many nuances of its text. To this end, in the spring of 1996, Trinh and I had a lengthy discussion of the making of *A Tale of Love*. We discussed sexuality, performativity, spectatorship, production, collaboration, and various other themes with regard to *A Tale of Love* and Trinh's other films.

GWENDOLYN FOSTER: *A Tale of Love* transgresses the borders between narrative film and experimental film. I read it as a postmodern performative enunciation of a nineteenth-century Vietnamese poem, "The Tale of Kieu." I was wondering how you might classify the film, if it even needed classification, and how those people who have seen the film are classifying it. It's been positioned as your "first narrative film." I am wondering how you feel about that.

TRINH T. MINH-HA: Yes, no doubt, the term is not mine and I don't consider *A Tale of Love* my first narrative film. One can see it as a natural extension of my previous work or one can see it as a different kind of performance, a new trajectory in directions similar to those taken by my earlier films. These have always resisted the reductive binaries set up between "fiction" and "documentary" films.

G.F.: Exactly. This brings up the issue of categorization.

T.M.H.: I've made it quite clear, in the writings and interviews I've published, that "experimental" is not a genre and "documentary" does not really exist since everything goes through fictional devices in film. Rather than reverting endlessly to these established categories, I would prefer to speak about different degrees of staged and unstaged material, or about different spaces of resistance—such as that of enriching meaning while divesting it of its power to order images and sound. I work with the tension these differences raise and the way they creatively or critically contaminate each other. This largely accounts for the difficulties my films kept on encountering in many exhibition venues, including those that claimed to support multicultural, independent, or alternative work. The films I've been making confront people in their normalized need to categorize, to make sense, and to know all. It is in this vein that *A Tale* also continues to frustrate easy consumption, although it certainly differs from the earlier films in its work process. For example, none of my previous films was scripted before the shooting, while in this film almost everything was scripted ahead of time, albeit in a form that was unusual for the actors and the crew.

G.F.: What was different about the way you worked with the actors and the crew on this film?

T.M.H.: The script I gave them had all the scenes, with storyboards that showed all the camera positions and movements, the framings, as well as the lighting designs for each scene. But there was no set order to these scenes. I wrote them both as a director and as an editor, so I was leaving room for the scenes to build on one another during the shooting and to find their own order in the editing phase. Since I did away with sequential order, the planning was at times very frustrating for the key organizing members, including the script supervisor, who is traditionally the continuity person. Working with a large crew in a limited time frame makes it almost impossible to improvise and to operate outside of the framework of traditional narrative filmmaking, in which the specific division of labor tends to become at times too rigid and constraining. However, most of the "department heads" of our crew had more than one role to fulfill, and I can't complain, for everyone did their best. The actors, for example, tried very hard to make their lines, their roles, and their precisely blocked movements all seem natural despite the quite "unnatural" nature of the script. I myself had to shift ground radically and to conceive of the space of "improvisation" other than as a space of spontaneous formation. The openings offered should then be found elsewhere than in the dichotomy of unscripted versus scripted work.

G.F.: One could read the film in the traditional linear narrative fashion in the sense that it centers on a heroine, Kieu, who is in love with writing. She's investigating "The Tale of Kieu" and working as a model. But as the film unfolds I see her as a figure who moves across narrative zones. I notice she often gazes at the viewer and speaks to us as she actively deconstructs the very narrative that she embodies. Toward the middle of the film, the narrative drive of the film becomes, I think, less and less linear. I'm referring to those sections of the film in which we watch her writing and daydreaming, thinking about writing and fantasizing. She makes me think of a "character zone," a very fluid zone in the sense that Bakhtin used that phrase. Do you see her that way?

T.M.H.: To some extent, yes. Most of the experimentation done in "narrative film" focuses on the structure of the narrative. Very few filmmakers have worked on the space of acting to stretch the dimension of the narrative. Marguerite Duras certainly contributed to calling into question narrative form by doing away with acting as impersonifying and representing. Her complex use of the voice (voice-over, voice offscreen; external, nonpsychological, noninteriorized voices) in relation to blank spaces, love, death, desire, and their absence-presence through the actors' bodies is unique. It is more common among experimental filmmakers to rupture the narrative by using nonlinear time and space, for example. But for me, since I've always worked at the limits of several categories, several narrative realms at once, it was not a question of simply rejecting linearity or doing away with the story.

G.F.: Yes, here we have many stories, many Kieus, many levels of narrative and at the same time there really is no unified narrative.

T.M.H.: You start out with a story and you realize, as it unfolds, that there's not really a story in the film. The thread created moves forward, criss-crossed and interlaced by other threads until it breaks with its own linearity; and hence, a story is told mainly to say that there is no story—only a complex, tightly knit tissue of activities and events that have no single explanation, as in life. Of course, a number of viewers tend to catch immediately onto the relationship between Kieu, the protagonist, and Alikan, the photographer, because what they see above all is a conflict between genders, cultures, economical and political positions (boss/employee; subject/object). The ideology of conventional narrative is, as Raul Ruiz puts it, based on the globalized central conflict theory; a theory that rules over both the film industries of the world and the political system of the United States as a dominant model nation. Fortunately however, for other viewers and myself, there is no real conflict in *A Tale*. Not only is the relationship with Alikan merely one among the three visualized in the film, but there are also many relationships other than the ones people tend to follow, especially those not dependent on actors and dialogues. These dialogues are further not real dialogues; they are written as story-spaces that are peculiar to each role designed, and despite their close interactions, they maintain their independent logic—not good-versus-bad logic, but only *different* ones.

Here the notion of fluid "character zone" raised in your earlier question is very relevant. I am thinking more specifically of the movements of the characters across dream states and reality on film. I could talk in dichotomies and say they are the landscapes of a person in love: internal and external, past and present, mythical and historical, literary and filmic. I could also see these movements as inscribing a multiplicity of narrative threads and narrative interfaces. An example is the night scene (in an industrial setting) toward the end of the film when Kieu is speaking to a man wearing a raincoat and a hat, whom we do not recognize as Alikan until either the last line of the scene or until we see Kieu, in the next day shot, waking up (in Juliet's court) and uttering his name with surprise. The same day shot with Kieu drowsing off (in Juliet's court) is seen somewhere toward the beginning of the film. So many things have happened in the film during this lapse of time that a multitude of questions may be raised as to both the nature of that night scene (is it a nightmare? a fantasy? a memory?) and the nature of the events that came before it. (Was she telling herself stories all this time? Or was the daydream dreaming her?) No single linear explanation can account for these narrative interfaces in which performer and performance, dreamer and dream are constituted like the two sides of a coin. One cannot say that she's simply moving in and out of fantasy and reality, but rather, that it's a different zone we are experiencing.

G.F.: Exactly. One of the things that I really liked about the film is that it obviously is a meditation on the discourse around the politics of women and objectification and voyeurism. As a viewer, I felt engaged in a performance that was voyeuristic and at the same time it made me critique that place of voyeurism. This must be provoking all sorts of responses from audience members. Can you talk about that?

T.M.H.: Yes, I think the film can offer the viewer a unique entryway when it is placed in the context of feminism; but if you miss that entryway, there are other possible ways to enter *A Tale,* because the voyeur has appeared quite prominently in a number of writers', filmmakers', and artists' works. One can look at the entire history of narrative in terms of voyeurism—how different forms of voyeurism are deployed in order to sustain narrative power, and how they are made to go unnoticed, especially among spectators who, unaware of their complicity as screen voyeurs, want to be "convinced" of what they see. In other words, the production of (unacknowledged) voyeurism and the consumption of realist narrative continue to feed on each other. It's difficult for me to tell right now how audiences are viewing the film because it has just been released. From the screenings I attended, its reception already oscillates between a very high discomfort and a very intense, enthusiastic response.

G.F.: Maybe even a bit of both. I do remember being a bit shocked that you were taking on what can be shown and what cannot be shown. I mean, we're looking at women being looked at and with all the discourse around women being reduced to their object status of to-be-looked-at-ness, this is transgressive space that you're moving into. And it is clearly an important counterstrategy. It made me constantly ask myself questions such as, How is Trinh, as a woman filmmaker, different in her representation of voyeurism? How can I negotiate the many different narrative strands of the film with relation to the questions of voyeurism and spectatorship? How is this moving the discourse of pornography further beyond rigid moralistically defined ideals?

T.M.H.: Right. Actually the film does not really show nudity in a pornographic way and it doesn't have any lovemaking scenes, for example. As a filmmaker has said it before, when it comes to lovemaking, all actors just start looking like all other actors. The way lovemaking scenes are realized on film remains quite homogenous throughout the history of commercial narrative. Knowing my background, it was perhaps unavoidable that you would ask how a feminist treatment of voyeurism could be different, but this is one way of approaching *A Tale*. I would say that the viewers' discomfort with it so far seems to be less easily locatable, perhaps because it takes time to articulate this discomfort, and there is no consensus among them as to where or what disturbs them. Some think it's the script; some, the lack of plot and unified storyline; others, the acting and the actors; and others yet, the explicit recognition of themselves being voyeurs.

A number of comments did focus on the acting, which some spectators find "hard to look at," "self-conscious," "distant," "odd," or they simply "didn't like the style." Informed viewers have invoked similarities with the films of Straub and Huillet or of Duras. What seems striking in the more negative comments is the fact that viewers differ markedly in their opinions about the specific actors: the one they really have a problem with is definitely not always the same (and this applies "democratically" to all five main actors of the film), and yet each sees in *one* and only one particular actor the unequivocal source of their discomfort. Several viewers have also divided the acting, in accordance with the setting and the characters, into three levels: more natural, more stylized, and in between the two, mid-stylized. By these comments, it seems likely to me that the viewer is uncomfortable because she or he feels some of the acute moments when the actors themselves are self-conscious. This is exactly what I was aiming for, although I was not sure what the exact outcome would be. *A Tale* does not fall squarely into the kind of film whose actors' deliveries sound deliberately *read* or monotonously flat because the artifice is clearly exposed as such. There are a number of films that work in that direction; Yvonne Rainer's films for example. In my case, I was experimenting with different effects in a slightly different space, and I didn't want the scripted lines to sound distinctly "read." I would let the actors try to make their deliveries as naturalistic as possible because I knew that the "dialogues" I wrote could not be entirely naturalized, although what ultimately resists being naturalized remains undefined and, hence, fascinating to me.

G.F.: I found great visual pleasure watching the scene in which the male photographer is blinded. I don't know if that was an allusion or not but it reminded me of something that nineteenth-century women writers do to heroes in Gothic romances. I was particularly thinking of *Jane Eyre*. I wondered if you were making an allusion or if I was just looking for connections to women writers?

T.M.H.: This is a wonderful reading. But for me, this was not a direct allusion because when I was creating it, I was doing it quite intuitively in relation to the whole context of voyeurism. It is important to note that in the scene you mentioned, both the man and the woman are blindfolded. The people working with me and some of the viewers who have seen the film have been really struck by the fact that for the first time neither can *see* each other.

G.F.: Yes, that scene is certainly one of the most transgressive images. It certainly destroys subject-object positionality as we know it. It is a staggering image. To look as a voyeur at both male and female who are bound with the veil feels oddly powerful yet self-conscious because we find ourselves surprised in our active gaze.

T.M.H.: On the one hand, it is a rupture with domination by eye because only touching prevails here in the relationship between the man and the woman. And the sense of touch is all the more heightened when sight is hindered. Vision and visuality have long been the domain in which male mastery is exerted, while the eroticism of the female body through touch is an area some feminists have reappropriated and theorized at length. On the other hand, one can say that the film is a trap for the gaze, and the gender line is not so clear cut. Except for Alikan, the other voyeurs in the film are women, and as you mention, the scene we discuss is one among those designed to call attention to the viewing space or to the spectator's own voyeurism. (If the actors can't see each other, then who's looking at them?) Finally, it is not just looking at the scene, but being put on the spot—the voyeur's encounter with his or her own gaze—that has the potential to make the viewers most uncomfortable, even though they may not recognize this and would rather find fault elsewhere.

Voyeurism in *A Tale of Love* is further coupled with the aesthetics and politics of the veil. Of course the veil and the headless female body are reflected in many ways in the film, both literally and metaphorically. Linked to voyeurism, it is framed in a whole fabric of relations. First, Alikan's love for everything that is veiled, including the *look* of the model. That the model should not "look back" while he shoots is certainly nothing new in photography. (The naturalistic formula we all abide by when shooting on location is: "Don't look at the camera, just go on with your activities as if I'm not there.") Looking back is also commonly experienced as an act of defiance, a perilous act that is historically feared for its ability to divest the Master of his power to possess and control. In many parts of the world, the unveiled woman is still the one who moves about "undressed." She who looks back rather than hide or be oblivious to her body and her sensuality is bound to provoke. And here we paradoxically link up with the other dimension of the veil: if Alikan uses all kinds of veiling devices, it is both to dispossess the model of her power to gaze and to prevent the image from falling into the realm of pornography. (In pornography, the nude often looks straight— provocatively and invitingly—at the camera.) The veil is oppressive, but it can also become a form of resistance; hence the importance of the scene in which both man and woman are blindfolded, and the necessity of also having women voyeurs in the film, as mentioned. The way we all partake in the politics and aesthetics of veiling is complex and often paradoxical.

The scene in which Kieu walks outdoors is therefore very important for me personally. I've noticed, for example, how in certain Middle Eastern cultures—this should apply to other contexts across nations as well—the streets continue to belong to men while the domestic realm remains women's domain. But this being said, I don't want to reiterate that binary opposition between public and private space as developed in certain feminists' work. Let's just say that since the street belongs to men, women have a different space. Whenever they go out into the street, for example, they go out only at certain hours of the day. The unspoken rule is that they shouldn't be seen too much in daylight and they shouldn't be seen at night, it should be somewhere in between. This is what I've noticed in Yemen. Between four and six P.M. the women come out in the street completely veiled. This is the time of the day when their veiled silhouettes are seen moving outside against the walls of the houses. So, for me, the scenes of women walking outdoors at night, the scene of Kieu walking by herself and a later scene in which the camera pans along with women outside on the street, is also a way of gesturing toward the whole history of veiling. The dark of night itself is a veil.

Even in progressive societies, a woman is not supposed to be alone, outside in the street if she comes, let's say, from a well-to-do family or if she has been "properly educated." The night belongs, actually, to those of the margins: sex workers, drug users, secret lovers, and so on. So the scenes of women walking outdoors can be liberatory, but they also remind us of the values of society and the restraints it puts on women in their movement. For how is a woman walking aimlessly alone at night looked at?

## HYBRID MIMICRY: PAM GRIER

The overdetermination of power/knowledge systems is supported by repression and underdetermination of a heterogenetic web of possibilities for resistance and its agents (such as hybridization and mimicry of Colonialist diagetic space). Often we simply miss the oppositional spatial politics of meaning making because we view ourselves through a prison of overdetermined captive order-of-things. As Baudrillard notes, in *Forget Foucault*, "force relations become easily trapped and deenergized by . . . the reverse challenge, with its includable simplicity [which] comes to an end only with power" (55). By reasoning in terms of force relations, we often miss real and theoretical challenges because they are not as visible as systems of essentialized power. Yet Postcolonial theorists locate counter-hegemonic practices in the forms of mimicry, hybrid ambivalency, code switching, signifying, and zones of intersubjective agency. Postcolonial agency is distinctly possible in the celluloid palimpsests of onscreen space, which can evoke *yet transform* the Colonial Plantocratic imagination.

Fortunately there are critical modes that don't depend on and reconstitute captive modes of spatiality. These modes embrace narrative space as more than a mirror of production. De Certeau, for example, notes that stories about space do not merely "exhibit the products of knowledge," they also emphatically "exhibit, on the contrary, the operations that allow it" (121). In this way, we can begin to see that even in the most seemingly overdetermined Colonialist project (the jungle film, the exploitation film, etc.), onscreen diagetic space *unproduces* Colonialism as much as it reproduces Colonialism. Characters are not flat essentialist reproducers of meaning, not simply contained or containable agents. They can operate in hybrid space as what Bakhtin termed "character zones" [*zony gereov*] (1981, 316). Drawing on the work of I. S. Turgenev, Bakhtin imagines the space of the character zone as fluid and rife with the possibility of agency, much in the same manner that Homi K. Bhaba evokes the "margin of hybridity, where cultural differences 'contingently' and conflictually touch . . . it resists the binary opposition of racial and cultural groups, sipahis and sahibs, as homogeneous polarized political consciousness" (1994, 207). Likewise, Bakhtin's character zones

> formed from the fragments of character speech [*polurec*], from various forms for hidden transmission of someone else's word, from scattered words and sayings belonging to someone else's speech, from those invasions into authorial speech of others' expressive indicators [ellipsis, questions, exclamations]. Such a character zone is the field of action for a character's voice, encroaching in one way or another upon the author's voice. (1981, 316)

In conjuring the prism of the hybridic character zone, we can begin to see examples of sites of resistance in a figure not unlike that described by Jenny Sharpe as the "mimic man" or Colonial subject, "a contradictory figure who simultaneously reinforces Colonial authority and disturbs it" (1995, 99). Pam Grier is a telling example of a mimic woman, whose appearances in seventies blaxploitation films are immersed in the Other's authorial voice and space. Nevertheless, Grier effectively exploits the agency of the exploitation film that seeks to capture her. Pam Grier coproduces her image as hypersexualized African American/supervixen and action heroine in films such as Jack Hill's *Coffy* (1973), Arthur Marks's *Friday Foster* (1975), Jack Hill's *Foxy Brown* (1974), Bob Kelljan's *Scream, Blacula, Scream* (1973), and Eddie Romero's *Black Mama, White Mama* (1972). Though the Black exploitation genre seeks to invoke a monologic discourse of White supremacy and White desire of the Other, neither Grier nor the genre can contain the counterhegemonics of Postcolonialism's project. Pam Grier's mimicry is characterized by that menace of mimicry described by Homi K. Bhaba: "Mimicry does not merely destroy narcissistic authority through the repetitious slippage of difference and desire. It . . . necessarily raises the question of the *authorization* of Colonial representations" (1994, 90). The blaxploitation genre attempts to contain the spectre of mimicry, which is one of the primary attributes of those zones of resistances buried in genres, tropes, and structures of embedded oppositionalities. Pam Grier's 1970s films exploit Pam Grier, but Grier exploits the narrative zone in a characteristic display of hybrid mimicry.

In *Coffy* (1973), Pam Grier is a young nurse who has lost her brother to drugs. The spectre of Grier, dressed as a super Black action heroine, hell-bent on destroying the system of "drugsploitation" of African Americans, operates in a zone of agency that meets the requirements of the genre: excessive display of the body of Pam Grier, especially the breasts of Pam Grier, in generic tropes of the Black female body that characterize the Black exploitation vehicle. Grier sports her beauty as a utility that can aid her on her quest for vengeance. The genre displays her beauty to redeploy the Colonialist fantasy of "eating the other," to paraphrase bell hooks. But beauty itself, Black beauty, can interrupt the intimacy of Colonialism as much as it can induce Colonial ambivalence. If "beauty refers to that about a thing which makes its existence not a matter of neutrality or indifference" (Farley, 80), Grier's beauty is superseded only by her ability to outsmart everyone around her, which is one of the most pleasurable tropes in her films. Coffy takes on hit-men, thugs, druglords, and king-pins and continually defeats them all. Characteristically, Black power, when "unleashed" in blaxploitation films, is overdetermined as an irrepressible, monstrous, "natural," and "primitive" urge that cannot be "tamed." As the voiceover in the film's trailer emphasizes, "*Nobody* sleeps when they mess with Coffy!" Black rage here is raised as an oppositional force to Colonialist ambivalence. The duality of Grier's positionality, White fear projection or agent of resistance to White patriarchal imperialism, confronts us with a question posed by Sara Suleri: "How can the dynamic of imperial intimacy produce an idea of nation that belongs neither to the colonizer nor the colonized?" (1995, 113). Or, as Stephen Slemon wonders: "Who or what acts oppositionally, when ideology or discourse or psychic processes of some kind construct human subjects?" (1995b, 52). Which Pam Grier is an agent of Colonial mimicry: the Pam Grier who (as Coffy, Friday Foster, Foxy Brown, or other characters) is repeatedly seen in victim tropes in scenes in which she is held prisoner, sexually abused, performing catfights, etc.; or the Pam Grier who overthrows the White supremacist social system that seeks to enslave her (and by implication the Black Other)?

It has to be both. Grier is an intersubjective agent of Postcolonial resistance. As an active interrogator and inhabiter of diagetic and extradiagetic screen space, Grier simply cannot be contained. She uses her body in a performative inter/rupture of the ethnographic genre of blaxploitation. She operates in the zone of performative enunciation where, Steven Shaviro reminds us: "Perception is turned back upon the body of the perceiver, so that it affects and alters the body, instead of merely constituting a series of representations, for the spectator to recognize" (50).

In *Friday Foster*, Grier is teamed with Godfrey Cambridge (who plays a private eye) in an espionage vehicle that centers around an assassination conspiracy plot against Black politicians. Here and elsewhere, Grier's speech is both hers and that of an/Other. Her use of dialogic speech is another trope of blaxploitation vehicles that marks the ambivalence of resistance. Grier's pronunciation of graphic street language is delivered in a deliberate, overdetermined manner that seeks to parody White constructions of Black language. Grier often enunciates these lines as if she is playfully rendering them in a Black voice mocking a White interpretation of Blackness. "I'm gonna shoot you, you dope dealing *motherfucker*," she screams at one of her adversaries, consciously playing to the audience in a self-reflexive manner. Her use of vocal inflection can be compared to the ethnographic subject's use of the Third Eye. Her "third voice" looks back as if to say, "I see you looking and listening to me and constructing my essential Blackness, but I will not be captured by your lens or your microphones."

Even in one of the most degrading blaxploitation vehicles of her career, *Foxy Brown*, Grier's performance is salvageable as a mimic who interrupts the violent spectacle of exploitational tropes. *Foxy Brown* is a hybridized rape-revenge film in which Grier, as Foxy, seeks revenge for the murder of her brother. Again Grier takes on the head of a crime ring, Miss Katherine, who runs a string of brothels. Miss Katherine routinely preys upon women of color and gets them addicted to drugs. Foxy goes undercover and tries to help out one of the enslaved prostitutes. As a result, Foxy is beaten, drugged, raped, and left in a closet. Here the narrative begins to trope itself after the rape-revenge film. Foxy destroys the crime ring, and graphically castrates Miss Katherine's lover, as she revels in a performative body of seemingly endless power, ability, and skills.

But often Pam Grier's 1970s films seem to evoke race in a manner described as "Jeffersonian" by K. Anthony Appiah. In *Black Mama, White Mama* (1972), in which Grier is chained to a White woman activist for most of the film's narrative, race is "invoked to explain cultural and social phenomena, in this case, the alleged political impossibility of a citizenship shared between White and Black races" (Appiah, 43). *Black Mama, White Mama* pits the characters of Lee Daniels (Pam Grier), against a blonde White woman, Karen Brent (Margaret Markov). The two women are chained together in a jungle prison camp. They escape, but they are

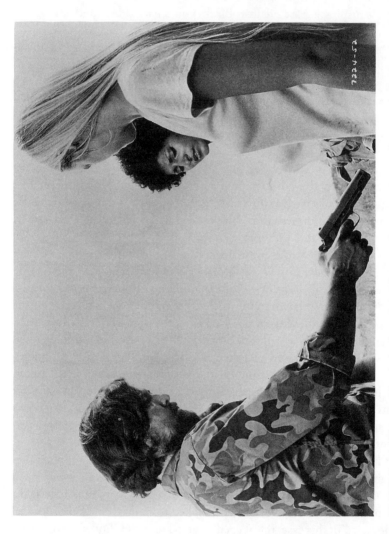

FIGURE 24. The ritualized display of the fetishized weapon in *Black Mama, White Mama.* Courtesy Jerry Ohlinger Archives.

unable to free themselves from their shackles; as signifiers of race and referents of gender, the women play out Plantocratic politics that stand between White and Black women. The impossibility of a shared citizenship between these women is marked by Grier's troped body as "naturally" more suited to beating off the savage Third World others, emissaries of the White Colonialists who do their bidding (again in the operation of an international conspiracy).

Markov is revealed as an impossibly stupid and physically incapable political activist. Her construction as a White female is tied to her "natural" inabilities and failings. Grier, on the other hand, is imbued with "natural" and "instinctive" traits that allow her to become a butch/femme Tarzana figure, one who can outwit and outmuscle the "primitive" forces of both the crime syndicate and the violent, ungovernable jungle they must survive in. But as Jane C. Desmond notes, "selling 'nature' is big business" (217). Grier is a natural at civilizing the jungle, a Black re-inscription of the White jungle goddess of serials and early jungle films. Here, however, the White woman is shown to be incapable in the role of "civilizer." Grier is an example of the re-representation of the Colonial subject within the discourse of the "menace of mimicry" as described by Bhabha: "The *menace* of mimicry is its *double* vision which in disclosing the ambivalence of Colonial discourse also disrupts its authority" (1994, 88). Thus, Grier's performativity, regardless of narrative troping, rejects a Kantian schema in which "women are merely the agents of beauty and style" (Bar On, 122).

If "the only weapon of power," as Baudrillard suggests, "is to reinject the real and the referential everywhere" (1994, 22), *Scream, Blacula, Scream* injects elements of Pan African spirituality into a narrative that disrupts the hegemonic codes of the White vampire tales that it hybridizes. This Pam Grier vehicle mimics White vampire films in its conception of the patriarch-as-vampire in the form of Blacula, or Dracula in race drag. However, this vampire legend pits Black cultural practices (voodoo) against White occultery. A sequel to *Blacula* (1972), which starred William Marshall as a Black Prince/Vampire who stalks the streets of L.A., *Scream, Blacula, Scream* pits Pam Grier, as Lisa, a "voodoo Priestess," against Blacula, who has predictably returned from his undead grave. Lisa rescues her boyfriend with her *voudon* rites, outwitting the Black Master vampire. The injection of "real" elements from African American cultural practices marks another conundrum of hybridization. Does the film reinject the real as a weapon of power, or does the film's application of racial characteristics simply characterize yet another White Colonialist correlation of biological race with essentialized characteristics? In a television interview in the late 1990s, Pam Grier asserted that these films were transgressive in their own way; she specifically cited the *voudon* practice in *Scream, Blacula, Scream* as a case of progressive politics, even though she quite readily recognized that blaxploitation vehicles were based on an inherent exploitation of Blackness. But resistances are not pure; they are always mediated. As Stephen Slemon suggests, "resistance itself is never *purely* resistance, never *simply* there in the text or the interpretive community, but it is always *necessarily* complicit in the apparatus it seeks to transgress" (1995a, 108).

## DOROTHY DANDRIDGE: RESISTANT BLACK GODDESS

Dorothy Dandridge, "the first truly integrated Black goddess" (84), in the words of Gary Dauphin, left a legacy of performances that suggests resistance, agency, and interventionist strategies. Dandridge's performances, from jungle Queen Melmendi in *Tarzan's Peril* (1951) to femme fatale in *Carmen Jones* (1954) and, most emphatically, as a slave aboard a slaveship in *Tamango* (1957), are triumphant performative displays of counter-hegemonics. Dandridge's performances may be read through the lens of de Certeau's theories of enunciation. Like Pam Grier, Dandridge uses the performative arena to speak near nonlinguistic and linguistic systems of hegemony. The power of enunciation is perhaps inherent in the performativity of the actor's profession, but it acquires specific political agency as it erupts through the body of Grier or Dandridge, who break through the largely absent Black woman figure in motion pictures and begin a project of resistance by their very presence on the screen. In speech-act theory, enunciation is the power-knowledge nexus of resistance and agency. As de Certeau writes, enunciation presupposes specificities:

Enunciation presupposes: (1) a *realization* of the linguistic system through a speech act that actualizes some of its potential (language is real only in the act of speaking; (2) an *appropriation* of language by the speaker who uses it; (3) the postulation of an interlocutor (real or fictive) and thus the constitution of a relational *contract* or allocution (one speaks to someone); (4) the establishment of a *present* through the act of the "I" who speaks, and conjointly, since "the

FIGURE 25. Dorothy Dandridge and Curt Jurgens in *Tamango*; the dialectics of the Master/Slave relationship. Courtesy Jerry Ohlinger Archives.

present is properly the source of time," the organization of a temporality (the present creates a before and an after) and the existence
of a "now" which is the presence to the world. (33)

As one of the few Black Goddesses of the silver screen, Dandridge
was well aware of the burden of representation that was applied to her,
thus she displayed a realization of the linguistic and discursive systems in
which she performed. As an actress, she appropriated the language of
another, but in appropriating the language she dialogizes her lines to great
effect. Thus, when she says in *Carmen Jones* "Nobody owns me except me
myself," in a scene with Harry Belafonte, her enunciation of this line performs it with multivalence and a hyperreality of meaning. As Dauphin
notes, the line "still draws applause" (84); the audience coperforms and
coproduces the enunciative power of Dorothy Dandridge as a hypereal
signifier.

Watching Dandridge's films, I perceive Dandridge as a living performer; and in a way, she *is* a living enunciator if we see her through the
lens of virtual reality. Thus, cinematic performativity establishes an eternal "I" and "now" for the viewer. This was made remarkably clear at a
screening of John Berry's *Tamango* (1957), which I saw during a retrospective of Dandridge's films at Film Forum in New York. The film was
greeted by a profuse amount of audience interaction, directed not only at
the screen persona of Dandridge, but also in offscreen conversations
between audience members. This was true of many of the film screenings
in the retrospective, but *Tamango* in particular evoked audience members
to tears and shouting, and left the audience shattered by the grim ending
in which a slave-ship uprising is ultimately crushed by the ship's captain,
played by Curt Jurgens, who murders a group of revolutionary slaves by
firing a ship's cannon directly into their midst.

I cite the audience inter/reaction here to demonstrate the possibilities for Postcolonial counterhegemonics and intersubjectivities that situate agency as a shared embodiment across subjectivities. Dandridge's performance evokes Carol Mavor's description of Merleau-Ponty's
"inside-out, outside-in structure of the glove (its reversibility) as a model
of the double-open space in which [she] performs" (Mavor, 81). In
*Tamango*, Dandridge reperforms the female slave as a sexually exploited
figure. Her character is soon torn between her relationship with the ship's
captain and her loyalty to the slaves held in the cargo hold below, along
with their leader, Tamango. When Dandridge's character finally aligns

herself with her own people, Dandridge's performance changes considerably. Suddenly she embodies a more sharply defined personae, her body gestures change, and she flies into a rage against the ship captain.

Few films even begin to allow the countertransgressive acts that erupt in *Tamango*. The Black-White hostility and the complexities surrounding Black female subjectivity with regard to Colonial sexual/power relations are rendered with a clarity that is only matched in its effectiveness by the hegemonic denial of the existence of the African personae existence in most narrative cinema. *Tamango* enunciates the unspeakable acts of Colonialism; beatings, shootings, rapes, enshacklement, captivity. The view of the Black bodies, chained to the vile slaveship, is not romanticized by the usual extradiagetic music of soothing spirituals. In *Tamango*, these scenes are underscored solely by natural sound, with only a few bars of dirgelike music as accompaniment. Many audience members found the "realism" of the film too harsh; a few left. Yet there was nothing overtly "realistic" about the film; *Tamango* seems "realistic" because it is one of the few films to deal with slavery in such a forthright manner. And unlike more conventional narrative films that treat the subject of slavery, *Tamango* refuses to offer the audience the safety and closure of an artificially "happy" ending.

Dandridge's performance in Byron Haskin's *Tarzan's Peril* (1951), is marked by a Third Eye of self-reflexivity that serves to displace the center of the film's Colonialist tropes. Dandridge plays a queen of the jungle, Melmendi, who is rescued by Tarzan, played by Lex Barker. The small role is important because it marks a possible location of an eruption of difference as an agent itself. In most Tarzan vehicles, Tarzan, the man of "Nature," is sexually bound to the White civilizer/sex goddess Jane. Yet in *Tarzan's Peril*, Tarzan seems far more interested in Melmendi than Jane. Melmendi and Tarzan's relationship is only one of the many interracial partnerships (onscreen and off) that Dandridge was involved in in the racially charged 1950s. Robert Rossen's *Island in the Sun* (1957) locates interracial love as a site of transgressive countertestimony, again in a jungle surrounding. As the first Hollywood film to romantically pair Black and White stars since the introduction of the Motion Picture Code, it was boycotted in the American South. In the film, Dandridge was paired with John Justin, while Harry Belafonte played opposite Joan Fontaine. In terms of counterhegemonic politics, the pairing of a White *woman* with a Black *man* was seen as a deeply transgressive act, in that it enunciated the practice of interracial love in a manner that directly threatened White male patriarchy.

Far more contained, and far less transgressive, are interracial pairings of White *men* with Black *women*, as in *The Decks Ran Red* (1958), in which Dandridge is the only woman aboard a ship of sexually voracious men. Dandridge's performance as the lush Black Goddess here and in *Carmen Jones* (1954) is charged with confidence and assurance. Filmed in color and Cinemascope in 1954 by Otto Preminger, *Carmen Jones* finally pairs a Black Goddess with a Black male, Harry Belafonte, with whom Dandridge was also paired in *Bright Road* (1953). While *Bright Road* is a safe (and containing) "problem" picture that centers around Dandridge as a school teacher and Belafonte as a principal, *Carmen Jones* offers us Dandridge as the performative Black Goddess who seduces the sexually clean-cut soldier Belafonte.

Perhaps one of the finest examples of Dandridge as performative enunciator and nexus of agency is in a little-known film, John Peyser and Robert Gist's *Murder Men* (1962), which was originally presented as an episode of the television series *Cain's Hundred* in the United States, and then expanded into a feature for European theatrical bookings. Amazingly, this film was denied a U.S. playdate of any kind until the summer of 1997; although crude in spots, the film contains one of Dandridge's most interesting late performances. In *Murder Men*, Dandridge plays a junkie night club singer who gets out of jail and tries to regain the love of her estranged husband, played by Ivan Dixon. Dandridge, by this point in her career, was known to be dependent upon alcohol and prescription drugs, so her performance in *Murder Men* is ripe with the menace of mimicry inherent in performing a character zone not too far from herself. One cannot help but read a metanarrative into the film, the metanarrative of Dandridge's overdose of antidepressants which took her life at the age of forty-two. But far from retreating into a performance that would suggest the trope of the tragic mulatto, Dandridge instead injects the real into the film's metatext of drug dependence and demonstrates that slavery to drugs does not inherently prevent counterhegemonic practices of the self. The cinematic and performative memory of Dorothy Dandridge itself is thus a counterhegemonic practice of Black memory and enunciative intervention in the decolonization of image politics.

# CHAPTER FIVE

# *Disciplining Discourse*

Perhaps a good starting point in my analysis of disciplinary discourse is to invoke the realm of the fetish cabinet, a memento of the lost continent or forbidden jungle of bourgeois intellectual life. The fetish cabinet, as Emily Apter notes, was popularized in the nineteenth century as a sort of private cabinet of curios, and it was "the atmosphere of the forbidden that transformed the cabinet into an architectural fetish in eighteenth-century literature" (1991, 39). Theoretical texts act as cabinet texts, disciplining fetishes for and around popular culture as text. In the libidinal economy of academic fetishism, servant texts serve master narratives on a number of levels in a fetishistic display that "displaces the boundaries between propriety and proprietorship" (Apter, 1991, 43). Judith Mayne problematizes film theorists' preoccupation with the origins of cinema as "primal scenes" of "primitivity," provoking a discussion of film theories captivity to the discourse of psychoanalytic theory as well as Colonialist empiricism. The cultural preoccupations of cinematic inquiry reperform the work of the fetish cabinet.

> The "scene" of "primitive" cinema is informed by a fascination with otherness, with the exotic, with all that is seemingly alien to Western culture and subjectivity. . . . That some film historians have focused on modes of spectatorship in their revision of the early cinema suggests that here, too, an implicit assumption has been made that early film viewers brought with them only a "primitive" capac-

ity to distinguish between illusion and reality. . . . Some film historians have understood not only early films but early viewers as captured within a naive, childlike state of reception.

The infantilism that inheres in the word *primitive* has a particularly strong psychoanalytic resonance in French, where "scène
primitive" translates as the "primal scene." While Noël Burch frequently refers to the early cinema as so many "primal scenes" of the
cinema, his psychoanalytic terminology functions in a more general
metaphoric sense, whereby the early cinema is a kind of "id" to the
"ego" of classical cinema. For some psychoanalytic critics in France,
however, the early cinema functions very literally to stage the primal
scene. (182)

## INSIDE THE FETISH CABINET

Bound to discursive jungles of these primal scenes, cultural critics, in
turn, appropriate texts and their readers as "primitive," thus fetishizing
consumer's spatial zones of primal scenes. de Certeau describes this
practice as the "ideology of 'informing through books'" (166), wherein
the critical "producers' claim to *inform* the population . . . the elite,
upset about the 'low level' of journalism or television, always assumes
that the public is moulded by the products imposed on it" (166).
Because "the film theorist sets out to subsume every aspect of cinematic
phenomena under the putative laws of his or her minimally customized
version of reality" (Carroll, 41), the film theorist attempts to contain
the "primitive" or "primal" subconscious of the colonized audience in a
symbolic sadomasochistic relationship. Binding meaning and capturing
the primal scene of the filmic apparatus and the spectator has been the
dominant structure in theoretical practices for so long that we forget
that the critic is her/himself dependent on a compulsive return to the
fetish cabinet. In this myriad of relationships, one can locate a complex
dependency. As Lynn Chancer comments, "The very act of binding
attests to this dependency, and provides another significant explanation
for the pleasure experienced in physically [or intellectually] restricting
the other" (1992, 48).

Stanley Aronowitz agrees with this assertion, noting that "contemporary social theory is deeply enmeshed in a debate about the relation
between social structure and agency" (116). Indeed, agency and subjec-

tivity are the cultural texts of the late twentieth-century fetish cabinet of academe. This quest for the seemingly lost continents of subjectivity and agency comes at the same time as the appearance of the "body without organs" (Deleuze and Guattari, 1987, 149), the "abolishment of subjectivity" (Baudrillard and Lotringer, 74), the "cyborg" of Donna Haraway, the "performing body" of Judith Butler, and the "posthuman bodies" of Halberstam and Livingston. The body is thus perceived as yet another lost continent by the Postcolonial critic, who often evokes the fetishized text of Foucault's *Discipline and Punish* in order to discipline that body.

As Foucault himself suggests, it isn't as if there has been no resistance to critical dominations. Criticism, like reading or watching a film, is always an act of *translation*, as Trinh T. Minh-ha and Walter Benjamin maintain. Translation draws us into fascination with the saturation of meaning in everything; we are surrounded by lost objects, lost continents, fetishes of popular culture. This is one of the pleasures of criticism, "the group quest for truth," as described by Dana Polan:

> Simplifying we might suggest that the humanist theory of education starts from a simple epistemological premise. One version of this theory is dissected in Richard Rorty's *Philosophy and the Mirror of Nature*: truths exist as objects in nature, and subjects come from without to know those truths through transparent media of discovery, and these knowing subjects enable others to know truth through pedagogic transmission. The university will inflect this model by inserting the knower into a social universe. The goal of knowing is not simply to *acquire* but to *give* to others—to profess; and the spirit of collegiality—of collegeness—exists so that the quest for truth becomes a group quest. (1993, 31)

Polan locates professors as a "subculture" but emphasizes that, like subcultures, we interact with society in a "multiplicity of ways" (1993, 38). We attempt critical translation, but we are always aware of the fact that translation is a slippery and dangerous event. We are willing hostages to master narratives, captives of language signifiers, yet drawn to the fountain of unproscribed meaning, always aware that

> Translation, to the extent that it disarticulates the original, to the extent that it is pure language and is only concerned with language, gets drawn into what he calls the bottomless depth, something

essentially destructive, which is in language itself. . . . The translation belongs to the afterlife of the original, thus assuming and confirming the death of the original. (Derrida, 84, 85)

Critical theory is both attractive and fun because it operates both
within and outside of states of reality. As Jean Baudrillard suggests, in a
discussion with Sylvere Lotringer, entitled "Forget Baudrillard," theory is
a captive body unbound in a void charged with meaning:

> It's possible that theory will implode, that it will absorb its own
> meaning, that it will end up at best mastering its disappearance. But
> it doesn't happen like that. We must manage to choke back the
> meanings we produce—which always tend to be produced. If a the-
> ory—or a poem, or any other kind of writing (it's not endemic to
> theory)—indeed manages to implode, to constitute a concentric
> vortex of implosion, then there are no other effects of meaning.
> Theory has an immediate effect—a very material one as well—of
> being a void. It's not so easy to create a void. And besides, there's
> catastrophe all around it. I don't see how theory and reality can go
> together. Can we implode in the real with charm? Without going all
> the way to suicide, we continually play on the process of disappear-
> ance in our relations to others. Not by making ourselves scarce, but
> by challenging the other to make us reappear. That's what seduction
> is, in the good sense. Not a process of expansion and conquest, but
> the implosive process of the game. (128–129)

Identification is at the center of many of the current debates about film
reception. It has been largely through the efforts of feminist, Postcolonial,
and Queer theorists that film studies has exploded with new theories of
identification that foreground the pleasures of class, race, and gender:
gay/lesbian/transgendered, postnegritudinal, and a multitude of spectatorship possibilities. Recently, the self-representation of film theorists is
challenged by the interdisciplinary nature of moving-image study.


## CONTAINING CRISIS

"Whither Film Studies?" and "Cultural Studies in Crisis?" were proposed
panels for a recent annual meeting of the Modern Language Association.

Such titles would seem to suggest a crisis of self-representation in the fields of Cultural Studies and Film Studies. Such a staged turf war, however, is probably more indicative of a tendency in academe toward the simultaneous embrace and distrust of interdisciplinary fields. Interdisciplinary studies sound hot and sexy on paper, but as many of us know, such fields represent hotly contested locations that disrupt academic hegemonies. If there is indeed a "crisis" in the area around Film Studies and Cultural Studies, it is an invented one. The scholarship in the area could not be more lively, aggressively interdisciplinary, and studded with academic "stars" from bell hooks to Homi Bhabha. Students are highly responsive to these new texts and approaches. After all, students are generally more comfortable with change. If the ground shifts under their feet, they are more inclined to dance. If the earth moves under our feet, we scholars tend to run for cover.

In *Disturbing Pleasures*, Henry Giroux describes how he works with the pedagogical tools of Cultural Studies in the classroom. Giroux and his students actively contest the boundaries of the cultural turf of high and low popular culture and film. In this work, he and his students become earth movers, disrupting the boundaries of passive spectatorial pleasures. In investigating the familiar and pleasurable images of television, movies, and other media, students find themselves sometimes angry in their disturbance of pleasure. Giroux revisits his well-known theories of pedagogy: as cultural workers, teachers must not only contest the ground upon which we walk, but we must also move students to begin to analyze their place in culture and in the educational institution. Giroux reminds students that they "inhabit a photocentric, aural, and televisual culture in which the proliferation of photographic and electronically produced images and sound serve to actively produce knowledge" (88). Thus, students begin to analyze their position in the classroom as well as their position as consumers of culture.

In the Cultural Studies classroom, students find themselves analyzing power/knowledge constructions, with an emphasis on race gender and Postcolonial gazing, in locations such as the Benetton ad campaign, the Disney empire, and films such as Garry Marshall's *Pretty Woman* (1990) and *Grand Canyon* (1991). The sound you hear, when the ground begins moving, is the sound of the "border intellectual" or the student herself, who is beginning the cultural work of questioning basic underpinnings of those pedagogies and icons that have sought to suppress her ability to question and engage in an active spectatorial and theoretical investigation.

This is evidence of the exciting work going on in college classrooms. It is not always easy, as Giroux notes; in fact, Cultural Studies is dependent upon a sort of dis/ease that comes from a reworking of the boundaries of pleasure.

Drawing on the work of Paolo Friere, Giroux calls for a rethinking of the importance of the "border intellectual" as he applies the term to the undergraduate and graduate student. Being a border intellectual is a disruptive but healthy enterprise. In disturbing pleasure, the student remaps the border of intellectual inquiry, thus challenging the rigid limits of academic locations of discourse. At their healthiest, intellectual border crossings in the classroom, and in the profession, should be as noisy as a construction work site. After all, the border crossings of Cultural Studies and Film Studies remake a sense of "home" in discourse. As Giroux writes, "to move away from 'home' is to question in historical, semiotic, and structural terms how the boundaries and meanings of 'home' are often constructed beyond the discourse of criticism" (143). Perhaps it should not be surprising then that Cultural Studies and Film Studies locate themselves as nomadic disciplines. Our home is the classroom, where it is ironically easier to move minds than it is to reassign allocations. *Disturbing Pleasures*, read against the backdrop of contested and shifting grounds within the profession, becomes all the more valuable as a pedagogical tool to bring with you into the classroom as an educator.

Marcia Landy's *Film, Politics, and Gramsci* rereads Gramscian pedagogical theory through the lens of Film and Cultural Studies. Landy revisits familiar terrain from the landscape of critical theory, centering her rereading of Gramsci around notions such as hegemony, the subaltern, the knowing subject, the cultural importance of folklore, and the politics of Othering. Landy finds in Gramsci a political approach to popular culture that is Marxist in nature, yet allows for cultural critics to find voices of subversion. For Landy, Gramscian politics are not situated around a reading of popular culture that sees it as a hegemonic evil enterprise that would seek to work against the powerless subalternated subject. This opens the field up to inquiries into disruptive gaps or contestatory sites in mass culture, whether they are found in music, literature, film, or television.

Some of the best reading in *Film, Politics, and Gramsci* includes a chapter on melodrama in the "women's film" of World War II Britain. Here Landy finds "complex instances not only of female socialization and sexual repression but of antagonism and resistance to prevailing norms"

(104). Landy is one of the first scholars in Film Studies to reread the films of Gainsborough studios, films that had been previously dismissed as melodramatic (read unimportant). Landy notes that the Gainsborough melodramas were often written, directed, and produced by women. Far from being unimportant or antifeminist, Landy sees their importance as vehicles designed to meet the needs for visual pleasure and fantasy for a mass female audience in Britain in the war years. In Landy's rereading of current popular filmmaking in Britain, she refutes critical dismissal of this period of filmmaking, which has been read as a rise in Colonial myth-making. Films such as John Boorman's *Hope and Glory* (1987) beckon to the comforts of better days gone past, but, Landy argues, movies such as Stephen Frears's *Prick Up Your Ears* (1987), for example, are "producing direct and transgressive images of homosocial relations capable of being extrapolated to the sexually repressive and puritanical" (144) period in which we find ourselves.

*Film, Politics, and Gramsci* ends with a chapter on the writing of Antonio Negri. Here, again, Landy reworks some of the most basic notions of cultural studies: the formation of knowledge, subjectivity, and Otherhood. Negri's ideas about subjectivity seem in some ways to be more politically expedient and timely than those of Gramsci. Negri, like the highly influential film theorists Deleuze and Guattari, views subjectivity through a poststructural gaze. Landy is drawn to Negri's notion of radical subjectivity, that which emphasizes plurality and mutability, thus agency. *Film, Politics, and Gramsci* reaches forward as much as it reaches backward, moving Marxist cultural theories into context with current popular culture and current theory.

In *Cultural Studies and Cultural Value*, John Frow, Professor of English at the University of Queensland, flatly admits that "Cultural Studies exists in a state of productive uncertainty about its status as a discipline" (7). This book is an important work in the field because it explores the history of Cultural Studies as an "antidiscipline." Frow reworks the critical territory around the questions of high/low culture and the central question of the "Other." It is interesting to note that, despite differences between British (or Australian) and American Cultural Studies, there is a certain sameness evident here. What is at stake in Cultural Studies, regardless of cultural difference, are the same questions. Who can speak for others? Who defines an Other? Can the subaltern speak? How do we define high and low forms of popular culture? How do we teach Cultural Studies?

I think this suggests a healthy attitude in the field and supports the very notion of a field of Cultural Studies. Although Cultural Studies rose to great popularity in Britain in the mid to late 1980s as a pedagogical and political tool, it has changed considerably. As the field becomes more and more broadbased and inclusionary, it is being redefined to move beyond notions of class determiners and is renegotiating itself around broader categories of gender, sexuality, race, and other crosscultural determiners. It seems possible that one of the reasons Cultural Studies may be having a bit of trouble defining itself in the United States is that Postcolonial American critics have a healthy skepticism of things Colonial.

## SUBJECTIVITY AT THE MARGINS: THE CINEMA OF SAFI FAYE

By foregrounding the body, and the subjectivity of African women's experience, the Francophone filmmaker Safe Faye engages in what feminist anthropologist Allison Jablonko terms "haptic learning, learning through bodily identification" (182). Moving across the boundaries of visual pleasure, both scopic and haptic, Faye carves out a space for the skin, the body, the uncontained and uncontainable vessel of subjectivity. The body as haptic and scopic is irreducible and yet embodied. As Jennifer Barker explains:

> The body as excess presents such a problem for current theories . . . that posit narration as cohesive, unambiguous *containment* of different and contradicting voices within the text. (68)

Thus Faye is similar to other Francophone women ethnographers who address assumptions behind narrative theory and ethnographic theory, as well as the larger issues around the representation of difference.

Safi Faye negotiates subjectivity, haptic space, and women's space in *Selbe et tant d'autres* (1982). Faye cautiously avoids the traditional ethnographic objectification and silencing of African subjects by strategically choosing to allow the self-representation of a speaking African subject. *Selbe* is a thirty-minute film that follows the daily routines and rituals of Senegalese women, in particular one woman: Selbe. Faye converses with Selbe, who simply tells her story as she incessantly works—cooking, cleaning, and selling—in order to provide for her family. Men are largely absent here because, in this region, men leave for temporary jobs in the city. For the most part, as viewers, we watch the body of Selbe. The film is an extraordinary example of cinéma vérité. It explores women's space and women's subjectivity in ways not usually seen in film.

Selbe is a film of excess. Excess of female subjectivity, pain, pleasure, work, and the routine. It is a film that demands a new way of looking at film because of its intense physicality, aurality, and spirituality. Selbe is a film of the body, and it demands that we rethink the way we experience the body in the spectacle of film, the apparatus of film, the implied objective-subjective power relationship of film spectatorship.

Kristin Thompson's essay on cinematic excess reminds us that "each film dictates the way it wants to be viewed," and that responding to a film's excesses can renew films' "ability to intrigue us by its strangeness" (141). Thompson adds, "it can also help us be aware of how the whole film—not just its narrative—works upon our perception" (141). Traditional film methodologies ignore facets of experiencing film through and with the body. Borrowing, then, from ethnography and phenomenology, I'd like to push the envelope of film reception to pave the way for my reading of Selbe's subjectivity and alterity. It is often assumed in film theory, for example, that the introduction of the film apparatus necessitates the obliteration of subjectivity, that the film "captures" and therefore objectifies and negates the subject. This is of course one way of looking at film, and certainly many ethnographics and documentaries conform to this schema; but perhaps we have missed opportunities for intervention, in formulating such a universalizing concept.

Jean-Louis Baudry proposes that theorists have been so intent on the characteristics of film image that they have not noticed that the apparatus, "in its totality includes the subject":

Almost exclusively, it is the technique and content of film which have retained attention: characteristics of the image, depth of field, offscreen space, shot, single-shot sequence, montage, etc.; the key to the impression of reality has been sought in the structuring of image and movement, in complete ignorance of the fact that the impression of reality is dependent first of all on a subject effect and that it might be necessary to examine the position of the subject facing the image in order to determine the raison d'être for the cinema effect. (312)

*Selbe* provides a case in point when the apparatus indeed positions the subject somewhere, as Henri Bergson puts it "halfway between the 'thing' and the representation" (9). Moving through the body, *Selbe* problematizes existing film theoretical models because experiencing the film moves us into a negotiation across our own haptic zones, our own experience of the body and Selbe's experience of Selfhood. As Paul Ricoeur puts it:

> The metacategory of one's own body overlaps with the passivity belonging to the category of other people; the passivity of the suffering self becomes indistinguishable from the passivity of being the victim of the other (than) self. . . . In a sharp-edged dialectic between praxis and pathos, one's own body becomes the emblematic title of a vast inquiry which, beyond the simple mineness of one's own body, denotes the entire sphere of *intimate* passivity, and hence of otherness, for which it forms the center of gravity. (Ricoeur 51)

Traditionally, the center of gravity has been located in the critic's ontological space, discounting any *performative* rupture across the filmic apparatus: performance of fluid identity negotiation. What is at stake here, then, is the whole notion of perception. Perhaps this is what Christian Metz was hinting at when he wrote "*The fact that must be understood is that films are understood*" (59). Understanding would necessitate facilitating perception of the body.

Selbe illustrates what Jennifer Barker terms "bodily irruptions" (57); when Western objectifying critical film discourse is "challenged by the presence of the physical body, which threatens non-compliance with, even subversion of, the film's organized system of meaning-production" (58). Or, as Michael Taussig suggests: "Might not the mimetic faculty and the sensuous knowledge it embodies be precisely this hard-to-imagine state wherein *the senses therefore become directly in their practise theoreticians?*" (98). Taussig, rereading Walter Benjamin's famous and oft-quoted work on subject-object relations in spectatorship, goes as far as suggesting that the camera can "create a new sensorium involving a new subject-object relation and therefore a new person" (24).

Before I consider this notion further, I want to challenge and rethink Walter Benjamin's thoughts on the ritual nature of artwork—in this case film—at the service of the aura as it is embedded in the fabric of tradition. I think the notion of the aura is particularly applicable to a cross-cultural reading of this Senegalese film because we must keep in mind, as Benjamin writes, that "to pry an object from its shell, to destroy its aura, is the mark of a perception whose 'sense of the universal equality of things' has increased to such a degree that it extracts it even from a unique object by means of reproduction" (225). For Benjamin, and many others, art works in the service of ritual and artwork can and should "never entirely [be] separated from its ritual function" (226).

Critically privileging the *ritual* nature of film breathes a whole realm of meaning into cross-cultural film studies. In the case of *Selbe*, it reminds us of the ritual nature of Selbe's performative acts, whether they be cooking, caring for her children, collecting mussels to sell in order to provide for her family, throwing pottery, interacting with her children, or telling her story. The ritual nature of film, in this case, is deeply significant. Far from destroying the original, or decaying the aura of subjectivity of Selbe herself, Safi Faye's film can be seen as, in Walter Benjamin's phrase, "meeting the beholder halfway" (222) between cultures, and perhaps across and between subjectivities.

Despite my optimistic rereading of Walter Benjamin here, despite my desire to read cross-culturally, I am again reminded of the problem of filmic (re)production. Are we only looking at a copy, a simulacrum, an aura of Selbe's body, Selbe's culture, Selbe's subjectivity? Can we only go halfway because of the decay of the aura, or, more precisely, because of the nature of film itself, as a reproducer of culture and ritual? The distance is palpable, and it is worth quoting Benjamin on this distance as it is present in the aura:

> The definition of the aura as a "unique phenomenon of a distance however close it may be" represents nothing but the formulation of the cult value of the work of art in categories of space and time perception. Distance is the opposite of closeness. The essentially distant object is the unapproachable one. Unapproachability is indeed a major quality of the cult image. True to its nature, it remains "distant, however close it may be." The closeness which one may gain from its subject matter does not impair the distance which it retains in its appearance. (245)

I'm distinctly aware of the problematic of the aura as it presents itself in cross-cultural readings of African women's films. For example, in writing on *Selbe*, N. Frank Ukadike credits Faye for conveying "female subjectivity" (114); yet he states that the film "depicts the men as village parasites—totally indifferent to familial bonds" (113). While I thoroughly agree with Ukadike's point on the depiction of female subjectivity, I can't make the jump to see *Selbe* as a misandrist text. While it is quite apparent (as Ukadike notes) that the men in *Selbe* do not help women in the daily chores, Safi Faye does indicate that these same men are undergoing terrific hardships of their own—lack of employment or long days in the field (in some cases)—and also terrific apathy and depression. In short, there are many reasons why they don't help the women, reasons that are culturally defined. There is of course the matter of traditional gender divisions in Serer culture, and no doubt these would be far more easily read by an African, particularly Serer, audience.

In a case like this, I submit that it is not so much that reproduction of images is decaying the aura of the subject, but critical intervention that is prying an object from its shell, ignoring African tradition. I run this same risk of course, but I hope to limit the nature of my cross-cultural reading by foregrounding Selbe herself as subject. This seems in keeping with Safi Faye's project, if we take into account the fact that it is Selbe who maintains a constant screen presence, as self, as speaker (acting and performing ritual functions, inhabiting her body in both the scopic and haptic zones of uncontainable subjectivity).

Safi Faye's statements in an interview with Angela Martin indicate her status as an observer-participant; a storyteller who presents "documents," and an artist who believes less in the categories of "fiction, documentary and ethnology" (18) than she does in the importance of maintaining and recording traditional African culture and the presentation of the individual subject:

> What I try to film is things which relate to our civilisation—a civilisation and a social organisation that one can differentiate from others. In a word: a typically African culture. And it's good that the inhabitants of a district are enabled to speak. OK, they're the problems, the sequences of daily life, but for me that's a very important choice. Because I don't know if my children will have the opportunity to see what I've seen, or what I try to know. It's for this reason that I make films about reality. A reality that has a tendency to disappear. Why? Because the old people, the carriers of history, of Africa, are disappearing. . . . We become culturally assimilated and we only know through writing and through films what our past and

our society were. And I try to make films not in the usual sense, but documents. . . . I give people a voice; they are enabled to speak about their own problems, to show their own reality, and I take a position within that. I situate myself on one side or another; my voice criticises what is open to criticism or I provide some small explanation, but that's all. And I'm paving the way for the possibility of future self-expression because it is only they who can appropriately speak about their problems. (18)

Giving people a voice can be distinctly problematic in ethnography, for as Bill Nichols notes,

the anthropologist/filmmaker usually disappears behind the optical vantage point when camera and filmmaker preside—a behind-the-scenes perspectival equivalent of the film frame's vanishing point. This disappearance, once valorized as part and parcel of observational respect for one's subjects but subsequently criticized as a masquerade of self-effacement that also effaces the limitations of one's own physicality in favor of omniscience and omnipotence, transforms first-hand, personal experience into third-person disembodied knowledge. (1994, 64)

Safi Faye's films enjoy a reputation for avoiding the traps of traditional ethnography because of her presence, sometimes on camera; but mostly off camera in the use of her onscreen presence as interviewer and observer-participant. Though Selbe herself does most of the talking, we can hear Faye's presence in the form of questions and comments.

As N. Frank Ukadike points out, in the American print there is an annoying British female voiceover that threatens to disembody Selbe's knowledge and subjectivity. This voice-over serves as a reminder of Colonialist film practice that does violence to the Colonialized Other. Not only does it almost completely destroy the filmmaker's intentions, but it keenly demonstrates how disembodied knowledge destroys the authority of others. The delivery of the British woman's voice-over is terribly downbeat and completely at odds with Selbe's own temperament of strength and determination. The voice-over is a fine example of the disembodied voice described by Bill Nichols, the voice that denies the subject a voice; a subjectivity. Here is a case that clearly supports Aihwa Ong's assertion that "for feminists looking overseas, the non-feminist Other is not so much patriarchy as the non-Western woman," and it is when Western feminists look cross-culturally, that they often seek to "establish their authority on the backs of non-Western women" (372).

The British female voice-over judges and objectifies Selbe to the point of tragedy (in the guise of feminism). Far from appearing as a speaking subject, Selbe is reduced to a Colonialized Other and her life is read through a prism of Western feminism. This is a very important point, because in the original version, Selbe is not an objectified presence. Mark Reid elaborates here on Faye's construction of an oppositional gaze:

> Faye does not agree with the closed status of the male gaze but views the male gaze as a matter of who is behind, who is in front of, and who belongs to the audience that participates in this relationship. In *The Passerby*, a 10–minute narrative film, she disrupts the male gaze upon female body parts by giving the female object a transitive quality and, thereby, both reversing the source of the gaze and providing an "other" meaning. A series of shot-reverse shots and point-of-view shots decenters the authority of the male point of view, as well as its discourse, and exposes the polyvalent quality of the male gaze. Thus, as early as 1972, Faye was constructing a Black womanist gaze to resist dominant viewing relationships. (1995, 65)

This Black womanist gaze is certainly a form of that "oppositional gaze" as defined by bell hooks (1992). Faye doubly emphasizes the oppositionality of Selbe's gaze because Selbe herself speaks directly to the camera as she stares at us. In this way, there are multiple oppositional gazes here. I suggest that his multiplicity of oppositionality serves to break down the distance of the aura, where distance is automatically presumed between spectator and spectacle. Susan Buck-Morss suggests, incidentally, that it is when "the gaze is returned" (194) that we can break down the aura. But the gaze is only one of the senses that moves the body of Selbe across the spectacle of filmic apparatus and suggests a new shared sense of haptic or embodied subjectivity. As Trinh T. Minh-ha notes, "we write, we think and feel—with our entire bodies" (1989, 36), and "thought is as much a product of the eye, the finger, or the foot as it is of the brain" (1989, 39). Safi Faye's camera moves with the body of Selbe. We are as much gazing at her feet, her working arms, her gathering shoulders, her various facial expressions as we are experiencing her spiritual and psychological resilience. Every gesture is indicative of the zones of the haptic and scopic, the skin, the experience of alterity. Turning to gestures, I recall Gilles Deleuze's words on female *gest*, or gesture, and its importance in filmic representations of women:

> The states of the body secrete the slow ceremony which joins together the corresponding attitudes, and develop a female gest which overcomes the history of men and the crisis of the world. (196)

The female gest is everpresent in *Selbe*, in mannerisms, movement, bodily function, and form. Selbe migrates across specularity and suggests autoethnological responses by somatic reflexivity. Selbe's gestures may be read in anthropological terms as "signs of memory" and "signs of resemblance" (MacDougall 262), wherein "a day's work or a short trip can now speak of a life's journey" (MacDougall 262). Feminist cultural anthropologist C. Nadia Seremetakis suggests that memory senses move not only through the body, but through objects and spaces. In the case of Selbe, the self is grounded in objects such as pottery, the village, the female space, and carried by *colportage*.

> Colportage has nothing to do with completed appearances and geometric closures; rather, in ornamenting the everyday with the sensibility of the different it cuts up the edifice of the routine and prosaic, it forms fragments and animates broken up pieces of multiple realities in transit. This is the migration of sensory forms via material artifacts, and the memory they leave behind. The traffic of exotic matter here is both literal and symbolic, actual and remembered; the transport (*metaphora*) of artifacts and narratives from one historical or cultural site to another is their metaphorization. Therefore colportage and its engagement with what can be shifted and altered is neither nostalgic nor realist. (220)

Viewed in this light, subjectivity can be perceived as a floating chain of sensory signifiers of experiential memory; here the memory of Selbe cleaning clay in water, throwing pots, moving through the village, supporting Henri Bergson's claims that subjectivity may be perceived as "a contraction of the real . . . which exists in theory rather than in a fact" (34). This is the body and subjectivity of women's living space, not unlike that seen in Trinh T. Minh-ha's films. Like Safi Faye, Trinh T. Minh-ha focuses on "the relationship between women and living spaces (or women and architecture) as the very site of difference on which both the Universal and the Particular (historical, cultural, political) are at play" (Minh-ha, 1992, 185). The representation of women's space in *Selbe* is thus both fluid and nomadic, as is the representation of subjectivity and alterity, but there is a profound resonance of the body and presence of Selbe herself, like an aura, that cannot be denied.

## LOST IN THE JUNGLE

But in the Colonial narratives of the 1950s, especially, Africa has become "the place where alienated American men go, a last frontier on a shrunken planet. Metaphorically, 'Africa' is the name of a drawer where the corporation man, secretly bored with family values, puts his secret (antifamily) fantasies" (Cameron, 138). Yet this metaphoric escape is achieved only at the price of endless wandering, a perpetual existence lived as slaves to narrative, and the bondage of film form. Useless quests often form the basis of many of these doomed escape narratives. In Samuel Newfield's *The Lost Continent* (1951), Cesar Romero, Whit Bissell, John Hoyt, Hugh Beaumont, and Sid Melton are dispatched at the height of Cold War hysteria to retrieve a lost rocket that has crashed deep in uncharted jungle territory. Much is made of the arduousness of the men's sisyphian quest, as they climb a seemingly endless series of mountains, battle stop-motion dinosaurs, barely escape the inevitable volcano, which conveniently explodes in the film's last reel, all in the service of conforming to the narrative requirements enforced by heterotopic fifties' culture. Cesar Romero, the carefree bachelor, leaves his date Hillary Brooke with little reluctance; in the jungle, he knows he will meet (once again) Acquanetta. Although the film is in black and white, when the explorers finally break through into the jungle's interior, the entire film suddenly switches to lush green tints, suggesting that the primordial rain forest has subsumed not only the jungle itself, but also the bodies of the men who now inhabit it.

In Richard Cunha's *She Demons* (1958), three men and a woman (Irish McCalla, who also starred as *Sheena, Queen of the Jungle* in the eponymous 1950s' television series), are shipwrecked on an uncharted jungle isle, where a mad Nazi scientist is determined to keep his wife eternally young by injecting her with a serum derived from the bodily fluids of young women. The women, however, lose all conventional aspects of beauty as a

FIGURE 26. "From beauty to beast": the transgressive hypostasis of *She Demons*. Courtesy Jerry Ohlinger Archives.

result of this process: "from beauty to beast!" the ads proclaimed. Kept in a wooden-staked holding pen, the disfigured women revolt in the last minutes of the film, ending the Nazi scientist's reign of cruelty.

In Jerry Gross's *Girl on a Chain Gang* (1966), a young woman in slave irons is menaced by a hulking brute clad in a leather vest holding a whip, but both, within the confines of the film, are equally enslaved by the grinding, inexorable certitude of the film's threadbare narrative, a series of predictable formulaic situations that entrap victim and victimizer equally within the locus of the filmic text. Debra Paget, in chains in Roger Corman's *The Haunted Palace* (1963): is she not equally a victim of the requirements of the genre film, as she is to Vincent Price's prefabricated dungeon? In Mario Bava's *Blood and Black Lace*, Cameron Mitchell is condemned to play the role of a masked sadist obsessed with possessing beauty through the agency of homicidal frenzy—specifically, his victims are high fashion models of the period, plucked from the international designer runways of Italy, France, and Germany. But as Mitchell, clad in a trench coat and a White mask, which covers his entire face, "escapes" with yet another victim, one cannot help but feel that all the participants in this film are equally trapped, equally entombed, by the circuitous, never-ending, constantly repeating living death of the commercial cinema's taxonomical domain.

Bela Lugosi, condemned to repeat endlessly the roles that destroyed his career, consigning his future as a theatrical Shakespearean actor in his native Hungary to evanescent oblivion, goes through the wearisome stations of the curse in Gordon Douglas's *Zombies on Broadway* (1945), a veritable catalogue of heterosexual S/M fetishes. The medical gaze is here cross-indexed with the narrative/generic bondage of Hollywood's typecasting regime, as Lugosi, a "Zombie expert," holds a young woman hostage, preparing her for a twilight existence as a cinematic zombie—a zone of semiconsciousness which, it might well be argued, already engulfs them both. In Albert Rogell's *You May Be Next* (1936), Douglass Dumbrille and his confederates display for the audience the figures of both men and women bound and gagged by the requirements of narrative exigency; as the title warns us, this haptic spectacle of bondage and confinement may soon include us, as well.

In George Archainbaud's *The Lost Squadron* (1932), out of work World War I fighter pilots Richard Dix and Joel McCrea are forced to accept an assignment working for mentally unbalanced Hollywood director Arthur von Furst (Erich von Stroheim), who is so jaded by the certainties of conventional narrative filmmaking that he stages a series of grisly plane crashes to increase audience interest in his film. As the "real-life" death toll mounts, von Furst tells his stunt pilots and cameramen before each take, "and remember, in case of a crash, keep grinding!" This is an apt metaphor, not only for the ceaseless flow of film through the camera necessitated by the persistence-of-vision illusion that informs the illusion of motion pictures, but also for the unrelenting demands of narrative exhaustion and replenishment, in which those who are captive remain so only to escape, and those who die must inevitably be restored to life with each new projection of the film. In Terence Young's *Zarak* (1957), Victor Mature stars as the leader of a group of outlaw tribesmen in British Colonial India. Much of the film's action centers on a series of ritualistic floggings, humiliations, and the undeniably homoerotic connection forged between outlaw Chieftain Mature and British Colonial officer Michael Wilding, as the two men become locked in an embrace of power and desire, made all the more surreal by the bizarre transgressive reinscription of Victor Mature in a racially "Othered" role.

In Walter Grauman's *The Disembodied* (1957), with Allison Hayes and Paul Burke, the body of the White intruder is held captive by those whom Hayes and Burke seek to exploit, and the power of indigenous religion is seen to be superior to the agency of Christian celebration. Mass crucifixions and ritual impalements similarly dominate the figurative landscape of the supposedly Biblical epic released in the United States in 1960 as, *The Sword and the Cross*, in which floggings, burnings at the stake, and other tortures of the body are literally the only thematic material the film contains. The film is, in fact, an Italian/Spanish 1957 production, originally titled *Le schiave di Cartagine*, directed by Guido Brignone, in which dubbing and the language of "postsychronese" are used to substantially alter the original film's intent, and highlight the various corporeal mutilations which have, through translation, become the focus of the film's action-as-narrative intent. In *Theodora, Slave Empress* (1954), directed by the prolific genre craftsperson Riccardo Freda (aka Robert Hampton), the film's protagonist, played by Gianna Maria Canale (who also starred in *Le schiavedi Cartagina*) is now the captive of a group of soldiers who pin her to the floor with spears, an image of figurative impalement and phallic penetration which became one of the generic requirements of the Italian historical epic film in the fifties and sixties.

In this, the figuration of the "heroic" Imperial male in these films is every bit as defined and intransitory as the roles women were consigned

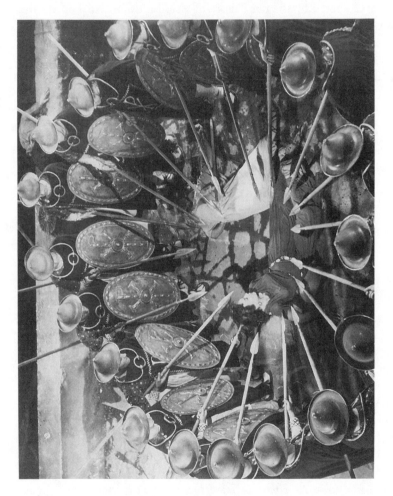

FIGURE 27. At spear's point; the female body as zone of fetishistic dis/ease in *Theodora, Slave Empress*. Courtesy Jerry Ohlinger Archives.

to play. Reg Park or Steve Reeves as Hercules (in *Hercules Conquers Atlantis* and *Hercules*, respectively) are bodies held captive by their bulging pectoral muscles, their scars of battle, their "beefcake" outfits that invite the male and/or female fetishistic gaze, even as they labor in the service of women who are equally constructed and traditionally gender defined. While most pronounced in these films, in which the physique of the performers literally transcends any requirements for conventional acting, in the Western, too, that most prolific of American genres, codes of masculinity and feminine behavior are rigidly defined. Spencer Gordon Bennet's *Calling Wild Bill Elliott* (1943) demonstrates that the most important skill that can be handed down from man to boy is the use of a gun to mark one's territory; in Ray Nazarro's *Blazing Across the Pecos* (1948), it is the rule of the gun, and the Black raiment of the malefactors within the film's narrative, which is the defining characteristic of the formulaic narrative.

In Christy Cabanne's *The Mummy's Hand* (1940), Tom Tyler as the Mummy is so entombed within the bandages that create his fetishistic bondage costume that he can literally be intercut with scenes from Boris Karloff in the same role from the 1932 original without detection; his bondage within the production of the film (as a walking simulacrum of a cine-memetic original) is mirrored by his position within the film's narrative, that of perpetual slave to the designs of high priest George Zucco, who commands the Mummy's eternal allegiance. Just as Dracula in Terence Fisher's *Dracula, Prince of Darkness* (1966) is attended by hypnotized slave Thorley Walters in the pursuit of "trophy-wife" Suzan Farman, the concept of men ruled by the commands of other men mimes the dominator/submissive labor dynamic of the corporate work environment, in which the dynamism of social agency is created almost solely through an inequality of power. This economy of power through control finds one of its most effectively disruptive burlesques in the two-reel shorts of The Three Stooges, in which Moe, Larry, and Curly are forever in search of a job, a wife, any increase in status that might ameliorate the pathetic circumstances of their marginal social existences. Yet in the creation of their comic personae, the Stooges forced themselves into a series of rigidly defined physical stereotypes. Moe's bowl haircut, Curly's perpetually shaved head, Larry's frizzy tufts of parted hair consign them to the margins of cinematic masculinity, as antimasculine, desexed males within an aggressively heterotopic, fetishized cinematic universe. Originally dismissed by contemporary critics as obvious and inane, The Three Stooges' shorts at their best are actually marvels of cultural disruption, as in the scene in which Curly inverts the typical vaudeville practice (still sadly prevalent even in the early 1930s) of Whites appearing in Blackface, by appearing in "Whiteface" much to the surprise of an African American security guard who confronts them.

## THE LIMITS OF EXPERIENCE

In all these films, what is sought is a "limit experience," not in the Foucaultian sense by any means, but rather in the most reductive sense of that phrase: an experience with strictly defined rules, regulations, and expectations. The suture of editorial syntax in these films thus functions as a series of delimiting markers to thoroughly inscribe, above all else, the *boundaries* of this shared cinematic space, the limits of the protagonist's transgression upon the spectator. When one speaks of "capturing" images, one is doing precisely that, entombing a series of artificially frozen visual hieroglyphs with which to adorn the sarcophagus of our shared cinematic memory, to be replayed at 3 A.M. on cable television, or in the endless corridors of human memory.

When the director shouts "That's a wrap!" at the end of the film, s/he directly acknowledges that the images being sought during production have indeed been wrapped up, preserved, captured for all time, captured for commercial resale as a commodified slave spectacle for the movie-going public. Packaged, branded, ritualistically wounded, and displayed for public consumption, the filmic star becomes a totemic enterprise across which is reinscribed the generic rules of classical narrative structure, or "closure" as the artificial suture of spectatorial dreams. Borrowing an ethnographic gaze, Larry Clark's *Kids* (1995) depicts an amoral, pansexual universe in which the threat of AIDS is omnipresent, and the protagonists lie, cheat, steal, and then drink and drug themselves into unconsciousness, only to awaken the next morning to repeat the cycle again. Only the spectre of disease haunts this barren/amoral landscape, in which Clark's characters seek above all else the embrace of death and personal oblivion. What is tomorrow? It is a zone of now-existence, a location of fabulation and impossibility? For the female and male protagonists of *Kids*, life exists solely in the eternal present. As Berkeley Kaite notes of this political gift-exchange of "loss, and surrender . . . between the masculine and the feminine" as articulated in the films we have just touched upon:

Because identification involves visual projection, loss, and surrender, and in this case the visual object oscillates between the feminine and the masculine, this represents more than the (repressed) pleasurable wish for a reunion with the original plenitude. That would be the death of the subject (Bataille: "Human beings are only united with each other through rents or wounds"). The pleasurable spectacle is the body which denies difference and yet resurrects it by proxy, through the surplus of (feminine, fetish) signifiers, to create the body textual. Does the fetish disavow difference? In "TV," as with all porn, it bestows virility on the body, making it a body, though still in its feminine writing, poised to penetrate and invade. Desire is not opposed to its correlative threat but may itself be threatening, involving as it does subjection and death ("la petite mort"), the consumptive expenditure of a small death. (134)

But such a politics of representation runs directly counter to the required tyranny of narrative causation, as defined by Maltby, in his discussion of the requirements of traditional Hollywood narrative:

The "sophisticated" viewing of a movie, on the other hand, can be an act of fatalistic, doomed resistance to the inevitability of its moralistic ending. In the early days of the Production Code, reformers often, if unfairly, castigated the industry for having "invented the perfect formula—five reels of transgression followed by one reel of retribution." But as the implementation of the Code developed, it insisted on an ever more coherent narrative, the very interrelatedness of which provided a defence against accusations of promoting immorality. Audiences "viewing against the grain" found themselves also viewing against the "stair-step" construction of narrative causation. (455)

And yet, with the increasing economic outlay inherent in the production of such heavily commodified spectacles as James Cameron's *Titanic* (1997), in which the narrative outcome of the film is literally known even before the first frame of the film is projected, both the public and producers seem to increasingly demand this specific narrative precertitude. In such a relationship between a financially "bound" producer and a predetermined, "prenarrated" audience, we can observe the power dynamic Lynn Chancer so accurately defines as an extension between the relationship of sadist/masochist into the realm of audience/purveyor of cinematic spectacle:

Yet, what is the underlying meaning of the sadist's desire and need to bind the masochist in the first place, the sadist's need to belittle the other in order to feel superior? For there can be no doubt . . . that the sadist requires a masochist to bind. That the sadist's power is possible only relative to the masochist's lack of it implies the former's extreme need and dependence upon the latter. (1992, 48)

This is the inherent domain of the visual in contemporary cinema; we, the willing captives/spectators, are the coproducers of the spectacle which so desperately seeks to enthrall us, and which so transparently depends upon our existence, acquiescence, and patronage for survival. For the cultural work of the formulaic cinematic experience is to recreate, and thus reenvision, the bonds and boundaries of our daily existence. We must be chained so that we can be free; bound so that we may be released. As John G. Cawelti notes:

formula stories affirm existing interests and attitudes by presenting an imaginary world that is aligned with those interests and attitudes . . . formulas resolve tensions and ambiguities resulting from the conflicting interests of different groups within the culture or from ambiguous attitudes towards particular values . . . formulas enable the audience to explore in fantasy the boundary between the permitted and the forbidden and to experience in a carefully controlled way the possibility of stepping across this boundary. This seems to be preeminently the function of villains in formulaic structures; to express, explore, and finally reject [although I would argue this last contention] those actions which are forbidden, but which because of certain other cultural patterns, are strongly tempting . . . we find a number of formulaic structures in which the villain embodies explicitly or implicitly the threat of racial mixture . . . formulas assist in the process of assimilating changes in values to traditional imaginative constructs. (35–36)

Genre films thus offer reassurance, and at the same time the strangely comforting spectacle of rupture. The expression of the "forbidden" (issues of Queer discourse, alterity, racial and social "Othering," and the like) are thus part of the dominant structure these films ultimately seek to uphold. We envy the villain (perhaps more than Cawelti suggests) because often it is the villain's desire to destroy the existing order which is most attractive to us, and simultaneously, the most personally liberating use of our own bodily experience. The Jungle Queen, that most transgressively unrealistic reinscriptive and inherently racist concept from the 1950s, and persisting even into the 1980s with such films as John Guillermin's 1984 remake of *Sheena, Queen of the Jungle*, is in one sense, at least, a figure of liberation and sexual power, as is Lucy Lawless in the teleseries *Xena, Warrior Princess*—a fantasy locus of postfeminist reconfiguration and desire.

Much in the same way that Barbara Cartland's endless series of romance novels invite us to recreate and reinvent the period of heterotopic White courtship into an endlessly halcyon rupture of perpetual precoital anticipation, or Dean Koontz's numerous novels involving serial killer protagonists permit us to vicariously and momentarily identify with the monstrous Other within us, so the films discussed in this volume are paradoxically works of polymorphous and perverse social, sexual, and racial taxonomy, and simultaneously visions of the self as Other that allow us to become more than spectators, but rather willing coproducers of the images that unspool upon the screen before us. We are captive bodies, in one sense: captive in the theater, captive within the social, racial, and sexual roles assigned to us by the dominant order, captive to generic standards and requirements of physical perfection either originating or inculcated by classical Hollywood cinema. Yet at the same time, through exploring these transgressive alterities, and projecting ourselves through the framework of the narrative onto the screen, we can achieve a paradoxical freedom through bondage that allows us to become "freed captives," aware of our enslavement while liberated by it. The lure of the forbidden is nascent, perpetual, and continually enticing. In embracing the challenge encapsulated in this reverse formulation of societal expectations, we can most fully apprehend the circumstances and opportunities of our own existence.

# WORKS CITED
# AND CONSULTED

——————————————— ∞∞ ———————————————

Abel, Elizabeth. "Black Writing, White Reading: Race and the Politics of Feminist Interpretation," *Critical Inquiry* 19 (Spring): 470–98.

Abelove, Henry, and Michele Barale. *The Lesbian and Gay Studies Reader.* New York: Routledge, 1993.

Alliez, Éric. *Capital Times: Tales from the Conquest of Time.* Georges Van Den Abbeele, trans. Minneapolis: University of Minnesota Press, 1996.

Allison, Dorothy. *Bastard Out of Carolina.* New York: Dutton, 1992.

Andrade-Watkins, Claire. "A Mirage in the Desert? African Women Directors at FESPACO," *Cinemas of the Black Diaspora.* Michael T. Martin, ed. Detroit: Wayne State University Press, 1995: 145–52.

Appiah, K. Anthony, and Amy Gutmann. *Color Conscious: The Political Morality of Race.* Princeton, N.J.: Princeton University Press, 1996.

Apter, Andrew. "Que Faire: Reconsidering Inventions of Africa," *Critical Inquiry* 19 (Autumn): 87–102.

Apter, Emily. *Feminizing the Fetish: Psychoanalysis and Narrative Obsession in Turn-of-the-Century France.* Ithaca, N.Y.: Cornell University Press, 1991.

Aronowitz, Stanley. *Dead Artists, Live Theories and Other Cultural Problems.* New York: Routledge, 1994.

Ashcroft, Bill, Gareth Griffiths, and Helen Tiffin, eds. *The Postcolonial Studies Reader.* London: Routledge, 1995.

Bad Object Choices, eds. *How Do I Look? Queer Film and Video.* Seattle, Wash.: Bay Press, 1991.

211

Bailey, F. G. *The Prevalence of Deceit.* Ithaca, N.Y.: Cornell University Press, 1991.

Baker, Peter. *Deconstruction and the Ethical Turn.* Gainesville: University Press of Florida, 1995.

Bakhtin, Mikhail M. *The Dialogic Imagination.* Michael Holquist, ed. Caryl Emerson and Michael Holquist, trans. Austin: University of Texas Press, 1981.

———. *Toward a Philosophy of the Act.* Michael Holquist and Vadim Liapunov, eds. Vadim Liapunov, trans. Austin: University of Texas Press, 1993.

Balibar, Etienne, and Immanuel Wallerstein. *Race, Nation and Class: Ambiguous Identities.* London: Verso, 1994.

Banta, Martha. *Taylored Lives: Narrative Productions in the Age of Taylor, Veblen, and Ford.* Chicago: University of Chicago Press, 1993.

Bar On, Bat-Ami, ed. *Modern Engendering: Critical Feminist Readings in Modern Western Theory.* Albany: State University of New York Press, 1994.

Barker, Jennifer. "Bodily Irruptions: The Corporeal Assault on Ethnographic Narration," *Cinema Journal* 34.3 (Spring, 1995): 57–77.

Barnes, Elizabeth L. "Mirroring the Mother Text: Histories of Seduction in the American Domestic Novel," in *Anxious Power.* Carol J. Singley and Susan Sweeney, eds., Albany: State University of New York Press, 1993: 157–72.

Baudrillard, Jean. *Forget Foucault.* Nicole Dufresne, trans. New York: Semiotext(e), 1987.

———. *The Illusion of the End.* Chris Turner, trans. Stanford: Stanford University Press, 1994.

———. *Seductions.* Brian Singer, trans. New York: St. Martins Press, 1990.

———. *Simulacra and Simulation.* Sheila Faria Glaser, trans. Ann Arbor: University of Michigan Press, 1994.

Baudrillard, Jean, and Sylvère Lotringer. "Forget Baudrillard," *Forget Foucault.* Phil Beitchman, Lee Hildreth, and Mark Polizzotti, trans. New York: Semiotext(e) 1987: 65–137.

Baudry, Jean-Louis. "The Apparatus: Metapsychological Approaches to the Impression of Reality in the Cinema," *Narrative, Apparatus, Ideology.* Philip Rosen, ed. New York: Columbia University Press, 1986: 299–318.

Bauer, Dale M., and Susan Janet McKinstry. *Feminism, Bakhtin, and the Dialogic.* Albany: State University of New York Press, 1991.

Beck, Henry Cabot. "Bad Girls," *Interview* (April, 1994): 62.

Benjamin, Jessica. "The Shadow of the Other (Subject): Intersubjectivity and Feminist Theory," *Constellations* 1.2: 31–51.

Benjamin, Walter. "A Short History of Photography," Stanley Mitchell, trans. *Screen* 13.1 (Spring, 1972): 5–26.

———. *Illuminations*. Hannah Arendt, ed. Harry Zohn, trans. New York: Schocken, 1968.

———. *Moscow Diary*. Gary Smith, ed. Richard Sieburth, trans. Cambridge, Mass.: Harvard University Press, 1986.

Bergson, Henri. *Matter and Memory*. Nancy Margaret Paul and W. Scott Palmer, trans. New York: Zone Books, 1988.

Bernardi, Daniel. "The Voice of Whiteness: D. W. Griffith's Biograph Films," *The Birth of Whiteness: Race and the Emergence of U.S. Cinema*. Daniel Bernardi, ed. New Brunswick, N.J.: Rutgers University Press, 1996: 103–28.

Bhabha, Homi K. *The Location of Culture*. London: Routledge, 1994.

Birdwhistle, Ray. *Kinesics and Context: Essays on Body Motion Communication*. Philadelphia: University of Pennsylvania Press, 1970.

Bizzell, Patricia, and Bruce Herzberg, eds. *The Rhetorical Tradition: Readings from Classical Times to the Present*. Boston: Bedford, 1990.

Blair, Hugh. *Lectures on Rhetoric and Belles Lettres*. Harold F. Harding, ed. Carbondale: Southern Illinois University Press, 1965.

Blanchot, Maurice. *The Writing of the Disaster*. Ann Smock, trans. New Bison Edition, Lincoln: University of Nebraska Press, 1995.

Blassingame, John W. *The Slave Community: Plantation Life in the Antebellum South*. New York: Oxford University Press, 1972.

Blau, Herbert. *The Eye of Prey: Subversions of the Postmodern*. Bloomington: Indiana University Press, 1987.

Bobo, Jacqueline. *Black Women as Cultural Readers*. New York: Columbia University Press, 1995.

Bogle, Donald. *Dorothy Dandridge: A Biography*. New York: Armistad, 1996.

———. *Toms, Coons, Mulattoes, Mammies, and Bucks: An Interpretive History of Blacks in American Films*. New York: Continuum, 1994.

Bordo, Susan. "Reading the Male Body," *The Male Body: Features, Destinies, Exposures.* Laurence Goldstein, ed. Ann Arbor: University of Michigan Press, 1994: 265–306.

Bordwell, David. "Contemporary Film Studies and the Vicossitudes of Grand Theory," *Post-Theory: Reconstructing Film Studies.* David Bordwell and Noël Carroll, eds. Madison: University of Wisconsin Press, 1996: 3–36.

Bordwell, David, and Noël Carroll, eds. *Post-Theory: Reconstructing Film Studies.* Madison: University of Wisconsin Press, 1996.

Bornstein, Kate. *Gender Outlaw: On Men, Women and the Rest of Us.* New York: Vintage, 1994.

Boundas, Constantin V., ed. *The Deleuze Reader.* New York: Columbia University Press, 1993.

Bowser, Eileen. *The History of American Cinema II: The Transformation of Cinema 1907–1915.* New York: Scribners, 1990.

Bowser, Pearl, and Louise Spence. "Identity and Betrayal: *The Symbol of The Unconquered* and Oscar Micheaux's 'Biographical Legend'," *The Birth of Whiteness: Race and the Emergence of U.S. Cinema.* Daniel Bernardi, ed. New Brunswick, N.J.: Rutgers University Press, 1996: 56–80.

Braun, Marta. *Picturing Time: The Work of Etienne-Jules Marey (1830–1904).* Chicago: University of Chicago Press, 1992.

Bright, Susie. *Susie Bright's Sexual Reality: A Virtual Sex World Reader.* Pittsburgh, Pa.: Cleis Press, 1992.

Brown, Helen Gurley. *Sex and the New Single Girl.* New York: Geis, 1970.

Bruno, Giuliana. *Streetwalking on a Ruined Map: Cultural Theory and the City Films of Elvira Notari.* Princeton, N.J.: Princeton University Press, 1993.

Buck-Morss, Susan. *The Dialectics of Seeing: Walter Benjamin and the Arcades Project.* Cambridge: MIT Press, 1989.

Burgher, Veronica. "Cities Gear for Annual Night Out," *Omaha World Herald* 132.257 (Friday, August 1, 1997): 33–34.

Butler, Judith. *Gender Trouble: Feminism and the Subversion of Identity.* New York: Routledge, 1990a.

———. "Performative Acts and Gender Constitution: An Essay in Phenomenology and Feminist Theory," in *Performing Feminisms: Feminist Critical Theory and Theatre.* Sue-Ellen Case, ed. Baltimore: Johns Hopkins University Press, 1990b: 270–82.

Buzzell, Linda. *How to Make It in Hollywood.* New York: HarperCollins, 1992.

Byg, Barton. *Landscapes of Resistance: The German Films of Danièle Huillet and Jean-Marie Straub.* Berkeley: University of California Press, 1995.

Bynum, Carolyn Walker. *Fragmentation and Redemption: Essays on Gender and the Human Body in Medieval Religion.* New York: Zone, 1991.

Cameron, Kenneth M. *Africa on Film: Beyond Black and White.* New York: Continuum, 1994.

Campbell, Edward D. C. *The Celluloid South: Hollywood and the Southern Myth.* Knoxville: University of Tennessee Press, 1981.

Carby, Hazel. *Reconstructing Womanhood.* New York: Oxford University Press, 1987.

Carrol, Noël. "Prospects for Film Theory: A Personal Assessment," *Post-Theory: Reconstructing Film Studies.* David Bordwell and Noël Carrol, eds. Madison: University of Wisconsin Press, 1996: 37–68.

Cartwright, Lisa. *Screening the Body: Tracing Medicine's Visual Culture.* Minneapolis: University of Minnesota Press, 1995.

Case, Sue-Ellen, Phillip Brett, and Susan Leigh Foster, eds. *Cruising the Performative: Interventions into the Representation of Ethnicity, Nationality and Sexuality.* Bloomington: Indiana University Press, 1995.

Castillo, Ana. *Massacre of the Dreamers: Essays on Xicanisma.* New York: Penguin, 1994.

Cawalti, John G. *Adventure, Mystery, and Romance: Formula Stories as Art and Popular Culture.* Chicago: University of Chicago Press, 1976.

Celebate Sluts, The. Unpublished, unrecorded. New Brunswick, N.J.: 1980–1982.

Chambers, Ross. *Story and Situation: Narrative Seduction and the Power of Fiction.* Minneapolis: University of Minnesota Press, 1984.

Champagne, John. "Stop Reading Films! Film Studies, Close Analysis and Gay Pornography," *Cinema Journal* 36.4 (Summer, 1997): 76–97.

Chancer, Lynn Sharon. "Prostitution, Feminist Theory, and Ambivalence: Notes from the Sociological Underground," *Social Text* 37 (11.4) (Winter, 1993): 143–72.

———. *Sadomasochism in Everyday Life: The Dynamics of Power and Powerlessness.* New Brunswick, N.J.: Rutgers University Press, 1992.

Chatterjee, Margaret. *Our Knowledge of Other Selves.* Bombay: Asia Publishing House, 1963.

Chatterjee, Partha. *Nationalist Thought and the Colonial World: A Derivative Discourse?* London: Zed, 1986.

Chaudhuri, Nupur, and Margaret Strobel, eds. *Western Women and Imperialism: Complicity and Resistance.* Bloomington: Indiana University Press, 1992.

Chow, Rey. *Writing Diaspora: Tactics of Intervention in Contemporary Cultural Studies.* Bloomington: Indiana University Press, 1993.

Cicero, Marcus Tullius. *De inventione.* H. M. Hubbell, trans. Cambridge, Mass.: Harvard University Press, 1949.

Cicero, Marcus Tullius. *Rhetorica ad Herennium.* Harry Caplan, trans. New York: Loeb Classical Library, 1954.

Cixous, Hélène. "The Laugh of the Medusa," *Signs* I, 1976: 875–93.

Cixous, Hélène, and Mireille Calle-Gruber. *Rootprints: Memory and Life Writing.* Eric Prenowitz, trans. London: Routledge, 1997.

Clark, Danae. *Negotiating Hollywood: The Cultural and Politics of Actor's Labor.* Minneapolis: University of Minnesota Press, 1995.

Clover, Carol J. *Men, Women, and Chain Saws: Gender in the Modern Horror Film.* Princeton, N.J.: Princeton University Press, 1992.

Cohan, Steven, and Ina Rae Hark, eds. *Screening the Male: Exploring Masculinities in Hollywood Cinema.* London: Routledge, 1993.

Collins, James. *Spinoza on Nature.* Carbondale: Southern Illinois University Press, 1984.

Cook, David A. *A History of Narrative Film* (2d ed.). New York: W. W. Norton, 1981.

Covino, William A. *The Art of Wondering: A Revisionist Return to the History of Rhetoric.* Portsmouth, N.H.: Boynton/Cook, 1988.

Crossette, Barbara. "What Modern Slavery Is, and Isn't," *The New York Times* (Sunday, July 27, 1997): Section 4: 6.

Dargis, Manohla. "'Thelma and Louise' and the Tradition of the Male Road Movie," in *Women and Film: A Sight and Sound Reader.* Pam Cook and Philip Dodd, eds. Philadelphia: Temple University Press, 1993: 86–92.

Dauphin, Gary. "Taking to Donald Bogle About Dandridge and Desire," *The Village Voice* (June 24, 1997): 84, 88.

Davis, Peter. *In Darkest Hollywood: Exploring the Jungles of Cinema's South Africa.* Athens: Ohio University Press, 1996.

de Certeau, Michel. *The Practice of Everyday Life.* Steven Rendall, trans. Berkeley: University of California Press, 1984.

de Lauretis, Teresa. *The Practice of Love: Lesbian Sexuality and Perverse Desire.* Bloomington: Indiana University Press, 1994.

————. "Through the Looking Glass," in *Narrative, Apparatus, Ideology: A Film Theory Reader,* Philip Rosen, ed. New York: Columbia University Press, 1986: 360–72.

de Man, Paul. *The Resistance to Theory.* Minneapolis: University of Minnesota Press, 1993.

De Marinis, Marco. *The Semiotics of Performance.* Aine O'Healy, trans. Bloomington: Indiana University Press, 1993.

Debord, Guy. *The Society of the Spectacle.* Donald Nicholson-Smith, trans. New York: Zone, 1995.

Deleuze, Gilles. *Cinema 1: The Movement Image.* Hugh Tomlinson and Barbara Habberjam, trans. Minneapolis: University of Minnesota Press, 1986.

————. *Cinema 2: The Time Image.* Hugh Tomlinson and Robert Galeta, trans. Minneapolis: University of Minnesota Press, 1989.

————. *Masochism: An Interpretation of Coldness and Cruelty.* Jean McNeil, trans. New York: Braziller, 1971.

Deleuze, Gilles, and Félix Guattari. *A Thousand Plateaus: Capitalism and Schizophrenia.* Brian Massumi, trans. Minneapolis: University of Minnesota Press, 1996.

Desmond, Jane C. "Performing 'Nature': Shamu at Sea World," *Cruising the Performative: Interventions into the Representation of Ethnicity, Nationality, and Sexuality.* Sue-Ellen Case, Philip Brett, Susan Leigh Foster, eds. Bloomington: Indiana University Press, 1995: 217–36.

Diawara, Manthia, ed. *Black American Cinema: Aesthetics and Spectatorship.* New York: Routledge, 1993.

Dijkstra, Bram. *Evil Sisters: The Threat of Female Sexuality and the Cult of Manhood.* New York: Knopf, 1996.

Dixon, Wheeler Winston. "'Femmes Vivantes' and the Marginalized Feminine 'Other' in the Films of Reginald LeBorg," *Cinefocus* 3, 1995: 34–41.

————. *The Films of Reginald LeBorg: Interviews, Essays, and Filmography.* Metuchen: Scarecrow, 1992.

————. *It Looks at You: The Returned Gaze of Cinema.* Albany: State University of New York Press, 1995.

Doane, Mary Ann. "The Clinical Eye: Medical Discourses in the 'Woman's Film' of the 1940s," in *The Female Body in Western Culture*, Susan Rubin Suleiman, ed. Cambridge, Mass.: Harvard University Press, 1986: 152–74.

———, ed. *Femmes Fatales: Feminism, Film Theory, Psychoanalysis.* New York: Routledge, 1991.

Dollimore, Jonathan. *Sexual Dissidence: Augustine to Wilde, Freud to Foucault.* Oxford: Oxford University Press, 1991.

Doyle, Jennifer, Jonathan Flatley, and Jose Esbeban Muñoz, eds. *Pop Out: Queer Warhol.* Durham, N.C.: Duke University Press, 1996.

Durkheim, Emile. *Readings from Emile Durkheim.* Kenneth Thompson, ed. Margaret A. Thompson, trans. London: Tavistock, 1985.

Dyer, Richard. "Monroe and Sexuality," in *Women and Film*, Janet Todd, ed. New York: Holmes and Meier, 1988a: 69–96.

———. "White," *Screen* 29.4 (Autumn, 1988b): 44–65.

Egan, Jennifer. "The Thin Red Line," *The New York Times Magazine* (July 27, 1997): 21–25, 34, 40, 43, 48.

Eliot, Mark. *Walt Disney: Hollywood's Dark Prince.* New York: Birchlane Press, 1993.

Ellis, Brian. *Truth and Objectivity.* Oxford: Basil Blackwell, 1990.

Erkkila, Betsy, and Jay Grossman, eds. *Breaking Bounds: Whitman and American Cultural Studies.* New York: Oxford University Press, 1996.

Esterberg, Kristin G. *Lesbian and Bisexual Identities: Constructing Communities, Constructing Selves.* Philadelphia: Temple University Press, 1997.

Fanon, Franz. *Black Skin, White Masks: The Experiences of a Black Man in a White World.* Charles Lam Markmann, trans. New York: Grove Press, 1967.

Farley, Wendy. *Eros for the Other: Retaining Truth in a Pluralistic World.* University Park: Penn State University Press, 1996.

Feinberg, Leslie. *Transgender Warriors: Making History from Joan of Arc to RuPaul.* Boston: Beacon Press, 1996.

Ferguson, Moira, ed. *The History of Mary Prince: A West Indian Slave, Related by Herself.* London: Pandora, 1987.

Ferguson, Russell, Martha Gever, Trinh T. Minh-ha, and Cornel West, eds. *Discourses: Conversations on Postmodern Art and Culture.* Cambridge, Mass.: MIT Press, 1990.

Finley, Karen. *Enough Is Enough: Weekly Meditations for Living Dysfunctionally.* New York: Poseidon, 1993.

———. "We Keep Our Victims Ready," *Shock Treatment.* San Francisco: City Lights, 1990: 103–44.

Fish, Stanley. *Professional Correctness: Literary Studies and Political Change.* Oxford: Oxford University Press, 1995.

Fitzpatrick, Tara. "The Figure of Captivity. The Cultural Work of the Puritan Captivity Narrative," *American Literary History* 3.1 (Spring, 1991): 1–26.

Flitterman-Lewis, Sandy. "Psychoanalysis," *New Vocabularies in Film Semiotics: Structuralism, Poststructuralism, and Beyond.* Robert Stam, Robert Burgoyne, and Sandy Flitterman-Lewis, eds. New York: Routledge, 1992: 124.

Forte, Jeanie. "Women's Performance Art: Feminism and Postmodernism," in *Performing Feminisms: Feminist Critical Theory and Theatre.* Sue-Ellen Case, ed. Baltimore, Md.: Johns Hopkins University Press, 1990: 251–69.

Foster, Gwendolyn Audrey. *Women Filmmakers of the African and Asian Diaspora: Decolonizing the Gaze, Locating Subjectivity.* Carbondale: Southern Illinois University Press, 1997.

Foster, Hal. *The Return of the Real: The Avant-Garde at the End of the Century.* Cambridge, Mass.: MIT Press, 1996.

Foucault, Michel. *Discipline and Punish: The Birth of the Prison.* Alan Sheridan, trans. New York: Vintage, 1979.

———. *The History of Sexuality.* Robert Hurley, trans. New York: Pantheon, 1978.

———. *The Order of Things: An Archeology of the Human Sciences.* New York: Vintage, 1973.

Fraleigh, Sondra Horton. *Dance and the Lived Body.* Pittsburgh: University of Pittsburgh Press, 1987.

Fraser, Nancy. "Beyond the Master/Subject Model," *Social Text* 37 (11.4) (Winter, 1993): 173–82.

Fried, Debra. "The Men in *The Women,*" in *Women and Film,* Janet Todd, ed. New York: Homes and Meier, 1988: 43–68.

Friedberg, Anne. *Window Shopping: Cinema and the Postmodern.* Berkeley: University of California Press, 1993.

Frow, John. *Cultural Studies and Cultural Value.* Oxford: Oxford University Press, 1995.

Fuchs, Cynthia J. "Michael Jackson's Penis," *Cruising the Performative: Interventions into the Representation of Ethnicity, Nationality, and Sexuality.* Sue-Ellen Case, Philip Brett, Susan Leigh Foster, eds. Bloomington: Indiana University Press, 1995: 13–33.

Fuss, Diana. *Identification Papers.* New York: Routledge, 1995.

Gaines, Jane. "White Privilege and Looking Relations: Race and Gender in Feminist Film Theory," *Screen* 29.4: 12–27.

Gallop, Jane. *Thinking Through the Body.* New York: Columbia University Press, 1988.

Garey, Juliann, and Bronwen Hruska. "They Shoot *Bad Girls,* Don't they?" *Us* 196 (May, 1994): 74.

Gibson, Pamela Church, and Roma Gibson, eds. *Dirty Looks: Women, Pornography, Power.* London: BFI, 1993.

Gilman, Sander. *Difference and Pathology: Stereotypes of Sexuality, Race and Madness.* Ithaca, N.Y.: Cornell University Press, 1985.

Giroux, Henry A. *Disturbing Pleasures: Learning Popular Culture.* New York: Routledge, 1994.

Goldstein, Laurence, ed. *The Male Body: Features, Destinies, Exposures.* Ann Arbor: University of Michigan Press, 1994.

Gordon, Linda. "On 'Difference,'" *Genders* 10 (Spring, 1991): 91–111.

Graf, Fritz. "Gestures and Conventions: The Gestures of Roman Actors and Orators," in *A Cultural History of Gesture.* Jan Bremmer and Herman Roodenberg, eds. Ithaca, N.Y.: Cornell University Press, 1991: 36–58.

Graff, Gerald. *Beyond the Culture Wars.* New York: Norton, 1992.

Haggard, Sir H. Rider. *Allan Quatermain.* London: Longmans Green, 1887.

———. *King Solomon's Mines.* London: Cassel, 1885.

———. *She.* London: Longmans Green, 1887.

Halberstam, Judith, and Ira Livingston, eds. *Posthuman Bodies.* Bloomington: Indiana University Press, 1995.

Hanna, Judith Lynne. *The Performer—Audience Connection: Emotion to Metaphor in Dance and Society.* Austin: University of Texas Press, 1983.

Hansen, Miriam. "Pleasure, Ambivalence, Identification: Valentino and Female Spectatorship," *Cinema Journal* 25.4 (Summer, 1986): 6–33.

Hanson, Ellis. "The Telephone and Its Queerness," *Cruising the Performative: Interventions into the Representation of Ethnicity, Nationality, and Sexuality.* Sue-Ellen Case, Philip Brett, Susan Leigh Foster, eds. Bloomington: Indiana University Press, 1995: 34–58.

Haraway, Donna J. *Simians, Cyborgs and Women: The Reinvention of Nature.* New York: Routledge, 1991.

Harris, Sharon M. "Early American Slave Narratives and the Reconfiguration of Place," *Journal of the American Studies Association of Texas* 21.3 (October, 1990): 15–23.

Hart, Constance. *The Handbook of Beauty.* New York: Dell, 1955.

Hebdige, Dick. *Subculture: The Meaning of Style.* New York: Methuen, 1979.

Herdt, Gilbert, ed. *Third Sex, Third Gender: Beyond Sexual Dimorphism in Culture and History.* New York: Zone, 1994.

Herrmann, Anne C., and Abigail J. Stewart, eds. *Theorizing Feminism: Parallel Trends in the Humanities and Social Sciences.* Boulder, Colo.: Westview Press, 1994.

Herron, Jerry, Dorothy Huson, Ross Pudaloff, and Robert Strozier, eds. *The Ends of Theory.* Detroit: Wayne State University Press, 1996.

Hewitt, Andrew. *Fascist Modernism: Aesthetics, Politics and the Avant-Garde.* Stanford: Stanford University Press, 1993.

Hollander, Elizabeth. "Subject Matter: Models for Different Media," *Representations* 36 (Fall, 1991): 133–46.

hooks, bell. *Black Looks: Race and Representation.* Boston: South End Press, 1992.

——. *Reel to Real: Race, Sex, and Class at the Movies.* New York: Routledge, 1996.

hooks, bell, and Andrea Juno. "Bell Hooks," *Re/Search* #13, 1991: 78–93.

Hubner, John. *Bottom Feeders: From Free Love to Hard Core, the Rise and Fall of Countercultural Heroes Jim and Artie Mitchell.* New York: Doubleday, 1992.

Hunt, Lynn. "Introduction: Obscenity and the Origins of Modernity, 1500–1800," *The Invention of Pornography.* Lynn Hunt, ed. New York: Zone, 1993: 9–45.

Irigaray, Luce. *I Love to You: Sketch of a Possible Felicity in History.* Alison Martin, trans. New York: Routledge, 1996.

Irvine, Janice M. "Regulated Passions: The Invention of Inhibited Sexual Desire and Sex Addiction," *Social Text* 37 (11.4) (Winter, 1993): 203–26.

Ivy, Marilyn. "Have You Seen Me? Recovering the Inner Child in Late Twentieth-Century America," *Social Text* 37 (11.4) (Winter, 1993): 227–52.

Jablonko, Allison. "New Guinea in Italy: An Analysis of the Making of an Italian Television Series from Research Footage of the maring People of Papua New Guinea," *Anthropological Filmmaking.* Rollwagon, Chur, eds. Harwood, 1988: 169–96.

Jacobs, Harriet Brent (Linda Brent). *Incidents in the Life of a Slave Girl.* San Diego: Harcourt Brace, 1973.

Jarratt, Susan. "Performing Feminism, Histories, Rhetorics," *Rhetoric Society Quarterly* 22.1 (Winter, 1992): 111–32.

Jay, Martin. "Photo-unrealism: The Contribution of the Camera to the Crisis of Ocularcentrism," *Vision and Textuality.* Stephen Melville and Bill Readings, eds. Durham, N.C.: Duke University Press, 1995: 344–60.

Johnston, Georgia. "Exploring Lack and Absence in the Body/Text: Charlotte Perkins Gilman Prewriting Irigaray." *Women's Studies* 21.1 (1992): 75–86.

Jones, John. *Wonders of the Stereoscope.* London: Jonathan Cape, 1976.

Kaite, Berkeley. *Pornography and Difference.* Bloomington: Indiana University Press, 1995.

Kaminsky, Stuart. "*High Noon,*" *International Dictionary of Films and Filmmakers Vol. 1,* Nicholas Thomas, ed. Chicago: St. James Press, 1990: 385–87.

Kaplan, E. Ann. *Looking for the Other: Feminism, Film, and the Imperial Gaze.* New York: Routledge, 1997.

Kaplan, Louise. *Female Perversions: The Temptations of Madame Bovary.* New York: Doubleday, 1991.

Kasson, John F. *Rudeness and Civility: Manners in Nineteenth-Century Urban America.* New York: Hill and Wang, 1990.

Kipnis, Laura. *Bound and Gagged: Pornography and the Politics of Fantasy in America.* New York: Grove Press, 1996.

Kirkham, Pat, and Janet Thumim, eds. *You Tarzan: Masculinity, Movies and Men.* New York: St. Martins Press, 1993.

Kolodny, Annette. "Letting Go Our Grand Obsessions: Notes Toward a New Literary History of the American Frontiers," *American Literature* 64.1 (March, 1992): 1–18.

Kroker, Arthur and Marilouise, eds. *The Last Sex: Feminism and Outlaw Bodies.* New York: St. Martins Press, 1993.

Lahue, Kalton C. *Bound and Gagged: The Story of Silent Serials.* New York: A. S. Barnes, 1968.

Landy, Marcia. *Film, Politics, and Gramsci.* Minneapolis: University of Minnesota Press, 1994.

Lane, Anthony. "Hercules," *The New Yorker* 72.19 (July 14, 1997): 27.

Laqueur, Thomas. *Making Sex: Body and Gender from the Greeks to Freud.* Cambridge, Mass.: Harvard University Press, 1990.

Lee, Jonathan Scott. *Jacques Lacan.* Amherst: University of Massachusetts Press, 1990.

Lefkovitz, Lori Hope, ed. *Textual Bodies: Changing Boundaries of Literary Representation.* Albany: State University of New York Press, 1997.

Leslie, Alan M. "A Theory of Agency," *Causal Cognition: A Multidisciplinary Debate.* Dan Sperber, David Premack, and Ann James Premack, eds. Oxford: Clarendon Press, 1995: 121–49.

Linnaeus, Carl. *Systema naturae per regna tria naturae secumdum classes.* London: Ray Society, 1911 (originally published in 1753).

London, Bette. "Mary Shelley, *Frankenstein* and the Spectacle of Masculinity," *PLMA* 108.2 (March, 1993): 253–67.

Long, Beverly Whitaker. "Performance Criticism and Questions of Value," *Text and Performance Quarterly* 2.2 (April, 1991): 106–15.

López, Ana M. "Are All Latins from Manhattan? Hollywood, Ethnography, and Cultural Colonialism," *Unspeakable Images: Ethnicity and the American Cinema.* Lester D. Friedman, ed. Chicago: University of Chicago Press, 404–24.

Lyotard, Jean-François. "Acinema," *Narrative, Apparatus, Ideology.* Paisley N. Livingston and Jean-François Lyotard, trans. Philip Rosen, ed. New York: Columbia University Press, 1986: 349–59.

———. *The Postmodern Condition: A Report on Knowledge.* Geoff Bennington and Brian Massumi, trans. Minneapolis: University of Minnesota Press, 1991.

Lyotard, Jean-François, and Jean-Loup Thébaud. *Just Gaming.* Wlad Godzich, trans. Minneapolis: University of Minnesota Press, 1994.

Macann, Christopher, ed. *Critical Heidegger.* London: Routledge, 1996.

MacDougall, David. "Films of Memory," *Visualizing Theory: Selected Essays from V.A.R. 1990–1994.* Lucien Taylor, ed. New York: Routledge, 1994: 260–70.

Malraux, André. *The Voices of Silence.* Princeton, N.J.: Princeton University Press, 1978.

Maltby, Richard. "A Brief Romantic Interlude: Dick and Jane Go to 3 1/2 Seconds of the Classical Hollywood Cinema," *Post-Theory: Reconstructing Film Studies.* David Bordwell and Noël Carrol, eds. Madison: University of Wisconsin Press, 1996: 434–59.

Marchetti, Gina. "The Threat of Captivity: Hollywood and the Sexualization of Race Relations in *The Girls of the White Orchid* and *The Bitter Tea of General Yen,*" *Journal of Communication Inquiry* 11.1 (Winter, 1987): 29–42.

Marin, Louis. "The Gesture of Looking in Classical Historical Painting," *History and Anthropology* 1.1 (November, 1984): 175–91.

Martin, Catherine Gimelli. "Orientalism and the Ethnographer: Said, Herodotus, and the Discourse of Alterity," *The Ends of Theory.* Jerry Herron, Dorothy Huson, Ross Pudaloff, and Robert Strozier, eds. Detroit: Wayne State University Press, 1996: 86–103.

Martin, Angela. "Four Filmmakers from West Africa," *Framework* 11, 1979: 16–21.

Mavor, Carol. *Pleasures Taken: Performances of Sexuality and Loss in Victorian Photographs.* Durham, N.C.: Duke University Press, 1995.

Maynard, Richard A. *Africa on Film: Myth and Reality.* Rochelle Park, N.J.: Hayden Book Company, 1974.

Mayne, Judith. *The Woman at the Keyhole: Feminism and Women's Cinema.* Bloomington: Indiana University Press, 1990.

McNay, Lois. *Foucault and Feminism: Power, Gender and the Self.* Cambridge: Polity, 1992.

Melville, Stephen, and Bill Readings, eds. *Vision and Textuality.* Durham, N.C.: Duke University Press, 1995.

Merleau-Ponty, Maurice. *The Visible and the Invisible.* Claude Lefort, ed. Alphonso Lingis, trans. Evanston, Ill.: Northwestern University Press, 1968.

Metz, Christian. *Film Language: A Semiotics of the Cinema.* New York: Oxford University Press, 1974.

————. "Problems of Denotation in the Fiction Film," *Narrative, Apparatus, Ideology.* Philip Rosen, ed. New York: Columbia University Press, 1986: 35–65.

Miller, Judith. "On Arts Day in the Capitol, Lobbyists Fight Cuts," *The New York Times* (Thursday, March 13, 1997): Section B: 2.

Miller, Nancy K. "Representing Others: Gender and the Subjects of Autobiography," *Differences* 6.1 (Spring, 1994): 1–27.

Minh-ha, Trinh T. *Framer Framed.* New York: Routledge, 1992.

————. *Woman, Native, Other: Writing, Postcoloniality and Feminism.* Bloomington: Indiana University Press, 1989.

Minsky, Rosalind. "Introduction: Psychoanalysis and the Unconscious," *Psychoanalysis and Gender.* Rosalind Minsky, ed. London: Routledge, 1996: 3–24.

Mitchell, Sally. *The New Girl: Girls' Culture in England, 1880–1915.* New York: Columbia University Press, 1995.

Morley, David, and Kuan-Hsing Chen, eds. *Stuart Hall: Critical Dialogues in Cultural Studies.* London: Routledge, 1996.

Morrison, Toni. *Playing in the Dark: Whiteness and the Literary Imagination.* Cambridge, Mass.: Harvard University Press, 1992.

Mulvey, Laura. "Visual Pleasure and Narrative Cinema," in *Narrative, Apparatus, Ideology: A Film Theory Reader,* Philip Rosen, ed. New York: Columbia University Press, 1986: 198–209.

Mudimbe, V. Y. *The Invention of Africa: Gnosis, Philosophy and the Order of Knowledge.* Bloomington: Indiana University Press, 1988.

Musser, Charles. *Before the Nickelodeon.* Berkeley: University of California Press, 1991.

Neuman, Shirley, ed. *Autobiography and Questions of Gender.* Portland: International Specialized Book Service, 1991.

Nichols, Bill. "The Ethnographer's Tale," *Visualizing Theory: Selected Essays from V.A.R. 1990–1994.* Lucien Taylor, ed. New York: Routledge, 1994: 60–83.

Obeyesekere, Gananath. *The Work of Culture: Symbolic Transformation in Psychoanalysis and Anthropology.* Chicago: University of Chicago Press, 1990.

Ong, Aihwa. "Colonialism and Modernity: Feminist Re-Presentations of Women in Non-Western Societies," *Theorizing Feminism: Parallel Trends in the Humanities and Social Sciences.* Ann C. Herrmann and Abigail Steward, eds. Boulder, Colo.: Westview, 1994: 372–81.

Orenstein, Gloria. *The Reflowering of the Goddess.* New York: Pergamon, 1990.

Paglia, Camille. *Sexual Personae: Art and Decadence from Nefertiti to Emily Dickinson.* New Haven, Conn.: Yale University Press, 1990.

Pietropaolo, Laura, and Ada Testaferri, eds. *Feminisms in the Cinema.* Bloomington: Indiana University Press, 1995.

Polan, Dana. *Power and Paranoia: History, Narrative and the American Cinema, 1940–1950.* New York: Columbia University Press, 1986.

————. "Professors," *Discourse: Journal for Theoretical Studies in Media and Culture* 16.1 (Fall, 1993): 28–49.

Poly Styrene and X-Ray Spex. *Germ Free Adolescents.* Middlesex, UK: EMI, 1979.

————. *Oh Bondage, Up Yours!* London: Virgin Records, 1980.

Post, Emily. *Etiquette.* New York: Funk & Wagnalls, 1945.

Quintilian, Marcus Fabius. *Institutes of Oratory.* H. E. Butler, trans. New York: Loeb Classical Library, 4 vols., 1921.

Ramus, Peter. *Arguments in Rhetoric Against Quintilian.* Carole Newlands, trans. James J. Murphy, ed. Dekalb: Northern Illinois University Press, 1986.

Rapf, Joanna. "Myth, Ideology and Feminism in *High Noon,*" *Journal of Popular Culture* 23.4 (Spring, 1990): 75–80.

Reid, Mark A. "Dialogic Modes of Representing African(s): Womanist Film," *Cinemas of the Black Diaspora.* Michael T. Martin, ed. Detroit: Wayne State University Press, 1995: 56–69.

————. "Rebirth of a Nation: Three Recent Films Resist Southern Stereotypes of D. W. Griffith, Depicting a Technicolor Region of Black, Brown and Gray," *Southern Exposure* 20.4 (Winter, 1992): 26–28.

————. *Post-Negritude Visual and Literary Culture.* Albany: State University of New York Press, 1997.

Reynolds, Nedra. "Ethos as Location: New Sites for Understanding Discursive Authority." *Rhetoric Review* 2.2 (Spring, 1993): 325–38.

Rich, B. Ruby. "At Home on the Range," *Sight and Sound* 3.11 (November, 1993): 18–22.

Ricoeur, Paul. *Oneself as Another.* Kathleen Blamey, trans. Chicago, University of Chicago Press, 1992.

Ritchie, Joy. "Confronting the 'Essential' Problem: Reconnecting Feminist Theory and Pedagogy," *JAC* 10.2 (Fall, 1990): 249–75.

Roach, Joseph R. *The Player's Passion: Studies in the Science of Acting.* Ann Arbor: University of Michigan Press, 1993.

Roof, Judith. *Come As You Are: Sexuality and Narrative.* New York: Columbia University Press, 1996.

Root, Deborah. *Cannibal Culture: Art, Appropriation, and the Commodification of Difference.* Boulder, Colo.: Westview Press, 1996.

Ronald, Kate. "Personal and Public Authority in Discourse: Beyond Subjective/Objective Dichotomies," in *Farther Along.* Kate Ronald and Hephzibah Roskelly, eds. Portsmouth, N.H.: Boynton/Cook, 1990: 25–39.

Rony, Fatimah Tobing. *The Third Eye: Race, Cinema and Ethnographic Spectacle.* Durham, N.C.: Duke University Press, 1996.

Rorty, Richard. *Philosophy and the Mirror of Nature.* Princeton, N.J.: Princeton University Press, 1979.

Ross, Kristin. *Fast Cars, Clean Bodies: Decolonization and the Reordering of French Culture.* Cambridge, Mass.: MIT Press, 1995.

Rowlandson, Mary. "A True History of the Captivity and Restoration of Mrs. Mary Rowlandson," in William Andrews, ed. *Journeys into New Worlds.* Madison: University of Wisconsin Press, 1990: 31–65.

Said, Edward W. *Culture and Imperialism.* New York: Knopf, 1993.

———. *Representations of the Intellectual.* New York: Vintage, 1994.

Schaefer, Eric. "The Obscene Seen: Spectacle and Transgression in Postwar Burlesque Films," *Cinema Journal* 36.2 (Winter, 1997): 41–66.

Schiebinger, Londa. *Nature's Body: Gender in the Making of Modern Science.* Boston: Beacon Press, 1993.

Schmitt, Jean-Claude. "The Ethics of Gesture," *ZONE 4: Fragments for a History of the Human Body.* Michel Feher, Ramona Naddaff, and Nadia Tazi, eds. New York: Zone, 1989: 129–47.

Schor, Naomi. "Female Fetishism: The Case of George Sand," in *The Female Body in Western Culture,* Susan Rubin Suleiman, ed. Cambridge, Mass.: Harvard University Press, 1986: 354–62.

Schwartz, Hillel. *The Culture of the Copy: Striking Likenesses, Unreasonable Facsimiles.* New York: Zone, 1996.

Sedgwick, Eve Kosofsky. *Epistemology of the Closet.* Berkeley: University of California Press, 1990.

———. "Queer Performativity: Henry James's *The Art of the Novel,*" *GLQ* 1.1 (Summer, 1993): 1–16.

Seltzer, Mark. *Bodies and Machines.* New York: Routledge, 1992.

Seremetakis, C. Nadia. "The Memory of the Senses: Historical Perception, Commensal Exchange, and Modernity," *Visualizing Theory.* Lucien Taylor, ed. New York: Routledge, 1994: 214–29.

Sharpe, Jenny. "Figures of Colonial Resistance," *The Post-Colonial Studies Reader.* Bill Ashcroft, Gareth Griffiths, and Helen Tiffin, eds. London: Routledge, 1995: 99–103.

Shaviro, Stephen. *The Cinematic Body.* Minneapolis: University of Minnesota Press, 1993.

Shohat, Ella. "Ethnicities-in-Relation: Toward a Multicultural Reading of American Cinema," *Unspeakable Images: Ethnicity and the American Cinema.* Ledter Friedman, ed. Chicago: University of Illinois Press, 1991: 216–50.

Silverman, Kaja. *Male Subjectivity at the Margins.* New York: Routledge, 1992.

Simon-Ingram. "Narrative Fatalism and Psychoanalytic Determination: Reading *Jacques the Fatalist* with *Dora,*" *Women's Studies: An Interdisciplinary Journal.* 19.1 (1991): 19–44.

Slemon, Stephen. "Unsettling the Empire: Resistance Theory for the Second World," *The Post-Colonial Studies Reader.* Bill Ashcroft, Gareth Griffiths, and Helen Tiffin, eds. London: Routledge, 1995a: 104–10.

———. "The Scramble for Post-Colonialism," *The Post-Colonial Studies Reader.* Bill Ashcroft, Gareth Griffith, and Helen Tiffin, eds. London: Routledge, 1995b: 45–52.

Slits, The. *Cut.* London: Island, 1979.

Snyder, Jane McIntosh. *The Woman and the Lyre: Women Writers in Classical Greece and Rome.* Carbondale: Southern Illinois University Press, 1989.

Sobchack, Vivian. *The Address of the Eye: A Phenomenology of Film Experience.* Princeton, N.J.: Princeton University Press, 1992.

Sontag, Susan. *On Photography.* New York: Farrar, Straus, and Giroux, 1977.

Sperber, Dan. *On Anthropological Knowledge.* Cambridge, Mass.: Cambridge University Press, 1982.

Spivak, Gayatri. "Can the Subaltern Speak?" *Marxism and the Interpretation of Culture.* Cary Nelson and Lawrence Grosberg, eds. Chicago: University of Chicago Press, 1988: 271–316.

Steele, Valerie. *Fetish: Fashion, Sex, and Power.* New York: Oxford University Press, 1996.

Stowe, Harriet Beecher. *Uncle Tom's Cabin.* New York: Penguin, 1981.

Straayer, Chris. "The Hypothetical Lesbian Heroine in Narrative Feature Film," *Multiple Voices in Feminist Film Criticism.* Diane Carson, Linda Dittmar, and Janice R. Welsch, eds. Minneapolis: University of Minnesota Press, 1994: 343–57.

Stoller, Robert. *Observing the Erotic Imagination.* New Haven, Conn.: Yale University Press, 1985.

Suleri, Sara. "The Rhetoric of English India," *The Post-Colonial Studies Reader.* Bill Ashcroft, Gareth Griffiths, and Helen Tiffin, eds. London: Routledge, 1995: 111–13.

Tasker, Yvonne. *Spectacular Bodies: Gender, Genre, and the Action Cinema.* London: Routledge, 1993.

Taussig, Michael. *Mimesis and Alterity: A Particular History of the Senses.* New York: Routledge, 1993.

Taylor, Lucien. *Visualizing Theory: Selected Essays from V.A.R. 1990–1994.* New York: Routledge, 1994.

Thompson, Kristin. "The Concept of Cinematic Excess," *Narrative Apparatus, Ideology.* Philip Rosen, ed. New York: Columbia University Press, 1986: 130–42.

Todd, Janet. *Women and Film.* New York: Holmes and Meier, 1988.

Tompkins, Jane. *West of Everything: The Inner Life of Westerns.* New York: Oxford University Press, 1992.

Ukadike, N. Frank. "Reclaiming Images of Women in Films from Africa and the Black Diaspora," *Frontiers* 15.1, 1994: 102–86.

Vigarello, Georges. "The Upward Training of the Body from the Age of Chivalry to Courtly Civility," *Fragments for a History of the Human Body.* Michel Feher, Ramona Naddaff, and Nadia Tazi, eds. New York: Zone 1989: 149–99.

Virilio, Paul. *The Art of the Motor.* Julie Rose, trans. Minneapolis: University of Minnesota Press, 1995.

Wallace, Edgar. *Sanders of the River.* London: Ward Lock, 1911.

Wallace, Michele. "The Hottentot Venus," *The Village Voice.* May 21, 1996: 31.

Warren, Charles. B*eyond Document: Essays on Nonfiction film.* Hanover, N.H.: Wesleyan University Press, 1996.

Waugh, Thomas. "Cultivated Colonies: Notes on Queer Nationhood and the Erotic Image," *Canadian Journal of Film Studies* 2.2/3, 1993: 145–78.

Weaver, Tom. *Science Fiction Stars and Horror Heroes.* Jefferson, N.C.: McFarland, 1991.

Weiss, Ken, and Ed Goodgold. *To Be Continued . . .* New York: Crown, 1972.

Young, Iris Marion. *Throwing Like a Girl and Other Essays in Feminist Philosophy and Social Theory.* Bloomington: Indiana University Press, 1990.

Young, John H. *Our Deportment or the Manners, Conduct, and Dress of the Most Refined Society Including Norms for Letters, Invitations, etc., etc., Also Valuable Suggestions on Home Culture and Training.* Detroit: F. B. Dickerson, 1980.

Weiss, Andrea. *Vampires and Violets: Lesbians in Film.* New York: Penguin, 1993.

Williams, Linda. "Film Body: An Implantation of Perversions," *Narrative, Apparatus, Ideology.* Philip Rosen, ed. New York: Columbia University Press, 1986: 507–34.

———. "Sisters Under the Skin: Video and Blockbuster Erotic Thrillers," in *Women and Film: A Sight and Sound Reader.* Pam Cook and Philip Dodd, eds. Philadelphia: Temple University Press, 1993: 105–14.

———. *Hard Core: Power, Pleasure, and the "Frenzy of the Visible."* Berkeley: University of California Press, 1989.

Willis, Sharon. "Hardware and Hardbodies, What Do Women Want?" A Reading of *Thelma and Louise,*" in *Film Theory Goes to the Movies.* Jim Collins, Hilary Radner, and Ava Preacher Collins, eds. New York: Routledge, 1993: 120–28.

Wilson, Harriet E. *Our Nig; or, Sketches from the Life of a Free Black.* New York: Random House, 1983.

Wilson, Judith. "Down to the Crossroads: The Art of Alison Saar," *Secrets, Dialogues, Revelations: The Art of Betye and Alison Saar.* Los Angeles: University of California Press, 1990: 41.

Wilson, Margery. *The Pocket Book of Etiquette.* New York: Colliers, 1937.

Zavarzadeh, Mas'ud. *Seeing Films Politically.* Albany: State University of New York Press, 1991.

# ABOUT THE AUTHOR

Gwendolyn Audrey is an Assistant Professor of Film and Cultural Studies in the Department of English, University of Nebraska, Lincoln. She wrote and directed *The Women Who Made the Movies*, an hour-long documentary on the history of women film makers, distributed through Women Make Movies in New York. Foster is also the author of *Women Film Directors: An International Bio-Critical Dictionary* (Greenwood Press), and *Women Filmmakers of the African and Asian Diaspora: Decolonizing the Gaze, Locating Subjectivity*, (Southern Illinois University Press). Her other forthcoming books include an anthology of criticism on director Chantal Akerman for Flicks Books, and *Troping the Body: Gender, Etiquette, Conduct, and Dialogic Performance* (Southern Illinois University Press).

# INDEX